This is the book we've all been waiting for! For years Sheryl Garrett has been the inspired leader of a movement to bring the highest quality financial planning to the middle income market. Now she tells us how to do it, soup to nuts, in her book, *Garrett's Guide to Financial Planning*.
George D. Kinder, CFP, author of *The Seven Stages of Money Maturity*.

This book, written by one of the industry's most innovative thinkers, is the ultimate guide to serving the largely untapped Middle Market efficiently and profitably.
Joel P. Bruckenstein, CFP, CFS, CMFC, co-author of *Virtual Office Tools for a High-Margin Practice: How Client-Centered Financial Advisors Can Cut Paperwork, Overhead, and Wasted Hours*

Sheryl Garrett worked in every type of financial services environment and then came up with a business model to do something no one thought could be done: provide fee-only financial advisory services to the middle class while making a good living. Her book tells you not only why the less-than-semi-affluent are great clients, but exactly how to find them and keep them satisfied.
David J. Drucker, MBA, CFP, co-author of *Virtual Office Tools for a High-Margin Practice: How Client-Centered Financial Advisors Can Cut Paperwork, Overhead, and Wasted Hours*

Sometimes the best clients are right under our nose: working Americans, whose financial decisions can be more critical to their future than the wealthy. Helping this market achieve financial independence is something every financial advisor can be proud of. For everyone who has ever wondered where to find new clients, Sheryl Garrett has come to the rescue. Here is a remarkably smart and solid plan to helping Americas retire with confidence.
Katherine Vessenes, JD, CFP, national speaker, and author of *Protecting Your Practice*

Sheryl Garrett is a pioneer, visionary and hero to middle Americans and the planners who serve them. This book is a gift.
Randy Gardner, LLM, CPA, CFP, MBA, co-author of *101 Tax Saving Ideas*

The Financial Industry and the Financial Planning business are both in the clutches of enormous change. Organizational realignment of structures and skills to better meet the public's needs is the order of the day. Sheryl Garrett's book is a common sense, clear view of the issues of the day, followed by a Peter Drucker-like analysis of Middle Market opportunities and practice management concepts. No one should miss this wonderful addition to the industry's body of knowledge.
Richard R. Lee Jr., CFP, CFA

Americans are searching for affordable financial guidance that is completely objective and relative to their particular needs. Sheryl is a pioneer in advocating and offering this kind of financial planning advice. Her book shares these years of experience and offers practical insights on how to offer hourly-based, affordable financial advice to anyone seeking such direction. The time has come for qualified financial planners to follow Sheryl's example and her book is the perfect "bridge" to that new practice model. This is a "must read" for any financial planner who wants to stay on the '"cutting edge" of the profession.
Paul Lemon, Integrated Financial Planning PC

Sheryl Garrett has revolutionized the financial advisory profession. She has taken the as-needed, fee-only financial advice model to the mainstream and proven that it works. This book paves the way for new models like ours and the tens of thousands of financial advisors who want to get quality, objective and affordable financial advice to all Americans.
Ron Peremel, CEO, myFinancialadvice.com

Sheryl Garrett makes a compelling case for financial advisors to serve middle American clients. Better yet, she goes on to teach you how to be successful in this huge market. A must-read for every financial advisor, especially those advisors new to the business.
Warren J. Mackensen, CFP, MBA, MS

One of the keys to the advancement and growth of the financial planning profession are new practice models to serve more people more efficiently. As a leader in this area, Sheryl has found some ways of building a profitable practice to serve the Middle Market. She freely shares her substantial knowledge and experience in a practical and useable way. For someone wanting to build a new practice today, this book is invaluable. The market she identifies is ready to harvest and she shows how to do it. The book is well organized and readable and is a road map to success!

J. Jeffrey Lambert, CFP

Sheryl is a leading financial services authority having built a successful firm of networking RIAs across the U.S to serve the Middle Market. Through this book she is passing her expertise on to other financial service professionals. A must read for those trying to understand the industry and interested in serving the Middle Market.

Richard Sincere, www.sincereco.com

Finally! Sheryl Garrett fills a gaping hole in the financial planner's bookshelf with her comprehensive, no-nonsense guide to fee-only financial planning for middle America. Drawing on her many years of experience successfully serving this market, insight from industry leaders, and market data, Ms. Garrett makes a compelling argument that the future of financial planning lies on Main Street, not just with the wealthiest 10% of America traditionally served by the industry. But the book doesn't stop there! Chock full of tips, one-pagers, and pointers to valuable outside resources, *Garrett's Guide to Financial Planning* also provides the tools that financial planners need to tap this underserved market profitably. It outlines the needs, preferences, and buying patterns of this new target client, and describes the practice model best suited for meeting them. Plus it includes Sheryl's time-tested best practices for getting noticed despite the marketing clutter constantly facing today's consumer. I devoured the entire book in two sittings, and I'm sure I saved myself months, if not years, of effort.

Sherrill St. Germain, www.newmeans.com

Garrett's Guide

to Financial Planning

How To Capture The Middle Market
and Increase Your Profits

The All-American Planner

By Sheryl Garrett

The
**NATIONAL
UNDERWRITER**
Company
PROFESSIONAL PUBLISHING GROUP

P.O. Box 14367 • Cincinnati, Ohio 45250-0367
1-800-543-0874 • www.nationalunderwriter.com

ISBN: 0-87218-621-0

Library of Congress Control Number: 2002112270

Copyright © 2002
The National Underwriter Company
P.O. Box 14367, Cincinnati, Ohio 45250-0367

DEDICATION

To my parents, Jack and Barbara Garrett, for their unconditional love and devotion. Thank you for giving me my entrepreneurial spirit – you gave me both the wings and the courage to fly.

To all those who have shared in and supported my life's passions. You know who you are and how much I appreciate you.

CONTENTS

ACKNOWLEDGEMENTS

This book would not have been possible without the professional contributions and unwavering dedication of my marketing communications consultant, Marie Swift. Since 1998, Marie's continued partnership, support and creative alliance has amazed and inspired me. She is my collaborator, coach, advisor and friend. Marie, I am grateful for your contributions over the years and look forward to many more.

I also wish to thank my editor, Sonya King, and the staff at National Underwriter Company for seeing the need and giving me the opportunity to write this book. My mission is to help make competent, objective financial advice available to anyone who seeks it. The National Underwriter Company shares this value. I thank them for their foresight, vision and professional partnership in this endeavor.

Bob Veres, thank you for recommending me for this project. Also, many thanks for being a very influential factor in my successful launch and development of The Garrett Planning Network, Inc. Your continued insights and contributions to me – and to the industry as a whole – are always on target and very much valued.

Jeff Rattiner, thank you for first convincing me that I should write professionally as a way to express my commitments and share my values. Thank you for publishing my first article, and for your insightful comments in the Foreword of this book.

To my colleagues and friends in the financial planning industry, thank you for your invaluable insights and ongoing support. Your wisdom and generosity continues to awe and motivate me.

JoEllen Fritz, Angie Herbers, Rosemary Danielson and Ryan Walker, thank you for keeping my businesses running smoothly while I was writing this book. You are the greatest staff anyone could hope for. Your continued support and dedication contributes to our mutual success;

your bright spirits and effervescent personalities make coming to work fun. Jamie Gfeller, Kansas State University intern, thank you for your assistance in gathering research for this project and for your volunteer efforts the past two years at Garrett Planning Network's "Pathways to Success" retreats.

Finally, to the members of The Garrett Planning Network, thank you for your faith in this mission, your enthusiasm and support for one another, and your passion to serve the Middle Market. You are the greatest group of people anyone could have the honor to lead.

FOREWORD

In an age of instant gratification, and with a buy-on-demand mentality, middle America is facing its biggest crises yet: the ability to continue operating the type of lifestyle these individuals have grown accustomed to during the '90s. With this prolonged bear market, and in a world where things are as uncertain as ever, middle America is facing a pressing need as we travel down the road of the 21st century — the continuance of staying power. How will middle Americans continue to pursue their habits of providing for themselves, their kids, their extended families, their employers and so forth? How will middle America find the right solutions to allow qualified individuals to help them pursue their financial necessities in order to ensure a better life for all of us?

In my practice, we focus on middle America. These clients have different wants and needs than other types of clients planners focus on. They are deeply concerned about the current financial environment and are beginning to display a fearful attitude for the first time in many years. They want answers now. They want the "perceived" certainty that has been missing since the end of the bull road for the foreseeable future. When advisors were earning 20% and higher annually for their clients, almost on a routine basis, their concerns were never immediate issues. Yet the world that we've been living in is far less certain for all of us. Much of what went on pre – 9/11 is not necessarily valid anymore. I find myself constantly assuring my middle American clients to continue holding firm on the same principles that got them there in the first place. A properly diversified portfolio, a long-term buy and hold strategy, dollar-cost-averaging, slow and steady growth towards wealth accumulation, and proper financial planning are all necessary to achieve success in arriving at the objectives agreed upon during the financial planning process. Getting to Point B from where they are at now (Point A) is always the critical issue.

Well, in talking with many advisors during my financial planning fast track and practice management training sessions, I find very few advisors pursing middle America as a viable client option. They respond that the reason they have not focused on this marketplace is that if they are going to spend time to develop planning and investment strategies for clients, they might as well go after the wealthier clients who can easily afford their services. As Tom Cruise stated in the movie "Jerry Maguire, "show me the money"! These clients are different than the high-income clients advisors are notorious for going after because in many cases, the same amount of work is involved, yet the payout could be substantially less. From the typical planner's mind, with a limited amount of time and from a cost-benefit standpoint, it does not make sense. How untrue! This marketplace is yearning for information. You need to deliver true and factual financial information and educate these clients to understand the importance of future independence and planning early. They are ripe, willing and able to go the distance. Your platform should be to educate middle America.

It worked for H&R Block. They educated middle America about the importance of having qualified individuals prepare their tax returns and it worked. They're nationwide and have just added financial services to their repertoire. We can't be so short-sided as to not see the opportunity that presents itself here. This is the information age and we need to provide advice in that arena to those middle Americans who desire it. Many of them are beginning to see the value in hiring a financial advisor. They know that in order for them to receive value added services, these clients are going to have to ante up for that service, like other professionals charge for theirs. Financial service professionals are another source of competent advisors that clients need to regularly deal with, just like CPAs, attorneys, and physicians. The numbers are showing that more middle Americans are paying for financial services and advice than ever before. Studies from the major planning membership and licensing organizations will confirm this.

In my mind, middle America holds the key to more successful planning opportunities for financial planners long-term. That's because they represent a significant number of potential clients. Just think about it — with 285 million Americans, and roughly 70% of them being classified as middle Americans, that translates into 105 million households. With 40,000 Certified Financial Planner® (CFP®) licensees nationwide, and another 200,000 self-proclaimed financial advisors serving the public, the odds of building up a practice are pretty strong. But the daunting question remains, why are planners continuing to ignore this marketplace?

With a void in the number of planners addressing middle America, there are many opportunities for all of us as financial advisors servicing this marketplace. They need help in all of the basic areas of insurance planning, education planning, investment planning, income tax planning, employee benefit and retirement planning, and estate planning. They will also be willing to compensate planners on a fee-only, commission-only, or some type of combination. Many large firms have already discovered this niche by providing the requisite training and resources necessary to get their reps up to speed on this market and this, in turn, has proved to provide a fine living servicing this clientele. It does take longer, but over time, the constant source for referrals and renewability factors is there. And I find that these clients are more likely to help their friends and family to get to the financial level they need than other types of clients.

Up to this point, no qualified advisor has written on how to aggressively penetrate this marketplace. It has truly been the lone missing educational component in our vast advisor encyclopedia of knowledge. However, after reading Sheryl Garrett's manuscript discussing this untapped market, and knowing about the high profile turn-key program she runs in Kansas City for advisors nationwide, I am convinced that by learning to fully understand this marketplace and instituting the appropriate game plan spelled out in this book, financial advisors will be able to tap into this hidden and potentially lucrative marketplace, before it becomes too widespread, and with today's advisors reaping the benefits from helping this important, yet over-looked, segment of our society.

Jeffrey H. Rattiner, CPA, CFP®, MBA, RFC
JR Financial Group, Inc.
Englewood, CO
August 25, 2002
Author of:
Getting Started as a Financial Planner (Bloomberg Press, 2000).
Rattiner's Financial Planner's Bible (John Wiley & Sons, 2002).

INTRODUCTION

LIFE LIKES TO BE TAKEN BY THE LAPEL AND TOLD,
"I AM WITH YOU KID. LET'S GO!"

– *Maya Angelou*

Thank you for reading *Garrett's Guide to Financial Planning: How to Capture the Middle Market and Increase Your Profits*. As you turn the pages of this book, it will become clear that I am passionate about spreading the word:

MIDDLE AMERICANS, DO-IT-YOURSELFERS, AND PEOPLE FROM ALL WALKS OF LIFE NEED AND WANT TO WORK WITH YOU!

As you read my thoughts and digest the information, please take the time to reflect on *your own* goals and dreams. Consider the possibilities and do not overlook this great opportunity. By tapping this large and lucrative market I call "Middle America" (which is actually much, much more than you may be thinking now – read on to find out why), not only could you make a *huge* difference for a host of appreciative clients, but you could also gain better balance in your own life while enjoying handsome profits and virtually no competition.

As an advisor and consultant involved in the financial planning profession since 1987, I've had the privilege of speaking with hundreds of financial planning practitioners and financial services professionals. As a staff planner, a financial services representative, an advisor to high net worth clientele, and now as an independent "All-American Planner," I've had the opportunity to walk in several sets of moccasins. I'd like to think I have a sense of some of the career decisions and the hard choices you've made (or are making now) as you've forged your own path in the financial planning/advisory business.

After serving a variety of clients in these assorted professional settings and roles for a number of years, I finally came to the conclusion that not only did I want to become an independent, financial planning entrepreneur, but that I wanted to be able to serve all people, regardless of net worth, income level or level of investable assets.

And so it was in 1997, when I was serving as Vice President and investment specialist at Stepp & Garrett, Inc., a Kansas City-based financial planning firm specializing in serving high net worth clients, that I determined to make a change. While I had enjoyed a high level of success, I eventually became convinced that the firm's focus on serving only affluent clients was too narrow to meet my personal objectives.

I always felt a sense of remorse when I had to turn potential clients away because they did not meet our client profile or account minimums. I grew up in a modest home and inherited honest, working-class values from my parents. While I'd achieved what some would consider a high level of success, there was always a tug at my heart when regular folk – like those I knew in my hometown and current community – called to inquire about my services. It was very hard to tell the hairdresser, the postman, the grocery store clerk, the church secretary, the video store-owner: "Sorry, you don't meet our minimums." Worse yet, I had no proven resource or other professionals to whom I felt comfortable referring them.

Obviously, they needed, and wanted help. Sometimes they just had a pressing question or two. Other times they needed validation and advice regarding the key choices they were facing. In some cases they needed one or two modules of a full financial plan; at other times, they needed a full financial plan. But I was unable to provide the assistance they needed due to the confines of my firm's service model.

This bothered me.

Was the photographer any less important than the corporate executive? Didn't the freelance writer need my help as much (or more) than the dot-com millionaire? Who could help my parents and townsfolk with their most important financial concerns?

In addition, as time wore on I began to feel increasingly burdened by the amount of responsibility and high level of ongoing commitment required to provide concierge level services. I'd carry a mental to-do list and be on call 24/7, even when I was on "vacation."

Eventually, I came to the realization that I wanted to serve "regular folk" and do-it-yourselfers, like me, whom I knew were being overlooked and/or underserved by the financial services industry. I knew I'd need to be extremely efficient with my time and service delivery, and effectively adapt my marketing strategy to reach this huge, untapped market.

But since 1998, I've proven that it can be done – and with stellar success.

With my new service model and practice focus, not only am I happier with the balance I have between my personal and professional lives, but I'm helping people who *truly appreciate me and the advice I provide*. I'm generating a good standard of living, similar to what a tax practitioner, attorney or family physician might generate, and I have enough time and mental freedom to enjoy my friends and family.

As I proved I could generate and sustain a professional standard of living – all the while serving the market I desired, and doing the work I loved – more and more planners wanted to find out how to tap the same market and realize success. I started mentoring other practitioners and formed a network for like-minded professionals.

Eventually, I added staff planners, a paraplanner and an administrator to my financial planning and client service team. Together, our mission is to offer professional, objective advice and quality financial planning services on a fee-only basis — not just to the wealthy, but to people from all walks of life. We happen to do this on an hourly, as-needed basis because that simply makes the most sense to us. But there are other service models that could also be a good fit for reaching out to and effectively serving the Middle Market and do-it-yourself consumer. And that's what this book is all about.

Join me, as we explore the boundless opportunities and joys of working with the Middle Market and do-it-yourself consumer. Whether or not you eventually join me and become an "All-American Planner," by reading this book you will:

- gain some fresh perspectives on the financial planning industry and the profession's evolution;

- learn about different practice models and opportunities;

- discover a host of financial planning resources; and

- glean key marketing insights.

I love hearing from other practitioners and would welcome your comments once you've completed reading the book.

So, let's get started – go to Chapter One now!

Sheryl Garrett, CFP®
www.GarrettFinancialPlanning.com
info@GarrettPlanningNetwork.com

Chapter 1

THE EVOLUTION OF FINANCIAL PLANNING

*IN A FEW HUNDRED YEARS, WHEN THE HISTORY OF OUR TIME WILL BE
WRITTEN FROM A LONG-TERM PERSPECTIVE, IT IS LIKELY THAT THE MOST
IMPORTANT EVENT HISTORIANS WILL SEE IS NOT TECHNOLOGY, NOT
THE INTERNET, NOT E-COMMERCE. IT IS AN UNPRECEDENTED CHANGE
IN THE HUMAN CONDITION. FOR THE FIRST TIME - LITERALLY -
SUBSTANTIAL AND RAPIDLY GROWING NUMBERS OF PEOPLE HAVE
CHOICES. FOR THE FIRST TIME, THEY WILL HAVE TO MANAGE
THEMSELVES. AND SOCIETY IS TOTALLY UNPREPARED FOR IT.*

– Peter F. Drucker

Financial planning was born out of the insurance industry in the late
1960's as a means to further identify clients' financial needs and to fulfill those needs with additional product offerings. Life insurance companies began to expand their proprietary product offerings to include
mutual funds, retirement plans and variable annuities. Over time, many
of the major life insurance companies evolved into the major financial
services companies we know today.

In the early years, financial services professionals were generally
captive agents of national insurance companies or brokers with major
wire house broker/dealers. Investment and insurance products were
limited to those branded by the respective company, and advisors were

restricted to the products offered by their employer. Commissions received on the sale of insurance and investment products compensated these advisors. In an attempt to better address the broad range of clients' financial planning needs, and to cross-sell additional products to their clients, advisors began to employ consulting and analysis techniques now known as the "financial planning process."

According to the CFP Board of Standards (see Figure 1.1), today's financial planning process consists of the following six steps:

1. Establishing and defining the client-planner relationship

2. Gathering client data, including goals

3. Analyzing and evaluating the client's financial status

4. Developing and presenting financial planning recommendations and/or alternatives

5. Implementing the financial planning recommendations

6. Monitoring the financial planning recommendations

As more agents and brokers began using the financial planning process with their clients, they felt hampered by the limited product offerings available through their captive broker/dealer relationships and they began to seek the freedom offered by independent broker/dealers. To this day, the majority of financial services professionals are affiliated with independent broker/dealers.

Along with the variety of product offerings that became available to the independently registered financial advisors came the flexibility to charge clients fees in addition to commissions. Advisors could receive compensation for their time and advice, regardless of whether products were sold or not. However, the majority of their compensation still came from commissions.

Figure 1.1

The Financial Planning Process
CFP Board of Standards (Modified to Third Person)

1. **ESTABLISHING AND DEFINING THE CLIENT-PLANNER RELATIONSHIP:** The financial planner should clearly explain or document the services to be provided to the client and define both the planner's and the client's responsibilities. The planner should explain fully how she will be paid and by whom. The client and the planner should agree on how long the professional relationship should last and on how decisions will be made.

2. **GATHERING CLIENT DATA, INCLUDING GOALS:** The financial planner should ask for information about the client's financial situation. The client and the planner should mutually define the client's personal and financial goals, understand the client's time frame for results and discuss, if relevant, how the client feels about risk. The financial planner should gather all the necessary documents before giving the client the advice needed.

3. **ANALYZING AND EVALUATING THE CLIENT'S FINANCIAL STATUS:** The financial planner should analyze the client's information to assess her current situation and determine what she must do to meet her goals. Depending on what services she has asked for, this could include analyzing her assets, liabilities and cash flow, current insurance coverage, investments or tax strategies.

4. **DEVELOPING AND PRESENTING FINANCIAL PLANNING RECOMMENDATIONS AND/OR ALTERNATIVES:** The financial planner should offer financial planning recommendations that address the client's goals, based on the information she provides. The planner should go over the recommendations with the client to help her understand them so that the client can make informed decisions. The planner should also listen to the client's concerns and revise the recommendations as appropriate.

5. **IMPLEMENTING THE FINANCIAL PLANNING RECOMMENDATIONS:** The client and the planner should agree on how the recommendations will be carried out. The planner may carry out the recommendations or serve as the client's coach, coordinating the whole process with the client and other professionals such as attorneys or stockbrokers.

6. **MONITORING THE FINANCIAL PLANNING RECOMMENDATIONS** – The client and the planner should agree on who will monitor the client's progress towards her goals. If the planner is in charge of the process, the planner should report to the client periodically to review her situation and adjust the recommendations, if needed, as her life changes.

Over the last decade, there has been a major movement within the financial services industry to increase fees as a percentage of revenues. Sales commissions for many products have declined substantially during this period. Independent financial advisors are finding that charging fees in addition to receiving commissions normalizes their cash flow and allows them to focus their energies on providing financial advice on any issue for which their clients need assistance. Client engagements are no longer based on transactions alone. Transactional engagements have evolved into long-term client-advisor relationships.

There has also been increased concentration on providing comprehensive financial advice. Many financial services representatives are evolving into financial planning professionals. They are embracing the value of comprehensive financial planning as a means to provide clients with better financial advice and more holistic solutions. Rather than providing advice and solutions for just one area of the financial planning process, they are focusing on clients' needs and objectives in all aspects of their financial lives.

One segment of the financial planning industry has migrated completely away from commissions. In this service model, 100% of the advisor's compensation is paid directly by the client. The "fee-only" compensation model is currently the fastest growing segment of the financial planning industry, and the trend is escalating. The primary reason for the popularity of fee-only advice is the relationship the advisor has with his or her clients. Consumers are becoming increasingly aware of the potential conflicts of interest between the compensation interest and affiliated business interests of their professional advisors. In recent years, the media has also been a strong advocate of the benefits of fee-only advice for consumers. This enhanced media coverage has fueled consumer interest in learning more about how their advisors are compensated, and fee-only planning options.

Fee-only advice is available for the traditional financial planning issues, such as: goal setting; cash flow planning; tax planning; investments and risk management; retirement planning; and estate planning. However, many fee-only practitioners have expanded their services and now include ongoing asset management, tax return and estate document preparation, trust services (and in some cases, concierge services), too.

In many cases, fee-only financial planners and independent advisors have become so successful, and comprehensive, in their service offerings that they have continually raised their minimum fees or assets under management requirements. As a result, most fee-only planners (in addition to a growing number of fee-based advisors) now target affluent and semi-affluent clients, exclusively. Many of these practitioners are no longer able to take on new clients, and their success is drawing more competition to this end of the marketplace. The competition consists of larger financial advisory firms with vast resources, brand names and relationships that facilitate the advisors' efforts to compete and serve the needs of more clients.

In two highly touted research papers by Undiscovered Managers, the authors addressed these issues and concluded that, "the business of providing financial advice to semi-affluent investors — is on the brink of a major evolution."[1]

The Undiscovered Managers' studies have been highly controversial. One of the fundamental controversies has centered on the definition used by the researchers concerning the financial advisory business. The Undiscovered Managers' reports concentrated solely on the investment advisory aspect of the financial planning process. Their research went on to compare the current climate in the financial advisory industry to that of the institutional money management industry 20 years ago. They concluded that the same trends that occurred within the institutional money management industry would most likely unfold in the next five to 10 years within the financial advisory industry.[2]

Unfortunately, the Undiscovered Managers' research equated *financial* advice with *investment* advice. This is a common misunderstanding for the public and the media alike. The financial planning industry also confuses *investment management* with *financial planning*. Investment advice is clearly a very important component of financial planning, but too many advisors and consumers confuse the two subjects. Investment advice and financial planning advice are not synonymous. Therefore, the conclusions drawn from this research should be taken only in the context they relate to the delivery of investment advice.

I fundamentally disagree with the statement in the Undiscovered Managers' report that reads, "[t]he financial advisory business — the business of providing financial advice to semi-affluent investors — is on the brink of a major evolution."[3] In my opinion the authors' contention that the financial planning business is the business of providing investment advisory services to semi-affluent investors is also flawed.

Actually, I see the financial advisory business as an evolving profession whose mission should be to provide the appropriate level of competent, objective financial advice to *any* individual seeking assistance. All consumers have the need to consult with a financial planning professional at one time or another. Competent, objective financial advice should not be reserved only for the wealthy.

The Undiscovered Managers' research leads to the conclusion that the future of the financial advisory business will be dominated by just a few large, institutional wealth management firms providing extremely comprehensive, one-stop-shopping advisory services to wealthy consumers. While this service model may be an important component of the future of the financial services industry, based on the limited number of Americans who desire and are able to afford this level of service, and the significant competition in this marketplace, we are still left with a vast, untapped opportunity to serve segments of the population that do not fit this model.

In this book, we'll explore these untapped markets, and answer such questions as:

– Who are these consumers?

– What services do they seek from financial planners?

- What business models effectively and profitably serve this marketplace?

- What are the specific financial planning needs and the appropriate strategies for serving these clients?

- How do we market to these consumers?

Let's begin by looking at the factors affecting the evolution of the financial planning industry, and how the desires and demands of the consumer are a fundamental part of this evolution.

WHAT'S DRIVING THE EVOLUTION?

Factors driving the evolution of the delivery of financial advice include the strong economy that we've been experiencing over the last several years, the availability and popularity of mutual funds, the 401(k) plan, and the insecurity of the Social Security system. The bull markets of the 1980's and 1990's also caused many consumers to become more interested in taking a proactive role in their personal finances.

There is significantly more publicly available information regarding personal finance than ever before. In fact, the two hottest topics in consumer journalism are personal health and personal finance. Personal finance publications such as *Kiplinger's Personal Finance*, *Smart Money*, *Worth* and *Mutual Funds* have made it possible for all consumers to learn more about their personal finances and to take a more proactive role in the management of their financial affairs.

The Internet has also made a significant impact in the availability of and access to financial information for all consumers. One report states that 70% of investors with at least $1,000,000 of investment assets get some of their investment news online.[4] The use of the Internet by average Americans is similarly popular.

Our society is busier than ever. We want to have more control, to make things simpler, more convenient and more efficient. The Internet has provided us with tools that can quickly and easily simplify our financial lives and provide us with greater control.

One area where we have seen tremendous growth is in investment assets in online brokerage accounts. Assets have grown from $27.7 billion dollars in 1995 to $754.4 billion dollars in 1999. In 2000, there were more than 11,500,000 online brokerage accounts. By 2004, the total dollars in online brokerage accounts is expected to reach 2.2 trillion dollars according to Cerulli Associates.[5]

Services such as Morningstar enable consumers to analyze individual mutual funds and portfolios of funds. Web-based services such as Financial Engines provide very sophisticated, yet user-friendly asset allocation tools that incorporate some of the most advanced financial simulation models available today. Software applications (e.g., Intuit's Quicken, Quicken Financial Planner and Turbo Tax) have empowered consumers by providing them with highly sophisticated tools to analyze and manage their personal finances. The result of the improvements in technology and access to information is that the cloak of mystery has been removed from the financial advisory business. *The playing field has been leveled.*

Many advisors in our industry are concerned about consumers' access to information. Although financial advisors were once the gatekeepers of financial information, we are no longer the only ones with access to the volumes of information, tools and resources needed by consumers. But professional advisors need not worry about job security – consumers still need help. They need trusted advisors that will work in their best interests to help them sort through the vast (and often confusing) amount of information, and make the best decisions for their personal situations.

The plethora of information available in the popular press, on the Internet and through publicly available financial software applications has actually provided financial advisors with *more*, not fewer, opportunities to assist clients. For example, the quality of the output from financial calculators or software programs is no better than the initial assumptions used in preparing the analyses. Most consumers are unskilled in determining appropriate assumptions to be used in these analyses (e.g., inflation rates, rate-of-return assumptions on asset classes and mortality expectations), let alone determining risk tolerance.

Most software applications utilize static averages in projecting cash flow over life expectancy. On the other hand, an educated advisor has access to and knowledge of probability analysis and modeling tools, such as Monte Carlo simulation. The output from a Monte Carlo simulation may reveal a low probability that the client would achieve success based on the assumptions they might employ in their projections. This is just one of the many areas where the advice of a qualified financial professional can be extremely beneficial to a client.

The amount of subject matter to be mastered in personal finance is enormous. It often takes professionals years to develop a level of expertise in most areas. The average consumer cannot be expected to understand, stay current on, or be able to incorporate the many appropriate options and strategies that may be available to them (presuming they even wanted to).

Consumers are rapidly recognizing the need for access to a trusted adviser — one who can help them weigh options and opportunities regarding their personal finances, and to assist them in appropriately planning their financial futures.

The Undiscovered Managers' research states that, "clients are better informed than in the past and are demanding better advice for their money." The report goes on to state that clients "still might not feel comfortable or capable of managing their own investments, but they will be far more able to evaluate the quality of service that they receive." [6]

As clients' needs and expectations of their advisors evolve, our industry and service offerings must evolve as well. Financial planning practitioners who embrace service models that meet the needs of informed consumers will benefit from "the information age."

Investment implementation options are also evolving. A growing number of consumers are investing directly in online brokerage accounts and with no-load mutual fund companies.

Indexing is now an option available to all consumers. The benefits of indexing are low costs and the simplicity of this investment strategy. An investor trying to replicate the returns of a market may do so simply by investing in an index fund.

Overseeing a portfolio of index funds can be simple, but determining the appropriate asset allocations may be more complex. Services such as Financial Engines now provide the average consumer with specific asset allocation strategies based on their stated tolerance for risk. Once the appropriate asset allocations have been determined, fund companies, such as Vanguard and Barclays iShares, make implementation of a passive asset allocation strategy simple and cost-effective.

Some investors who embrace a long-term buy and hold asset allocation strategy may no longer feel it necessary to pay a professional investment advisor to implement a passive investment strategy. However, many consumers still need validation from a professional to confirm the appropriateness of their asset allocations and analytical decisions with regard to their overall financial objectives.

Other important factors that have aided in the evolution of the financial planning profession are the public awareness and professional development activities of the CFP Board of Standards, the Financial Planning Association (FPA) and the National Association of Personal Financial Advisors (NAPFA). One of the primary missions of the FPA is to raise public awareness of the need for financial planning for all Americans. Financial planning is extremely valuable for all people, regardless of whether they employ a professional advisor or whether they are do-it-yourselfers. The financial planning process is the basis for making smart financial decisions. All consumers, and our society as a whole, will benefit from making smarter financial decisions.

TRADITIONAL FINANCIAL PLANNING TARGET CLIENTS VS. TYPICAL AMERICAN CONSUMERS

The typical target client of the traditional financial planner may be described in broad terms as a "delegator." While the delagator's composite may not include "old money" (i.e., an inheritance), and they may not necessarily be wealthy, these clients do enjoy sufficient resources as well as a desire to outsource many of the day-to-day services associated with an organized and successful life. The delegator client may happily pay for lawn mowing and gardening services, catered or convenience meals delivered to their home, a live-in nanny, custom-tailored clothing, luxury vacations, etc.

Characteristics of a "delegator" in a financial planning relationship are as follows:

- *Desires a permanent, ongoing engagement* with their advisor

- Is interested in, and willing to *delegate management of their financial affairs* to their advisor

- *Has money to invest* or immediate insurance needs

- Provides their advisor with a *long-term source of revenue*

While the above characterizations summarize the qualities of the client that most financial planners consider representative of their target market, this client is definitely not the "typical consumer."

The "typical" consumer may be described in broad terms as a "validator." While the validator's composite may include some of the characteristics described above, validators do not have the resources or the desire to outsource many of the day-to-day services that delegators tend to outsource. The validator client may prefer to: do his own lawn mowing and garden care; cook large batches of food and divvy them up in the freezer as convenience foods; create a babysitting co-op for childcare; shop sales at department stores; and purchase off-the-rack clothing. This client may also enjoy camping instead of going on a cruise, etc.

Characteristics of the "validator" in a financial planning relationship include:

- *Needs professional advice, periodically,* but not on a permanent and ongoing basis.

- Is *not interested in, or willing to, delegate* the management of their financial affairs to an advisor.

- Is aware of, and *may be sensitive to, potential conflicts of interest.*

- Is *cost sensitive,* but recognizes that there is no "free lunch." They are willing to pay for value when they see it.

- Has most of their investment assets in qualified retirement plans; *seeks investment advice, but not ongoing management* of these assets.

- Seeks empowerment, education and *validation of their decisions.*

If we had to split the country into just two groups, most of America would fall into the validator category, not the delegator category. I contend that the majority of Americans do not meet the definition of the "traditional" target financial planning client – that is, the delegator described above. In the following chapters, we will explore the needs of "typical" consumers – the validators – including what they want from a financial advisor, and the practice models that can profitably and effectively serve these clients.

Figure 1.2

Client Composites

Typical Target of Traditional Financial Advisor	Ideal Client for Planners Seeking Untapped Market
Broadly defined as a Delegator	Broadly defined as a Validator
Convenience-oriented	Value-oriented
Willing to delegate research, implementation and management of financial affairs to advisor	Willing to do some research, but does most implementation and monitoring on own
Desires and is willing to pay for a permanent, ongoing engagement with advisor	Does not desire, or is not willing to delegate management of financial affairs to an advisor
Willing to pay for services desired	Cost-sensitive / thrifty
Desires some education, wants to understand process, but willing to defer to advisor	Seeks empowerment, education, validation of their decisions
Wants ongoing services; Provides advisor with a long-term source of revenue	Needs professional advice periodically; Provides advisor with one-time or repeat business
Can afford and is willing to outsource a variety of household services	Does not have desire or resources to outsource most household services
Minority of Americans	Majority of Americans

ENDNOTES

1. Hurley, *et al.*, *The Future of the Financial Advisory Business and the Delivery of Advice to the Semi-Affluent Investor*, p. 1 (Undiscovered Managers, September 1999). See also Slowik, *et al.*, *The Future of the Financial Advisory Business Part II: Strategies for Small Businesses*, (Undiscovered Managers, September 2000).

2. Id. at p. 3.

3. Id. at p. 1.

4. See HNW at: http://www.hnw.com/newsresch/hnw_market/internet.jsp.

5. *The Internet and Financial Product Distribution*, pp. 75-81 (Cerulli Associates, Inc., 2000).

6. Hurley, *et al.*, at 17-18.

Chapter 2

THE FORGOTTEN MIDDLE MARKET

UPPER CLASSES ARE A NATION'S PAST; THE MIDDLE CLASS IS ITS FUTURE.

– Ayn Rand

When we say "Middle Market," what exactly do we mean? Is this term based on an income range, as in "middle income" Americans? Is it based on a mindset, as in "the middle class"? Is there a difference? Or is it something more?

While the financial services industry, economists, social scientists and the public at large may differ in their definitions of what "Middle Market" means, when asked to describe their families' income, wealth and social status, most Americans will answer with the non-descriptive label of "middle class." But exactly what does this mean?

Actually, it may be easier to define what the Middle Market is *not*. The authors of the Undiscovered Managers' reports define "semi-affluent" as those with net worths ranging from $1,000,000 to $10,000,000. This demographic represents about 2% of American households. Given this definition, one might define the "affluent" as those with $10,000,000 to $50,000,000 of net worth, and the "wealthy" as those individuals whose net worth exceeds $50,000,000.[1] The poverty line is also definable — according to the

U.S. Department of Health and Human Services, the 2002 Poverty Guideline for a family of four is approximately $18,000. This demographic makes up almost 12% of American households.[2]

According to the best-selling book *The Millionaire Next Door,* there were approximately 3,500,000 millionaire households in the United States in 1999, and 95% of these millionaires had a net worth between $1,000,000 and $10,000,000.[3] Cerulli Associates has defined clients with investable assets ranging from as low as $500,000 to as high as $5,000,000 as the "mass-affluent." Their statistics reveal that as of 1999, approximately 11.5% of all U.S. households fell within this demographic.[4]

I define "middle America" as individuals who fall somewhere between the broad definitions of poverty and semi-affluent – strikingly, this is about 86% of all Americans. My definition utilizes net worth rather than just household income. Bert Whitehead of Cambridge Advisors, LLC (a network of fee-only financial planners who target and serve the Middle Market) defines a "middle American" as "anyone who works for a living...or anyone who *has had* to work for a living." Both definitions clearly illustrate that "middle America" is mainstream America.

Based on after-tax, annual household income, most studies agree that the middle class is grouped around the national average (with the lower and upper ends of this range representing the 20th and 90th percentiles of the population), and accounts for 70% of U.S. households. This definition includes all sources of income. But annual income is just one criterion for defining "middle class." Other factors, such as educational level, occupation, family background and social status, should also be included.

Interestingly, the National Center for Opinion Research states that 36% of people earning less than $15,000 a year consider themselves "middle class." Among those with incomes between $35,000 and $50,000 a year, 50% identify themselves as "middle class." While 71% of individuals earning in excess of $75,000 a year described themselves as "middle class," statistically those persons earning over $75,000 per year are technically high-income households.[5] Most people earning around $75,000 a year would argue that they are not high-income, but statistically they are in the top 20% of all households.

Clearly, our concept of "middle class" and the statistical definition of "middle income" are different. While middle income may be statistically defined as the middle 70% of household incomes in the United States, keep in mind this is an average of *all* households in America regardless of geography, number of wage earners, members per household or employment status.

But from community to community and from household to household, "middle income" implies different things. For example, in rural mid-America, a widowed retiree living on $36,000 per year, who owns her own home, and has a government pension and health insurance for life is considered to be financially secure. However, that same $36,000 annual income would barely sustain a family of four living in the San Francisco Bay area.

A young professional just graduating from college may technically earn a low-to-medium starting salary, but as he matures in his career this individual may make an income of $75,000 per year, or more. This person will likely see himself as middle- or upper middle class based on his professional credentials and reputation, rather than his income.

Clearly, "middle class" is really a *mindset*. And I am convinced that it is a very healthy mindset for our financial planning clients to have. Individuals who think of themselves as middle class often have more realistic expectations for their financial lives. Fundamentally, they want the same things as their wealthier counterparts – that is, they want to enjoy life, provide for their families, and retire with financial security someday. And while the not-yet-affluent and never-will-be-affluent may have fewer options and strategies available to them than the wealthy, typically they also have less complex financial planning situations. With the right attitude, conviction and guidance, they can — and will — achieve their financial goals.

For the purpose of building wealth, *income doesn't matter as much as how much you save and what you do with the wealth you have accumulated.* For that reason, I'd much rather work with a client who earns $40,000 a year and saves 15% of her income than a client who earns $400,000 a year and can't seem to make ends meet.

In their insightful book, *The Millionaire Next Door,* Thomas J. Stanley, Ph.D. and William D. Danko, Ph.D. reported that most of the millionaires they profiled either *think* or *have thought* of themselves as middle class Americans. The majority of those studied live in middle class neighborhoods, drive middle class vehicles, and enjoy the same hobbies and activities (and sometimes even the same occupations) as their middle class neighbors.[6] While these individuals have accumulated net worths in excess of $1,000,000, their millionaire status has not changed who they are. *Net worth is only a measure of the success one has had in managing his or her money.*

Stanley and Danko found that affluent people typically follow a lifestyle that is conducive to accumulating money. They found seven common denominators shared by those who successfully build wealth. These are:

1. They live well below their means.

2. They allocate their time, energy and money efficiently, and in ways that are conducive to building wealth.

3. They believe that financial independence is more important than displaying high social status.

4. Their parents did not provide "economic outpatient care."

5. Their adult children are economically self-sufficient.

6. They are proficient in targeting market opportunities.

7. They chose the right occupations.[7]

There are an estimated 105,000,000 middle income households in the United States today. As we learned from the profiles in *The Millionaire Next Door*, most millionaires are "self-made" millionaires. Of the 105,000,000 middle income households in the United States, many of these individuals, with good financial management, will become the future "millionaires next door."

Stanley and Danko go on to report that:

"[M]ORE THAN TWENTY-FIVE MILLION HOUSEHOLDS IN THE UNITED STATES (APPROXIMATELY 17%) HAVE ANNUAL INCOMES IN EXCESS OF $50,000; MORE THAN SEVEN MILLION (LESS THAN 5%) HAVE ANNUAL INCOMES OVER $100,000. BUT IN SPITE OF BEING 'GOOD INCOME' EARNERS, TOO MANY OF THESE PEOPLE HAVE SMALL LEVELS OF ACCUMULATED WEALTH. MANY LIVE FROM PAYCHECK TO PAYCHECK." [8]

Millionaires, on average, invest nearly 20% of household realized income each year. Most invest at least 15%. Most don't become millionaires until they are fifty years of age or older. Most are frugal. "And few could have ever supported a high-consumption lifestyle and become millionaires in the same lifetime." [9]

The above research shows that regardless of income, individuals who (1) live well below their means, (2) allocate their time, energy and money efficiently, and in ways conducive to building wealth, and (3) believe that financial independence is more important than displaying high social status, can achieve financial independence.

Very few practitioners in the financial services industry have elected to target clients with household incomes of $75,000, even though that group accounts for fully 20% of household income in the United States. Instead, many practitioners have set their client income threshold at $100,000. But individuals in this group account for only 5% of the population, and competition for these clients is fierce. As minimum income levels are set even higher above $100,000, there are fewer and fewer households to target, and the market opportunity drops precipitously.

Where do you what to spend your energies in developing a clientele? Targeting the same market niche that every other financial advisor in the country is targeting? Or would you rather be developing a practice that can effectively meet the needs of those Americans who are currently being ignored or underserved by the financial planning community?

My ideal clients are the "Millionaires Next Door" — but 5 to 20 years *before* they reach their millionaire status. It is their attitude and conviction that makes them my ideal clients. We will explore other characteristics that make these individuals the largest untapped market for financial advisors in America.

While middle income consumers are obviously a large segment of the untapped market, there are many more smaller segments of mainstream America that have yet to be adequately served. As we focus on the target markets of traditional financial advisors, we will uncover these untapped opportunities.

As stated in Chapter 1, most financial advisors are looking for clients who are willing to delegate management of their financial affairs. However, as Stanley and Danko revealed, most millionaires make their own investment decisions. They employ the expertise of legal and tax professionals only when necessary, and few delegate management of their personal finances.

"According to a recent survey by Forrester Research, 35% of all investors are "delegators," which means they choose to put their money in the hands of a professional.[10] Another 55% are "validators" who want to control their own finances, but occasionally need an advisor's guidance." The remaining 10% are known as "do-it-yourselfers," but many do-it-yourselfers will also seek validation when needed.

Robert Klapper, vice-president of Schwab AdvisorSource has stated:

"DO-IT-YOURSELFERS HAVE NO DESIRE TO SEEK INVESTMENT ADVICE. THEY LIKE BEING IN CONTROL. DELEGATORS ARE PEOPLE WHO WANT HELP MANAGING THEIR PORTFOLIOS, AND ARE WILLING TO GIVE SOMEONE ELSE DISCRETIONARY CONTROL. VALIDATORS FALL SOMEWHERE IN BETWEEN DO-IT-YOURSELFERS AND DELEGATORS. THEY KIND OF KNOW WHAT THEY ARE DOING, BUT FEEL THAT THEY COULD USE SOME OUTSIDE HELP, PERHAPS IN THE FORM OF A ONE-TIME FINANCIAL PLANNING CONSULTATION." OFTEN, HE SAYS, "PEOPLE SHIFT BETWEEN THESE CATEGORIES AT DIFFERENT POINTS IN THEIR LIVES."[11]

In the December 2001 *Cerulli Edge* newsletter, Cerulli Associates reported that the volatility in the stock market was a contributing factor to an increased demand for financial planning among what they define as "mass-affluent" clients. They stated that:

"IN THE BULL MARKET OF THE 1990'S, A SIGNIFICANT NUMBER OF INVESTORS (MANY OF WHOM WERE NEW TO INVESTING) FELT CONFIDENT IN THEIR ABILITY TO MAKE FINANCIAL DECISIONS ON THEIR OWN AND ADOPTED A SELF-DIRECTED APPROACH. THEY OPENED ACCOUNTS WITH ONLINE BROKERAGE PROVIDERS AND TOOK ADVANTAGE OF ONLINE FINANCIAL PLANNING TOOLS. EVIDENCE OF INVESTOR CONFIDENCE WAS ILLUSTRATED BY A 1999 SURVEY CONDUCTED BY THE CERTIFIED FINANCIAL PLANNER (CFP) BOARD OF STANDARDS IN WHICH 33% OF UPPER-INCOME AMERICANS FELT CONFIDENT THAT THEY COULD MAKE FINANCIAL DECISIONS WITHOUT PROFESSIONAL HELP. THIS SENTIMENT HELPED FUEL THE ONLINE BROKERAGE MOVEMENT, AS ONLINE BROKERAGE TRANSACTIONS TOTALED 82.3 MILLION, ACCOUNTING FOR 38% OF TOTAL EQUITY TRADES CONDUCTED ON THE NYSE AND [THE] NASDAQ AT ITS PEAK IN THE FIRST QUARTER OF 2000."[12]

One fact that isn't revealed in these statistics is that the majority of self-directed investors use mutual funds and qualified retirement plans rather than individual stocks to implement their portfolio strategies. So individual investors make up a significantly higher percentage of equity transactions then these statistics indicate. Individual investors also receive little or no guidance from professional financial advisors.

Cerulli Associates goes on to report:

"IN THE SECOND QUARTER OF 2000, THE INTERNET BUBBLE BURST — LEAVING INVESTORS NOT ONLY QUESTIONING THEIR INVESTMENT CHOICES BUT ALSO RE-EVALUATING THEIR ABILITY TO EFFECTIVELY MANAGE THEIR FINANCES. THE CFP PREDICTS THE PERCENTAGE OF DO-IT-YOURSELF INVESTORS [WILL] DROP, AS THE STRATEGY APPEARS TO BE LOSING POPULARITY. THIS IS CONSISTENT WITH CERULLI'S LONG-HELD BELIEF THAT SELF-SERVICE INVESTING HAS PLATEAUED AND IS NOW ERODING. WITH THE STOCK MARKET CONTINUING ITS DOWNWARD SPIRAL THROUGH 2000 TO 2001, MANY FINANCIAL PLANNING FIRMS ARE REPORTING A JUMP IN THE NUMBER OF NEW CLIENTS SEEKING ASSISTANCE TO RECOVER FROM THE RECENT MARKET DOWNTURN AND REBUILD THEIR SAVINGS."[13]

Cerrulli Associates continues:

"INVESTORS ARE NOT JUST LOOKING TO DIVERSIFY THEIR PORTFOLIOS AND LIMIT THEIR EXPOSURE TO TECHNOLOGY STOCKS; THEY ARE SEEKING FINANCIAL PLANNING ASSISTANCE. INVESTORS INCREASINGLY WANT TO WORK WITH AN ADVISOR TO CREATE A PLAN TAILORED TO HELP THEM REACH THEIR OVERALL FINANCIAL GOALS. THIS BODES WELL FOR ADVISORS WITH FINANCIAL PLANNING EXPERTISE, AS MORE INVESTORS WANT PROFESSIONAL ADVISORS ACROSS A BROAD RANGE OF INVESTMENT TOPICS, INCLUDING STARTING COLLEGE SAVINGS PROGRAMS, MANAGING RETIREMENT PORTFOLIOS, ESTABLISHING ESTATE PLANS AND PURCHASING APPROPRIATE LIFE INSURANCE POLICIES."[14]

I find this excerpt from *The Cerulli Edge* newsletter to be thought-provoking, but debatable. The authors have drawn the conclusion that individuals who've had access to low-cost investment execution and who've grown comfortable with implementing their own investment decisions are now permanently scared away from their do-it-yourself strategy. I feel that this is a very narrow viewpoint of the psychology of individual investors.

Do-it-yourselfers have been empowered with information and resources that have enabled them to research and implement their investment strategies at a very reasonable cost. Many of these individuals have also learned some very important lessons over the last few years. Hopefully, they've learned that excesses in the marketplace will eventually be corrected, and that they can't predict the market. Do-it-yourself investors have discovered that they actually do need assistance in determining the appropriate asset allocations and investment strategies to fulfill their financial objectives. However, this doesn't mean that they can't implement those strategies themselves using the low-cost techniques they've discovered over the past few years.

Thus, I argue that the do-it-yourselfer will remain a do-it-yourselfer and the validator will remain a validator. Validators have recognized the need for periodic financial guidance, but they'll continue to implement the recommendations of their advisors themselves. They desire to manage their own investment portfolios. They'll seek the advice of qualified consultants to validate their approaches, strategies and decisions *when they feel it is appropriate*.

As stated in the *Cerulli Edge* article, do-it-yourselfers have recognized the need for professional guidance. Unfortunately, for many of these individuals there are very few palatable options available today for working with professional advisors because (as stated in Chapter 1) the majority of financial advisors want to work with clients who are willing to *delegate* management of their financial affairs to advisors.

THE CHARLES SCHWAB STORY

We can learn a great deal about the psyche of the individual investor by studying the evolution of the discount brokerage powerhouse, Charles Schwab & Company. The cover story of the May 27, 2002 issue of *Barron's* stated:

"WHEN WALL STREET PROS MUSE ABOUT THE FINANCIAL INSTITUTION OF THE FUTURE, THEY RARELY FAIL TO MENTION CHARLES SCHWAB. SINCE ITS FOUNDING IN 1974, THE BROKER HAS BEEN AT THE LEADING EDGE OF A SERIES OF INDUSTRY TRANSFORMING CHANGES. STARTING WITH DISCOUNT COMMISSIONS IN THE 'SEVENTIES, THE ABILITY TO TRADE DIFFERENT MUTUAL FUNDS IN ONE PLACE IN THE 'EIGHTIES, AND INTERNET-BASED TRADING IN THE 'NINETIES, SCHWAB SEEMED TO BLAZE THE TRAIL THAT COMPETITORS INEVITABLY FOLLOWED." [15]

Charles Schwab founded his company based on a strategy of being different. He wanted to be seen as the "un-broker." His goal was to provide great service without pushing products or making specific investment recommendations. Do-it-yourselfers and many validators now had a broker who would provide them with just what they wanted and nothing more — great execution and service at a low cost.

The bull market of the 1990's saw the addition of Schwab's no-fee OneSource program. Through OneSource, investors could consolidate holdings in a number of outside mutual funds in their Schwab account. New customers arrived in droves, but many of these investors were less sophisticated than the typical Schwab account holders. In response to the needs of its expanding customer base, Schwab has continually added services and tools to assist these less sophisticated investors while at the same time providing higher-end advisory assistance to its traditional clientele.

Schwab has enjoyed continued success in determining marketplace trends and capitalizing on those trends. In just 25 years after its founding, Schwab's market capitalization surpassed that of Merrill Lynch, the long-time industry leader. Daniel Leemon, Schwab's Chief Strategy Officer, attributes their success to the fact that they have extensive customer research, and he states that, "Where we're going... is the direction in which our customers are leading us." [16]

Figure 2.1

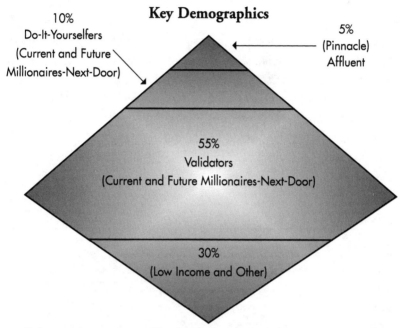

Taking a lesson from Charles Schwab & Company, we as planners should determine what the public wants from financial advisors and then deliver it to them. Remember, there are an estimated 105,000,000 middle income households in the United States. A good number of these "middle Americans" (and even some "millionaire-next-door" types) are "validators" – people who will seek out and pay for financial planning services and advice when needed to ensure they are making sound decisions. Of the 105,000,000 middle income households in the United States, many of these individuals – with your help and continued good financial management – will become the *future* "millionaires next door."

Instead of chasing the top 5% of the population, as most financial planners and advisors are prone to do, why not go where the greatest market opportunities are? Do you want to spend your energies competing in an already crowded marketplace (i.e., the affluent), targeting the same market niche that every other financial advisor in the country is targeting? Or would you prefer to develop a practice that can effectively meet the needs of those Americans who are currently being ignored or underserved by the financial planning community – and help *the rest* of America?

In Chapter 3, we will explore the various financial planning service models now prevalent with Middle Market practitioners, and for which middle Americans these service models are best suited. As we will discover, there are service models that can effectively and profitably meet the needs of virtually all consumers. Then, in Chapter 4, we will provide reasons why you should consider catering to the Middle Market and discuss why you should become an "All-American Planner."

ENDNOTES

1. Hurley, et al., *The Future of the Financial Advisory Business and the Delivery of Advice to the Semi-Affluent Investor,* pp. 8, 9 (Undiscovered Managers, September 1999).

2. U.S. Department of Health and Human Services, "Annual Update of the HHS Poverty Guidelines," 67 Fed. Reg. 6931 (2-14-02).

3. Thomas Stanley, Ph.D., and William Danko, Ph.D., *The Millionaire Next Door,* p. 13 (Simon & Schuster, 1996).

4. *The Cerulli Edge,* p. 13 (Cerulli Associates, Inc., December 2001).

5. *National Center for Opinion Research* (2000).

6. Stanley and Danko, pp. 8, 9-12, 302.

7. Id. at p. 4-5.

8. Id. at p. 2.

9. Id. at pp. 9, 11, 33, 34.

10. Lewis Braham, "Online Advice: Remote – and Reassuring," *BW Online* (May 28, 2001); http://www.businessweek.com/magazine/content/01_22/b3734024.htm.

11. Marla Brill, "Do you need a financial advisor," *Brill's Mutual Funds Interactive;* http://www.fundsinteractive.com/marla4.html.

12. *The Cerulli Edge* at p. 14.

13. Id.

14. Id.

15. Erin Arvedlund, "Schwab Trades Up: As It Expands With its "Lexus" Line, the Discounter's Own Shares Look Like a Buy" *Barron's,* p. 19 (May 27, 2002).

16. Jeffrey M. Laderman, "Remaking Schwab," *Business Week,* p. 122 (May 25, 1998).

Chapter 3

PRACTICE MODELS SERVING THE MIDDLE MARKET CLIENT

IT IS CHANGE, CONTINUING CHANGE, INEVITABLE CHANGE, THAT IS THE DOMINANT FACTOR IN SOCIETY TODAY. NO SENSIBLE DECISION CAN BE MADE ANY LONGER WITHOUT TAKING INTO ACCOUNT NOT ONLY THE WORLD AS IT IS, BUT THE WORLD AS IT WILL BE....

– Isaac Asimov

There are many styles, approaches and practice models used in the financial planning industry today. All of the practice models discussed in this chapter are utilized in serving the Middle Market. We will elaborate on the primary advantages and disadvantages of each model with regard to their effectiveness in meeting the needs of Middle Market financial planning clients.

Practice models are often defined initially by their compensation structure. The primary compensation structures include commission-only, fee and commission, fee-offset, and fee-only. For the sake of clarification, I wish to define these compensation structures. I will then elaborate on the commonalities of the service models and the clientele served by each model. Primary advantages and disadvantages of each model in serving the Middle Market will also be summarized.

COMPENSATION STRUCTURES DEFINED

- ### COMMISSION-ONLY

  Commission-only advisors receive all compensation from the recommendation and implementation of insurance and/or investment products.

- ### FEE AND COMMISSION (OR FEE-BASED)

  Advisors are compensated directly by the client to perform certain services, such as drafting a financial plan. Advisors also receive compensation from third parties for recommending and implementing insurance and/or investment products.

- ### FEE-OFFSET

  Clients are quoted a flat fee for services to be rendered. Advisors may receive compensation from third parties for implementing investment recommendations. Commissions received are applied toward the quoted flat fee. If the quoted fee exceeds the commissions received, the client pays the balance of the fee directly to the advisor.

- ### FEE-ONLY

  The National Association of Personal Financial Advisors (NAPFA) defines "fee-only" as advisors who "are compensated solely by fees paid by their clients and do not accept commissions or compensation from any other source."[1]

SERVICE MODELS: COMMONALITIES AND DIFFERENCES

Commission-Only

Decades ago, most financial services professionals were compensated exclusively by commissions generated from the sale of investment and insurance products. However, as discussed in Chapter 1, the financial planning profession is evolving toward comprehensive personal financial planning.

In an excerpt from the *White Paper on the Regulation of Financial Planners*, Jonathan R. Macey states that a financial planner is "someone who prepares individualized analyses of financial position and family situation, who assists in determining economic goals, and who formulates plans for clients to achieve their economic goals. In short, a financial planner develops plans that address all financial aspects of the individual's life."[2] Macey goes on to state that "[t]he breadth and scope of the advice given by financial planners is what distinguishes them from other, more specialized participants in the financial services industry."[3]

Financial services professionals who are compensated on a commission-only basis are the "specialized participants" to whom Macey refers. The commission-only advisor's relationship with his or her client is generally transaction-based. When the client has a specific investment or insurance need, the advisor implements appropriate products to fulfill specific needs.

Financial services professionals who are compensated on a commission-only basis will generally limit the comprehensiveness of their advice to the subjects for which they can be compensated.

Advisors who are compensated only when they can implement specific investment and insurance products may find it difficult to justify holding themselves out as financial planners and offering comprehensive financial planning services. As Macey says, "a financial planner develops plans that address *all* financial aspects of the individual's life" (emphasis added).[4]

Some commission-only professionals will, however, provide everything from case analysis to investment and insurance advice without a fee. They take their chances that the ideas they present to the client will be implemented. If the ideas are not implemented, they are not compensated for their work. A Life and Qualifying Member of the Million Dollar Round Table, John Moshides, told sales trainer Leo Pusateri, president of New York-based Pusateri Consulting and Training, that he had spent an enormous amount of his time in insurance and planning over the years, without ever asking for a fee. "We took our chances and hoped for closure," he said. "Our hit rate is high, but we've never been fully compensated for all the hard work and true value we have been providing to our clients."[5]

These specialized participants are usually happy to help Middle Market individuals who may not meet other advisors' account minimums, or assist individuals who do not want to turn over their assets for management. "Specialized participants" include financial services professionals who sell life, health, disability and long-term care insurance products, annuities, stocks, bonds, mutual funds and other securities, mortgages and real estate investments.

Examples of who can be considered a "specialized participant" include: an agent for Northwestern Mutual Life or American Family Insurance; a stockbroker with Merrill Lynch or UBS PaineWebber; a registered representative with Edward Jones or H&R Block Financial Advisors; a realtor with Century 21 or Better Homes and Gardens; or a mortgage broker with First National Financial Corporation or First Alliance Mortgage.

As I mentioned before, commission-only advisors fulfill critical roles in the financial planning process. For example, when a client wishes to do any of the following, she may seek the assistance of a specialized participant, the majority of whom are compensated on a commission-only basis:

- Implement a bond portfolio

- Purchase a portfolio of individual stocks

- Secure long-term care, auto, homeowners or disability insurance

- Buy real estate

- Obtain a mortgage

These specialized participants frequently work in tandem with comprehensive financial planners to assist clients in implementing their financial plans.

Essentially, there are two types of activities that clients may need or request: planning advice and implementation. Both are separate and distinct, and both have value. The planner may do the analysis and plan formulation, and then recommend that the client either:

1. Implement the plan on his or her own;

2. Engage the planner's services to assist with the implementation of the plan; or

3. Work with a specialized participant to provide the plan's implementation.

Pros and Cons of the Commission-Only Service Model

There are distinct advantages to working in the commission-only model:

- Most notable is the significant revenue opportunity that can be achieved in a relatively limited amount of time.

- The initial training and licensing required to transact business can be obtained fairly quickly.

- Minimal or no ongoing client service is required with transactional exchanges.

- Many financial services professionals prefer to specialize rather than maintain the broad knowledge base required of comprehensive financial planners.

The disadvantages of the commission-only model include:

- Transactionally-compensated financial services professionals must continually market their products or services; thus, a significant amount of time must be devoted to prospecting on a regular basis.

- There is no compensation paid until a sale is made.

- "Cold calling" is the name of the game, at least initially. Successful sales professionals are gifted with these skills, or they must learn them.

- Many Americans are inherently distrustful of sales people.

For the financial services company representative, one of the biggest obstacles is the last point stated above – that is, many Americans are inherently distrustful of sales people. And, while most financial services professionals have their clients' best interests at heart, they may have an ongoing negative perception to overcome. In many instances, they may not get the benefit of the doubt.

In addition, competition for investment assets and insurance business is at an all-time high. Consumers are bombarded with personal finance articles and advertisements highlighting insurance and investment options with low or no commissions. Other disadvantages are that the Middle Market provides limited opportunity for large initial sales and repeat business, and competition has also caused commission rates to fall.

Consumer finance journalists often see themselves as public defenders and they have drawn attention to the potential abuses in our industry. Journalists often make bold statements when writing for the masses. When writing an article on selecting a financial advisor, consumers are told to inquire about education, experience, credentials and potential conflicts of interest.

Consider this excerpt from an article in the *Washington Post* written by personal finance columnist, Jane Bryant Quinn:

"THERE'S NOTHING WRONG WITH COMMISSIONS PER SE. IF YOU GET ADVICE, YOU SHOULD EXPECT TO PAY FOR IT. BUT COMMISSIONS PRES-

ENT A CONFLICT OF INTEREST THAT YOU SHOULD KNOW ABOUT. A COMMISSIONED SALESPERSON, FOR EXAMPLE, MAY SELL YOU AN EXPENSIVE FINANCIAL PRODUCT WHEN THERE ARE CHEAPER ONES THAT WOULD DO A BETTER JOB. FEE-ONLY PEOPLE DON'T FACE THAT TEMPTA-TION — ALTHOUGH NOTHING GUARANTEES THAT THEY'LL GIVE YOU GOOD ADVICE.

ALWAYS ASK PLANNERS WHAT THEY'LL EARN FROM YOUR BUSINESS, SO YOU'LL KNOW WHAT FINANCIAL SERVICES COST. COMMISSIONED SALESPEOPLE SHOULD BE WILLING TO SAY.

IF THEY SAY YOU PAY NOTHING, WALK AWAY. THEY DO INDEED EARN SOMETHING, AND IT COMES FROM YOUR INVESTMENT IN VARIOUS WAYS. IF THEY'LL LIE ABOUT THAT, WHO KNOWS WHAT ELSE THEY'LL LIE ABOUT?" [6]

As a result of the media's continued educational efforts, journalists and prospective clients are now often more comfortable with an advisor whose compensation has little or nothing to do with the implementation of recommendations.

One of the most crucial characteristics of a successful financial planner is, of course, to be regarded as a trusted advisor. Unfortunately, commissioned-based financial professionals must overcome inherent distrust before they can become someone's trusted financial advisor.

Fee and Commission (or Fee-Based)

As I mentioned above, advisors who are compensated only when they implement specific investment and insurance products may find it difficult to hold themselves out as financial planners and offer comprehensive financial planning services. They generally limit their advice to subjects for which they can be compensated. However, as Jonathan Macey articulated, "a financial planner develops plans that address *all* financial aspects of the individual's life" (emphasis added).[7]

To ensure that adequate time and energy can be allocated to analyzing and providing recommendations for all aspects of a client's financial life, most advisors now charge fees in addition to receiving commissions.

Adding fee revenue to the compensation structure has not been a painless transition for many practitioners. For many years, clients received financial planning advice and did not pay a separate fee for that advice. The practitioner's compensation was built into the insurance premiums and investment products purchased by clients. Many clients may not have recognized exactly how, or how much, their advisor was being compensated because they did not actually write a check to the advisor. Many clients viewed commissions as a cost of doing business.

However, with the proliferation of no-load mutual funds, discount brokerage firms and the direct marketing of insurance products, the financial services industry has changed drastically over the last several years. Financial services companies are now marketing directly to consumers. At the same time, there has been enormous growth in the number of consumer finance articles, publications, newsletter services and websites providing advice to clients regarding these products and services.

Consumers are now much more aware of the availability of no-load and low-load insurance and investment products. Traditional commission rates have been falling in response to these market forces. As a result, many financial planning practitioners have added fees to their compensation structures to:

1. Offset declining commission rates;

2. Enable their businesses to provide a steady level of service and advice; and

3. Provide themselves with compensation for all areas of their advisory practice.

Currently, the majority of financial planners are compensated through a combination of fees and commissions. However, fees represent the fastest growing portion of most practitioners' total compensation. The majority of fee revenue is charged in the form of a retainer based on a percentage of assets, which the advisor manages. Some fee- and commission-based financial planners charge a flat fee that is determined by estimating the number of hours required to prepare a financial plan. They may also receive commissions upon the implementation of their clients' financial planning recommendations.

This practice model can be tailored to suit ongoing supervisory relationships or periodic engagements. An annual retainer is best suited for ongoing supervisory relationships, while the hourly or project-based engagement is best suited for periodic engagements.

Most practitioners prefer to work with clients on an ongoing, long-term basis because these long-term engagements provide a continual revenue stream for the advisor; they also relieve some of the marketing and prospecting burden.

With retainer clients, the financial planner is responsible on a continual and ongoing basis to provide oversight and advice to clients regarding their financial lives. This service can be very appropriate for clients wishing or needing to delegate the management of their financial affairs to their advisor. Conversely, most do-it-yourselfers and validators (see Chapter 1) are not interested in or willing to pay for the services of a full-time financial planner. Furthermore, many Middle Market consumers do not have enough manageable investment assets to justify the fees charged for continual and ongoing investment supervision.

In the *2001 FPA Staffing and Compensation Study of Financial Planning Practitioners*, the accounting firm of Moss Adams revealed that average revenues for solo practitioners ranged from $1,458 to $2,634 per client, and the average revenues in practices employing more than one professional ranged from $2,683 to $5,708 per client.[8] These revenues consisted of both fees and commissions, with the majority of fee revenue coming from assets under management.

Challenges of a Fee-Based Practice

- It often takes years for an advisor to establish and manage a profitable retainer-based practice. The labor involved in providing comprehensive financial planning and investment advisory services on an ongoing basis dictates that a typical financial planner may only be able to effectively serve 50-100 clients. These clients must be delegators, with needs that will allow the advisor to generate annual revenues averaging between $2,000 and $5,000. The survey respondents of the FPA *Staffing and Compensation Study* indicated that approximately 40% of gross revenues went toward overhead expenses.[9] Therefore, a practitioner who is limited to serving 50-100 clients must maintain fairly substantial average revenue per client.

- The advisor under retainer must be ready, willing and able to assist clients on a continual and ongoing basis. Some of my colleagues pride themselves on being available to their clients 24 hours a day, 7 days a week. However, this can put substantial pressure on the advisor when several clients need their attention at the same time. The advantages of continual and ongoing revenue can, at times, be outweighed by the continual and ongoing responsibilities of servicing retainer clients. As a result, most practitioners offering retainer services have found it necessary to employ and manage support staff.

- Many consumers are reluctant to enter into long-term contractual arrangements for financial planning services. Their reluctance might be due to unfamiliarity with, or distrust of, the advisor. They might question the value of professional financial advice. Their reluctance might be the result of the long-term contract itself. Some people are "tire kickers" – that is, they want to have professional experience with the advisor before turning over control of their investment portfolios to a planner. Others want periodic or as-needed advice, and they'll never be interested in a retainer arrangement.

Ongoing or Project–Based Services

All consumers have questions about their personal finances at one time or another. For delegators able to afford and justify the expense of a full-time financial advisor, there are those practitioners who offer ongoing retainer engagements. However, for the multitude of Middle Market consumers who are not the target clients for the retainer model, there are advisors who offer their services on a periodic or as-needed basis.

Few financial planners limit their practices to periodic or as-needed advice; therefore, they must balance the demands and responsibilities of managing retainer engagements while augmenting their services with periodic or project-based engagements. I advocate using either the retainer service model *or* the as-needed service model, rather then trying to provide both. The clients served, the services provided, the marketing functions and the administrative responsibilities can be unique to each model. In my experience, practitioners who focus on working with clients exclusively on a retainer- or a project-basis will be most efficient and profitable.

The project-based advisor may enter into 100 or more engagements per year. I refer to these projects as "engagements" rather than "clients" because, over time, the practitioner will be re-engaged to provide services to clients they have worked for in the past. Services are provided on an as-needed basis rather than on a continual and ongoing basis. Clients are responsible for contacting the advisor with questions or service issues for which they need the advisor's guidance.

Project-based advisors generally do not require minimum revenues per engagement; this greatly expands their prospective client base. However, given that no minimum revenue per client is required, the advisor must generate a significant volume of engagements each and every year. Initially, the marketing activities required to develop this practice model will be substantial. However, referrals should also be much more plentiful for the project-based advisor then the retainer-based advisor. Established financial planning practitioners receive the majority of their new business by referrals from existing clients. Because the project-based advisor has worked with substantially more consumers then the retainer-based advisor, they have more potential referral sources.

I have also discovered that clients of retainer-based advisors may be reluctant to refer their advisor to others. This reluctance may be a result of the minimum fees imposed by the advisor. Clients may be concerned that those whom they would refer may not qualify for, need, or elect to pay for the services they themselves deem appropriate and justified. A few clients might be concerned that they could offend someone by even suggesting that they need a full-time financial advisor.

Again, the media has played a large part in consumer awareness of the costs associated with employing a full-time financial advisor and paying for ongoing services. Consider this excerpt from an article in the *Wall Street Journal* by popular personal finance columnist and author, Jonathan Clements entitled, "Some Advice Worth Paying For: Most Planners Cost Too Much."

"You need a hand, but you don't want to pay an arm and a leg. The bull market of the 1990s gave many folks the confidence to invest on their own. Now that confidence has collapsed along with share prices, battered investors are looking for help.

But even if you hire a talented adviser, you could do more harm than good, because the cost of the adviser may offset any improvement in your portfolio's performance.

Indeed, if you're going to use an adviser and still earn healthy gains, I believe you need to stick with one of the low-cost alternatives. True, you may miss out on the heavy-duty handholding that traditional advisers offer. But given the cost savings, that seems like a small price to pay."[10]

Mr. Clements then goes on to list several low-cost options for obtaining financial planning services and/or investment management and advice.

In general, and as a tie-in to Mr. Clements' thoughts, I believe that the project-based advisor incurs less resistance obtaining engagements and referrals due to the fact that this type of advisor requires less commitment on the part of the client. A consumer can hire the advisor for a limited engagement and, if satisfied, they can re-engage him or her for additional services as needed. In a project-based scenario, the client does not need to feel that he or she is captive to the advisor's services. It's like visiting the dentist. If the dentist does a good job and the client has grown to like and trust him, the client will return periodically and re-engage his services. Clients who are happy with the service they have received will tell their friends about the professionals on their service team, including their dentist, accountant, personal trainer, financial advisor, etc.

Project-based advisors are able to tailor their services to the specific, immediate needs of the client. They cater to do-it-yourselfers and validators desiring periodic, as-needed advice.

Most practitioners embracing this model provide investment advice, but few of them manage money. This may appeal to the consumer who is either unwilling, or reluctant, to delegate the management of their investment portfolio.

However, fee- and commission-based advisors, regardless of whether they work under a retainer or on a project-basis are still receiving a portion of their compensation from commissions. Thus, they must still overcome the inherent distrust many consumers have of the advisor whose compensation is directly impacted by implementation decisions.

Pros and Cons of Broker/Dealer Affiliations

Commission- and fee-based advisors are typically independent financial services entrepreneurs who affiliate with independent broker/dealers (e.g., Financial Network Investment Corporation, Linsco/Private Ledger, Raymond James Financial Securities, Investor's

Capital, or Securities America) for back office and corporate level support such as:

- Securities and insurance analysis/recommendations

- Training and conferences

- Marketing support and ideas

- Securities custody and transaction clearing services

These independent, fee- and commission-based advisors own their own companies. In order to provide fee-based services to their clients, they may be registered as their own investment advisory firms with their state's Department of Corporations or the Securities and Exchange Commission (SEC). (Or, they may be required to register as investment advisors through their broker/dealers and their broker/dealers' SEC registration, depending on their broker/dealers' rules.)

In order to offer their clients a range of insurance, securities and investment vehicles and accept the corresponding commissions, these fee- and commission-based advisors must also pass various securities licensing examinations and become "registered representatives" of the broker/dealer. The broker/dealer screens and approves for sale a host of products (typically, there are thousands of choices, but not the whole range of the marketplace). The broker/dealer may also have a sales or production minimum that must be satisfied to maintain registered representative status.

Once the client has purchased the recommended product, the planner's commissions are debited from the client's total investment or insurance premium. The investment or insurance company pays the commission to the broker/dealer, who then passes down a portion of the commission to the registered representative. The percentage of the commission and/or fee that the broker/dealer pays to their registered representatives is called a "payout." Securities and insurance transactions clear through third-party resources, such as First Trust Corporation, which may provide additional reporting and online account viewing services. (The third-party resource is chosen and approved by the broker/dealer.)

Because broker/dealers incur some liability for the communications and operational processes of their registered representative, these advisors are required to run all of their advertising, marketing materials and client communications through their broker/dealer's compliance department for review, comment and approval. Most broker/dealers also require advisors to pay a portion (commonly 10%) of their fee revenue back to the broker/dealer for supervisory expenses. In addition, there may be branch office inspections by the broker/dealer's compliance department (in addition to any other inspections and compliance audits that proceed from routine or other triggers from the SEC or the state's Department of Corporations).

Clearly, the requirements for being a registered representative of a broker/dealer include both advantages (e.g., back office support, marketing assistance, compliance supervision) and disadvantages (e.g., corporate level rules, sales/production quotas, "selling away" conflicts, burdensome compliance rules, payout rates on product implementation, and fee revenue sharing). These are the trade-offs that exist if the advisor wishes to provide both independent, fee-based services and to accept commissions when his recommendations are implemented.

Fee-Offset

In theory, this compensation structure seems like the best of all worlds. The commissions received upon the implementation of investment advice are applied toward the total fee for all services rendered. However, the apparent simplicity of this model breaks down when you get into the details. It may be one of the most equitable compensation structures, but it can also be very difficult to explain to clients. Commissions received from the sale of insurance products may not be "rebated" to the client. Actual "payouts" on many investment products cannot be determined in advance. Therefore, upon the initial engagement, the client does not know for how much they might have to write a check.

The few financial planners who work on a fee-offset-basis generally work with clients on a retainer-basis when managing money. They may also provide project or as-needed advice on a very limited basis.

As explained above in the fee- and commission-based section, these individuals are usually independent financial services professionals on the financial planning side of their business, and registered representatives with one of the independent broker/dealers on the product implementation side of their business.

The major disadvantage of this business model (in addition to needing to overcome potential objections from clients concerning the acceptance of commissions) is that it is a fairly complex compensation structure that may be difficult to explain to clients.

Fee-Only

There are as many different ways to determine a fee as there are to earn a commission. Planners working under the "fee-only" model may employ a formula approach, such as 1% of assets under management, 0.75% of net worth, 2% of income, or any combination of the above. Commonly, fee schedules decline as assets, net worth or income rises. Occasionally, fee schedules decrease, and then level off over time to represent the additional work involved in the early years of the relationship. Other practitioners provide their services for a flat fee that is determined based on the anticipated time involved and complexity of the case. These are the most common types of fee structures utilized by those offering retainer services on a fee-only basis.

Determining the appropriate fee for services to be rendered over time can be quite challenging. No one formula will be equitable for all clients. However, fee schedules do have their advantages. During the initial meeting with a prospective client, the practitioner will have access to the information required to plug into the formula and quote a fee. The quoted fee may or may not be representative of the complexity of the client's situation or the amount of time required to prepare the plan. (The advantage is the simplicity of coming up with a number/quote because its a formula and the planner has the variables that go into the calculation.)

The fee-only approach has earned praise from the AARP, the Consumer Federation of America and leading journalists, all of whom regard the fee-only structure as being good for consumers. Quotes from journalists posted on NAPFA's web site[11] include:

"FINANCIAL PLANNERS WHO TAKE COMMISSIONS HAVE A BUILT-IN CONFLICT OF INTEREST...EVEN WITH DISCLOSURE, MY CHOICE WOULD BE A FEE-ONLY PLANNER."

Jane Bryant Quinn, Newsweek

"START WITH THE GENERAL PRACTITIONER...A FINANCIAL PLANNER (WHOSE) COMPENSATION SHOULD BE FROM FEES ALONE."

Money

"THE MOST IMPORTANT MATTER IS HOW THE PLANNER IS COMPENSATED. HIRE THE PLANNER WHO...HAS NO FINANCIAL STAKE IN (YOUR) INVESTMENTS."

Forbes

"THINK OF FINANCIAL PLANNERS AS MONEY CONSULTANTS. THEIR JOB IS TO LOOK OUT FOR YOUR MONEY'S BEST INTERESTS, NOT TO SELL YOU STUFF. YOU SHOULD PAY A PLANNER FOR HER TIME, EITHER AN HOURLY RATE OR A FLAT FEE. THEY ARE CALLED FEE-ONLY PLANNERS, AND THEY HAVE NO FINANCIAL INCENTIVE TO RECOMMEND ONE INVESTMENT OVER ANOTHER."

Barbara Loos, author of I Haven't Saved a Dime, Now What?!

Fee-only planners pride themselves on minimizing conflicts of interest regarding compensation. However, opponents of fee-only planners argue that basing one's fee on the percentage of assets under management will motivate the advisor to take control over as many of the client's assets as possible. For instance, a planner could face the dilemma of providing objective advice regarding the merits of funding a Section 529 college savings plan or paying off one's mortgage with investment assets. This decision will impact the advisor's compensation just as much as the advisor who is compensated by commissions upon the sale of an investment or insurance product.

While the media has been a big proponent of fee-only planning in recent years, they have also voiced their concerns about the value of an assets under management scenario. Consider these excerpts from respected consumer journalists:

"FOR YEARS, FEE-ONLY FINANCIAL PLANNERS HAVE DISPARAGED COM-MISSION-CHARGING BROKERS AND PLANNERS. THEIR ARGUMENT: COMMISSIONS GIVE ADVISERS AN INCENTIVE TO TRADE CLIENTS' ACCOUNTS AND TO RECOMMEND THOSE PRODUCTS THAT PAY THE FATTEST COMMISSIONS.

BUT AS MUCH AS I AGREE WITH FEE-ONLY FINANCIAL PLANNERS, THESE FOLKS HAVE A PROBLEM OF THEIR OWN. THEY ARE JUST WAY TOO EXPENSIVE. FEE-ONLY ADVISERS TYPICALLY SNAG 1% OF A CLIENT'S ACCOUNT EACH YEAR, EQUAL TO $10,000 ON A $1 MILLION PORTFOLIO.

MOREOVER, THESE ADVISERS OFTEN RECOMMEND MUTUAL FUNDS, WHICH MIGHT CHARGE 1% IN ANNUAL EXPENSES, BRINGING THE TOTAL COST TO 2% A YEAR. RESULT? IF YOUR PRE-COST ANNUAL RETURN IS 8%, YOU WILL LOSE A QUARTER OF YOUR GAIN TO INVESTMENT COSTS."[12]

Jonathan Clements, Wall Street Journal

"NO-COMMISSION ADVICE IS A GOOD IDEA, BUT IT'S POSSIBLE TO OVERPAY A FEE, TOO. MANY PLANNERS CHARGE 1 PERCENT OF THE VALUE OF YOUR ASSETS A YEAR: $5,000 A YEAR ON A $500,000 PORTFOLIO, FOR EXAMPLE. IF ALL YOU ARE GETTING IS ASSET ALLOCATION, 1 PERCENT IS PRETTY DARNED PRICEY."[13]

Linda Stern, Newsweek

I have yet another concern with respect to basing fees on a percentage of assets under management. If we tie our fees to investment portfolios, clients may view us as money managers instead of financial planners. Comprehensive financial planners must have knowledge of all subject matter relating to personal finance. Many financial planners don't have the time or expertise to successfully compete against professional money management firms with regard to the management of investment portfolios.

The majority of financial advisors who provide asset management services also perform labor-intensive portfolio accounting functions for their clients. They often produce quarterly investment portfolio performance reports. Along with these performance reports, advisors include their quarterly invoice. Quarter after quarter clients receive the message that they are paying for investment advice, rather than for financial planning services. As financial planners, we educate our clients that our objective is to assist them in achieving their financial goals over the long term. Yet quarter after quarter, we focus their attention on the short-term performance of their investment portfolios.

Fee-Only, Hourly or Flat-Fee

Some fee-only financial planners charge a flat fee for a specific project to be preformed. Others charge by the hour. Most hourly planners provide clients with an estimated fee range when quoting fees. Project-based and hourly fee models can provide a very equitable engagement for both the client and the advisor. However, the practitioner must have experience and full knowledge of the scope of the project in order to accurately estimate the amount of time required to complete the project. Practitioners new to hourly billing often underquote because they do not adequately estimate the complexity of the case or the amount of time that will be involved. On the other hand, the engagement rate for new practitioners is often very high, and this provides them with a lot of experience. Experience is, of course, how we all learn and grow. Presuming the advisor accurately tracks and monitors her time, she will become proficient at estimating and quoting fees under the hourly model.

In recent years, the media has been advocating fee-only *hourly* planning as a cost-effective option for the Middle Market and do-it-yourselfers. Consider these article excerpts:

> "...A NEW BREED OF PLANNER OFFERS SOPHISTICATED, À LA CARTE ADVICE AT REASONABLE HOURLY RATES, ALLOWING EVEN NEW INVESTORS THE OPTION OF LOW-COST ANSWERS TO SPECIFIC QUESTIONS."[14]

Mary Rowland, MSN Money Central

> "I THINK HOURLY PLANNERS MAKE A LOT OF SENSE FOR BEGINNERS AND OTHERS WHO CAN'T AFFORD THE UP-FRONT COST OF A COMPLETE PLAN, AS WELL AS FOR DO-IT-YOURSELFERS AND OTHERS WHO WANT TO GET A FINANCIAL EDUCATION."[15]

Mary Rowland, Bloomberg Wealth Manager

> "[F]INANCIAL ADVISERS ARE A QUIRKY BUNCH, AND THEIR INVESTMENT RECOMMENDATIONS TEND TO REFLECT HOW THEY'RE COMPENSATED, WHAT THEIR BACKGROUND IS AND WHAT SORT OF A COMPANY THEY WORK FOR. ... I WOULD SHY AWAY FROM USING COMMISSIONS TO COMPENSATE A BROKER OR PLANNER. ... MANY BROKERAGE FIRMS AND FINANCIAL PLANNERS WILL INSTEAD MANAGE A CLIENT'S ACCOUNT FOR AN ANNUAL FEE, EQUAL TO MAYBE 1% OF THE ACCOUNT'S VALUE. ... IF YOU PAY A PERCENTAGE OF ASSETS, YOUR ADVISER NO LONGER HAS AN INCENTIVE TO CHURN YOUR ACCOUNT OR PUT YOU IN INVESTMENTS THAT GENERATE THE HIGHEST COMMISSIONS. THESE FEE ARRANGEMENTS, HOWEVER, DON'T ELIMINATE ALL CONFLICTS OF INTERESTS. ... IF ADVISERS CHARGE A PERCENTAGE OF ASSETS, THEY CAN SEE THEIR INCOME SLASHED IF CLIENTS MOVE MONEY INTO 529 COLLEGE-SAVINGS PLANS OR BUY AN IMMEDIATE ANNUITY. ... WITH AN HOURLY FEE, YOU ELIMINATE VIRTUALLY ALL CONFLICTS OF INTEREST. ... IF YOU CAN FIND AN ADVISOR WHO CHARGES JUST AN HOURLY FEE, THAT MAY BE THE BEST WAY TO GO."[16]

Jonathan Clements, Wall Street Journal

> "THE PAST DECADE HAS SEEN A BIG PUSH AMONG PLANNERS TO TARGET HIGH-NET-WORTH CLIENTS. THEREFORE, MANY PLANNERS HAVE A

MINIMUM ASSET REQUIREMENT — TYPICALLY, $100,000. CONSIDERING THAT U.S. HOUSEHOLDS HAVE A MEDIAN NET WORTH OF $40,000, THAT LEAVES A LOT OF FOLKS IN THE COLD. LUCKILY, MIDDLE CLASS CLIENTS HAVE ALTERNATIVES ...PLANNERS WHO WORK PRIMARILY WITH THE $100,000-AND-UNDER INCOME SET, CHARGING HOURLY FEES FOR PERIODIC ADVICE."[17]

Nkiru Asika Oluwasanmi, Smart Money

Trends in Fee-Only Planning

All in all, fee-only financial planning is the fastest growing segment of the planning profession. The majority of fee-only financial planners also manage money on a continual and ongoing basis for their clients. There are also many fee-only advisors who manage money exclusively.

The FPA indicates that approximately 20% of their members are fee-only advisors. Unfortunately, we have found no statistics on the actual number of fee-only financial planners. NAPFA is the largest group of purely fee-only practitioners in the country, with approximately 850 members. Their definition of "fee-only" (stated above) drastically limits the number of potential members. One of the criteria for membership in NAPFA is that all compensation must be paid directly by the client. No third party compensation is permitted.

The statistics provided by the FPA (indicating that 20% of their members are fee-only) probably include fee-only money managers and fee-based financial planners who offer a fee-only option. Financial planners who offer both a fee-only option and fee- and commission-based services are tailoring their compensation structures in an attempt to satisfy the needs and desires of clients. However, I feel the most significant reason for charging on a fee-only basis is the removal of potential conflicts of interest related to compensation. Therefore, offering fee-only as an *option*, rather than *exclusively*, leads some clients to question the objectivity of the compensation structure as well as the recommendations.

Consumers engage financial planners to help them simplify their financial lives and attain their financial goals. They want trusted advisors who will listen to them, objectively evaluate their situations, and develop affordable and simple financial plans. Some clients need and want to delegate the implementation and monitoring responsibilities of their financial plans and investment portfolios to their advisors. However, many clients, particularly those in the Middle Market, do not have financial situations complex enough to justify having full-time financial advisors. Unfortunately, there are not nearly enough competent, objective advisors offering their services on a periodic or as-needed basis to meet the demands of the general public.

As stated above, the fastest growing segment of the financial planning industry is fee-only. One indication of public demand for fee-only advice is the volume of consumer inquiries received by the National Association of Personal Financial Advisors (NAPFA). In 2001, NAPFA received almost 30,000 inquiries to their consumer response program. On the other hand, the Financial Planning Association (FPA), with over 30,000 members, received only slightly more than NAPFA. Both organizations are very active in public awareness. However, the public appears to be responding much more favorably to NAPFA's message.

As noted earlier, the press also carries the fee-only torch. Over the last few years, the publishers of *Worth*, *Mutual Funds* and *Medical Economics* magazines have produced lists of top financial advisors in the country. The majority of the advisors named in these publications are fee-only. I am not implying that these lists are scientifically compiled or in any way exhaustive. However, consumers are obviously getting the message that the majority of the best financial advisors in the country work exclusively on a fee-only basis.

Many fee-only financial planners select this compensation structure for philosophical reasons. Others feel that they have an overwhelming marketing advantage by working on a fee-only basis. We all know outstanding financial advisors who are compensated in many different ways. But, it's becoming apparent that consumers seeking a financial planner are actively seeking out fee-only advisors. All financial advisors must market their services and themselves. However, most NAPFA members I know report that their marketing activities are minimal or nonexistent; instead, consumers are seeking them out.

I frequently receive phone calls and e-mails from consumers stating they sought advice from a fee-only advisor only to discover that they did not meet the advisor's client profile. Middle Market consumers frequently do not have adequate assets or income, or sufficiently complex financial situations to justify the minimum fees imposed by many fee-only advisors. These consumers have read the same publications discussing the advantages of working with a fee-only advisor as their affluent counterparts. Unfortunately, there are not enough fee-only financial planners offering services on a periodic or as-needed basis to meet the needs of the general public. Herein lies the greatest opportunity for reaching these "untapped Middle Markets."

In order for our industry to truly evolve into the profession of financial planning, I feel we must separate our compensation from the implementation of insurance and investment products and the investment portfolio. Our still-emerging profession must develop practice models that will enable *all* consumers to benefit from professional financial advice.

Middle Market consumers are beginning to seek out fee-only financial planners, and this trend will continue. However, most Middle Market consumers do not qualify for, will not justify the costs of, and possibly don't need the services of a full-time financial advisor. But *all* consumers periodically have questions about their personal finances and they need access to competent, objective advisors who can work with them on their terms.

These are the reasons I so strongly advocate the fee-only, hourly-as-needed service model. To me, it is simply the most effective and equitable way to serve people at all levels of income and net worth, while meeting the widest variety of client needs.

Whether or not you choose to serve your clients on a fee-only hourly basis as I do, my primary mission in writing in this book is to increase mainstream America's access to competent, objective financial advice that is tailored to meet their specific needs and budgets. I hope to inspire other practitioners to become "All-American Planners." In the following chapters we will explore ways to efficiently – and profitably – serve the Middle Market.

In Chapter 4, I'll address some of the myths that surround serving the Middle Market and do-it-yourself investors. I'll also present reasons why more financial planners should consider catering to this appreciative, and still virtually untapped, Middle Market. We'll get into financial planning basics for the middle income client in Chapter 5, and then cover a variety of marketing communications strategies in Chapter 6.

ENDNOTES

1. *Why Select a Fee-Only* Advisor, National Association of Personal Financial Advisors (NAPFA), at: http://www.napfa.org/ConsumerServices/whyfee.htm.

2. Jonathan R. Macey, *White Paper on the Regulation of Financial Planners*, Financial Planning Association, pp. 4-5 (April 2002), *quoting* John P. Moriarty & Curtlan R. McNeilly, *Regulation of Financial Planners*, §§2.01, 2-1 (West Group, Vol. 29 Securities Law Series, 2001).

3. Id.

4. Id.

5. Bill Pusateri, guest columnist, "A Fee-Based Journey – Too Old for New Tricks?," *The Referral Minute* (Bill Cates, Referral Coach International, 2002), at: Bill Cates@ReferralCoach.com. The Million Dollar Round Table is the premier association for the world's best sales professionals in the life insurance-based financial services business. The Top of the Table designation is reserved for the top producers from the MDRT group.

6. Jane Bryant Quinn, "Don't Get Burned by Fee-Only Planners," *Washington Post* (January 28, 1997) at: http://www.washingtonpost.com/wp-srv/business/longterm/quinn/columns/012897.htm.

7. Macey, at p. 5.

8. Moss and Adams, LLP, *2001 FPA Staffing and Compensation Study of Financial Planning Practitioners*. pp. 6, 11.

9. Id. at p. 2.

10. Jonathan Clements, "Some Advice Worth Paying For: Most Planners Cost Too Much," *The Wall Street Journal*, p. D1 (August 7, 2002).

11. See http://www.napfa.org/Media/Press/ar_misc.htm; and http://www.napfa.org/ConsumerServices/consumers_brochures.htm.

12. Jonathan Clements, "Some Advice Worth Paying For: Most Planners Cost Too Much," *Wall Street Journal*, p. D1 (August 7, 2002).

13. Linda Stern, "It's Time for a Checkup," *Newsweek*, p. 67 (April 1, 2002), *quoting* NAPFA member, Gary Schatsky.

14. Mary Rowland, "Financial Advice for the Little Guy," MSN Money Central (April 1, 2002), at: http://www.moneycentral.com/content/P20066.asp?.

15. Mary Rowland, *Bloomberg Wealth Manager* (July 3, 2002).

16. Jonathan Clements, "Think Picking Stocks is Tough? Try Selecting a Financial Adviser?" *Wall Street Journal*, p. D1 (May 22, 2002).

17. Nkiru Asika Oluwasanmi, "Ten Things Your Financial Planner Won't Tell You," *Smart Money* (December 18, 2001) at: http://www.smartmoney.com/consumer/index.cfm?story=tenthings-january02.

Chapter 4

WHY YOU SHOULD CONSIDER CATERING TO THE MIDDLE MARKET

MY BASIC PRINCIPLE IS THAT YOU DON'T MAKE DECISIONS BECAUSE THEY ARE EASY; YOU DON'T MAKE THEM BECAUSE THEY ARE CHEAP; YOU DON'T MAKE THEM BECAUSE THEY ARE POPULAR; YOU MAKE THEM BECAUSE THEY'RE RIGHT!

– Fr. Theodore Hesburgh, Former President, University of Notre Dame

There are numerous reasons why I advocate tailoring your services to the Middle Market. Strategic business factors include:

- **VAST OPPORTUNITY:** The majority of the untapped opportunities are in the Middle Market. There is little or no competition in this market. The overwhelming majority of the American population – approximately 70%-88% of all Americans – falls within the Middle Market definition, so the opportunity is truly vast.

- **NEED AND AWARENESS:** The average consumer's awareness of their need for professional guidance, with regard to the management of their personal finances, is greater than ever. The need – and the awareness of the need – is already there.

- **EASE OF MARKETING:** Marketing efforts are aided greatly by the fact that the media loves objective advisors who cater to their readers (most of whom are middle Americans). Opportunities for referrals are also greatly enhanced since the majority of today's independent financial advisors are targeting a more affluent clientele. Professionals who choose to target and serve the affluent, exclusively, can become your best allies and referral sources. They need other trusted advisors to whom they can refer the prospective clients that don't fit into their service model.

But, while the strategic business factors noted above are important, the *most important* reason I advocate catering to the Middle Market is the:

- **SENSE OF SATISFACTION:** The sense of personal satisfaction and enjoyment one can receive as an independent, trusted advisor to middle America is unequalled in my opinion. In building this profession of financial planning, our predecessors had the foresight to recognize that our moral responsibility as a profession is to help clients make smarter financial decisions by utilizing the financial planning process, and I wholeheartedly agree with this goal. Working with the underserved Middle Market can provide a great sense of personal and professional fulfillment.

VAST OPPORTUNITY

As I mentioned in Chapter 2, the majority of financial planners target an affluent clientele. The wealthy represent only about 2% of American households. Furthermore, the majority of financial planners target delegators, exclusively, which further narrows the opportunity base for those competing for clients within that segment of the population. According to Forrester Research, only 35% of all investors are delegators.[1] Regardless of the fact that not all Americans are investors, this statistic reminds us just how enormous the untapped Middle Market is.

As explained in Chapter 2, "middle income" may be statistically defined as 70% of all households in the United States. This means there are an estimated 105,000,000 middle income households in the United States today, yet – amazingly – most of these people are not target clients of typical financial planners today!

Compare the numbers and consider the opportunity:

- 105,000,000 middle income households (or 70% of the American population)

versus

- 7,000,000 affluent households (less than 5% of the American population)

As baseball movie "Bull Durham" star Susan Sarandon said, "hit 'em where they ain't." In other words, find the open spots on the field and target your energies there. Why follow the herd and target a narrow market when there is a vast, untapped market waiting for you? Why compete where the competition is most fierce when you can stand out as being unique by simply working with regular folk? I contend that it's easier to develop a service model that can effectively and profitably provide financial planning advice to middle Americans.

EVEN LESS COMPETITION IN THE *FEE-ONLY*, MIDDLE MARKET ARENA

There's even less competition for the Middle Market in the world of *fee-only* financial planning. Consumers are beginning to seek out the advice of fee-only financial planners. More and more, they're recognizing the benefits of paying a professional directly for advice. Consumers are becoming increasingly aware of, and more knowledgeable about, the value of hiring a professional when they need guidance in a variety of areas – whether it be legal, medical, or other professional services – and they are increasingly willing to pay directly for that advice.

As explained in Chapter 2, the press is one of the strongest advocates of fee-only financial planning (we'll revisit this topic in Chapter 6). The media can be your greatest partner in spreading the word to consumers about the benefits of working with a competent and objective advisor. The public is hungry for more information, understanding and wisdom regarding money management. Consumer finance journalists will continue to play a major role in the development and public awareness activities of our newly emerging profession.

MIDDLE MARKET SENSIBILITIES

Middle Market consumers have limited resources and, therefore, must make cost-effective decisions regarding how they spend their money. As the authors of *The Millionaire Next Door* revealed, millionaires generally "believe that financial independence is more important than displaying high social status."[2] You can't spend it all now and still have it working for you in the future. With regard to achieving financial independence, income doesn't matter as much as what one saves and how one invests and protects one's wealth.

If most Americans are ever to achieve financial independence, they must embrace frugality. They must learn to live below their means. They must also become good stewards of their resources, whether that be with regard to consumer purchases, major expenditures (e.g., purchasing a home), or prudently investing and protecting the assets they have accumulated.

Frugal people are not likely to justify spending hundreds or even thousands of dollars, year after year, for professional financial planning advice unless they *know* they will come out ahead. Who's to say that the informed consumer, now making sound financial decisions — with the occasional guidance of a competent, objective advisor — won't end up wealthier?

There is so much quality, publicly-available personal finance information available these days that a consumer who's willing to do his homework can now have access to, and gain knowledge about, financial planning matters that were once reserved for the highly-trained (and highly paid) financial services professionals.

And now there are advisors – "All-American Planners" – who cater to these validators and do-it-yourselfers!

As financial planners, we warn clients about excesses in mutual fund expenses, brokerage commissions, mortgage closing costs, insurance commissions, credit card rates, etc. The frugal advisor will guide her clients toward cost-effective alternatives, while at the same time assisting her clients in achieving financial independence.

ADDING VALUE BY MEETING IMMEDIATE NEEDS

Some advisors are discovering that they must continue to add services to ensure that their clients will perceive them as being a good value. One way to enhance your perception so that clients will deem your services a good value is to charge an hourly or project-based fee, and to provide advice or guidance that is focused *exclusively* on *the most immediate* issues facing the client at the time.

I have a lot of colleagues who refuse to take on a new engagement unless it starts out with a comprehensive financial plan. While I would love it if everyone could afford, and desired, to engage their advisors in comprehensive planning, realistically, however, many people can't afford and often don't require a truly comprehensive financial plan. I strongly advocate a comprehensive approach to financial planning for all clients, but at my firm the most we provide is what I call, "basic-yet-comprehensive financial planning services." We also offer advice on any portion of the client's financial situation that most needs assistance *now.*

Some advisors pride themselves on analyzing every segment of a client's financial situation to the "nth" degree. Unfortunately, most middle Americans can't – and I argue don't — need to pay for that level of analysis. As many of my clients have said to me over the years, "I'm not that complicated!"

Working in the Middle Market requires the planner to know when "enough is enough." It's our job as planners to help clients allocate their resources for the maximum utility. We have to step back and ask ourselves, "What would I do or provide if this were a beloved family member for whom I feel responsible?" When posed like that, we often find ways to be of significant help to our clients without using every tool and technique known to a CFP®.

As mentioned earlier, many consumers don't want or won't hire a full-time financial advisor. But all people have questions or concerns about their personal finances at one time or another. By allowing clients to engage us – one project at a time – they can access professional advice as their budgets and cash flow allows.

FRUGAL CLIENTS, FRUGAL PLANNERS

The "Millionaire Next Door" is a *self-made* millionaire. Typically, these individuals did not achieve millionaire status until after they were 50. They were originally middle income Americans. And most importantly, they were, and continue to be, frugal.

The majority of financial planning professionals target upper-income and upper-net worth clients who are willing to spend $2,000 or more annually for ongoing financial advisory services. When those advisors receive inquiries from consumers they cannot profitably or effectively serve, they benefit from referring those persons to a trustworthy advisor who can and *wants* to serve that type of client.

I have a dear colleague who would be bored to death with the level of financial planning subject matter I deal with on a daily basis. He most enjoys the challenge of technically difficult planning strategies and opportunities. He really loves complex cases. Thank goodness there are quality advisors out there who love this part of the business. I occasionally run into clients needing this level of sophistication, and I'm relieved to know advisors who specialize in these complex areas. My practice would drive him to distraction with the volume of meetings and personalities. Correspondingly, the depth into which he delves would give me a migraine. Each practice compliments the other. We are in no way competitors. My colleague and I have each recognized and passionately embraced the markets we serve.

PRIMARY REFERRAL SOURCES

Established financial planning professionals (like the colleague I described above) can become your primary referral sources, rather then your competition. Successful financial advisors who work exclusively with affluent clients are greatly relieved to know that there are competent and objective advisors willing and able to serve the Middle Market. High profile, top-end financial planners receive a lot of inquiries from people they would like to be able to help (I know, I used to be one of them). Taking on every client who comes their way would drive some practitioners to distraction and put some practices out of business. However, the top-end planners can help by referring individuals who do not fit their target client profile to professionals — like you and me — who want to work with these clients.

When I initially established my hourly, as-needed practice, successful wealth managers directed the majority of my new business to me. Now, the media and my clients are the most significant part of my sales force. Remember, the larger your client base, the more potential referral sources you have.

The press also makes it possible for us to gain exposure to the masses. I find that there are several primary factors that result in journalists contacting me (I'll elaborate more on these in Chapter 6), but the primary reason they do so is that they need a "quotable" resource – that is, someone who can speak to their readers (most of whom are Middle Market Americans).

THE MIDDLE MARKET IS A MEDIA-FRIENDLY STORY

Here's an example of a "quotable" quote from a recent article by Jonathan Clements in the *Wall Street Journal*:

> *"'I DON'T BELIEVE MOST AMERICANS NEED A FULL-TIME FINANCIAL ADVISER,' SAYS FINANCIAL PLANNER SHERYL GARRETT. 'BUT THEY DO NEED SOMEBODY WHOM THEY CAN CALL FOR ADVICE ON OCCASION.' DETRACTORS CARP THAT CHARGING BY THE HOUR DOESN'T WORK, BECAUSE CLIENTS ARE RELUCTANT TO PICK UP THE PHONE. MS. GARRETT'S RESPONSE? SHE ARGUES THAT THE TICKING CLOCK MAKES CLIENTS MORE FOCUSED. 'WHAT I HAVE FOUND IS THAT PEOPLE GET THEIR ACT TOGETHER BEFORE THEY CALL,' SHE SAYS. 'WE DON'T WASTE TIME ON IDLE CHIT-CHAT.'"[3]*

While the above quote is a bit bold, it is also honest and authentic. More importantly, it's the kind of quote the consumer press likes. I knew going into that interview that I would need to be able to differentiate myself and my services – and to say something "quotable."

Regarding the media's need for someone who can speak to their readers (most of whom are Middle Market Americans), here are some stories that should illustrate key points to remember:

The business editor of a major metropolitan newspaper once told me that when her new reporters get an assignment to interview a high-profile financial advisor they are, at least initially, extremely excited. However, after interviewing some of these high-profile advisors, they become disenchanted with much of our industry. Why? Because they find out that they personally could never hire any one of these advisors.

Consider this summary from an article called "Mixed Messages" in *Investment Advisor* magazine, in which Assistant Managing Editor, Karen Hansen Weese, laments:

"IT OCCASIONALLY STRIKES ME HOW MANY OF THE PLANNERS I TALK WITH EVERY DAY WOULDN'T ACCEPT ME AS A CLIENT BECAUSE OF THE AMOUNT OF MONEY I DON'T HAVE."[4]

The most stunning interchange the writer ever had was with a planner who said:

"IN THE WORLD OF FINANCIAL PLANNING FIRMS, THERE ARE BMWs AND THERE ARE FORDS. I HAVE BUILT MY PRACTICE FOR PEOPLE WHO DRIVE BMWs....I DON'T DENY THAT THERE ARE PEOPLE WHO DRIVE FORDS, ... BUT, WELL, THERE ARE OTHER PLANNERS OUT THERE FOR THEM."[5]

When the writer said she drove a Ford, and was actually quite fond of it, the advisor no doubt felt a bit embarrassed. Later in the article, Ms. Weese mentioned me, my practice, and a handful of other advisors who are focused on "serv[ing] the not-so-rich with hourly fees."[6] "[A]ll kinds of professionals, from accountants to attorneys, psychiatrists to consultants, charge by the hour," Weese wrote. "Perhaps it's time to give hourly fees a second look."[7]

Over the years, I've heard many similar comments from the professional journalists I've worked with. When M.P. Dunleavey contacted me regarding an article she was writing for MSN MoneyCentral titled "You're Never too Poor to Plan," I learned that her assignment was to find several financial advisers who were able to offer her, personally, an affordable financial plan and personalized, objective advice. While I won't share any of the details we discussed during our telephone conversations, I will share this excerpt from the resulting article:

"I'VE ALWAYS WANTED A FINANCIAL ADVISER. PREFERABLY AN OLDER PERSON WITH SPECTACLES AND A SYMPATHETIC SMILE, WHO WOULD DEVISE CUNNING STRATEGIES FOR ME TO MANAGE MY MONEY FOR THE REST OF MY LIFE. THE FANTASY ALWAYS FALLS APART WHEN I REMEMBER THAT I HARDLY HAVE ANY MONEY TO MANAGE. WHAT FINANCIAL PLANNER WORTH HIS SALT WOULD BE WILLING TO HELP ME

INVEST MY MEAGER ASSETS WHEN THERE ARE RICH FOLKS SUFFERING FROM LACK OF A TAX SHELTER?

THE FINANCIAL PLANNING WORLD IS A-CHANGING. FOR THE FIRST TIME, THE BUZZ ISN'T ABOUT BIG, WEALTHY CLIENTS, IT'S ABOUT THE LITTLE GUY. YOU AND ME. THE FREE, THE PROUD, THE BROKE.

NOW YOU CAN GET YOUR FINANCIAL PLANS DONE CAFETERIA-STYLE. AND IT'S CHEAP. OR IT CAN BE. WITH A LITTLE MUSCLE, I DUG UP FOUR FINANCIAL ADVISERS WHO WERE ABLE TO OFFER ME A PLAN FOR $500 OR LESS. CONSIDERING THAT THE TYPICAL FEE IS UPWARD OF $2,000, THAT'S A BARGAIN.'" [8]

Journalists are professionals, regardless of whether we agree or disagree with their journalistic stylings. Everybody wants to feel valued and respected. If journalists sense that they aren't important enough to be your client, they may determine that you're not the appropriate person to be their resource partner. On the other hand, if you're tailoring your services to the Middle Market, professional journalists should be more eager to speak with you.

A great deal of your success in marketing to the middle can come from positioning yourself as a trusted and valuable resource for the mainstream media.

INDUSTRY SUPPORT, ADVICE FOR *ALL* AMERICANS

One of the missions of the Financial Planning Association (FPA) is to raise public awareness regarding the importance of financial planning for all people. The National Association of Personal Financial Advisors (NAPFA) has also gotten very active in researching effective fee-only practice models that serve the Middle Market. They are currently sharing this information at NAPFA's Basic Training Conferences. Every NAPFA conference now has at least one significant practice management session geared toward serving the Middle Market on a fee-only basis. Some of the most successful fee-only advisors share their insights and practice management tips during these sessions.

FPA has been offering a "Bridge the Gap" session at their national conference for the past few years, as well. At the "Bridge the Gap" session, newer financial planners and financial planning students (or veteran planners who might be interested in the subject matter) learn practical information from experienced, successful financial planners on how to develop a financial planning practice and where to find financial planning career opportunities. More often than not, Middle Market, fee-only services are discussed at some length.

Thus, two of the most prominent organizations in the financial planning industry feel that providing competent and objective financial advice to *all* Americans is part of what will make us a truly respected profession. I wholeheartedly agree. How many of the other professions (law, medicine, accountancy, psychology, etc.) have members who elect to serve only the wealthiest 10% or 20% of Americans? The answer: all of them do. And all professionals certainly have the right to serve any particular market niche they choose. But none of the other professions so blatantly underserves the Middle Market as does the financial planning profession. Yet, the Middle Market is the part of our population that may need us most.

HIGH-LEVEL OF JOB SATISFACTION

The primary reason I choose to cater to the Middle Market is for job satisfaction. I really enjoy working with average Americans who are interested in taking a proactive role in the management of their personal finances. These individuals are often interested in enhancing their education, developing a better understanding of, and gaining more wisdom regarding their financial options and opportunities. They seek an advisor who can listen to them, communicate with them, and relate to their position in life.

I personally get the most satisfaction from being able to provide an average American with the type of solutions that can appreciably enhance their lives. I can make a significant difference in the lives of middle Americans. When I worked for wealth management firms in the past, there were occasions with certain clients when I felt more like a personal financial secretary than a valued, respected professional financial advisor.

Clients often tell me that they have been searching for a financial advisor like me, but their searches were initially very frustrating. Several clients have stated they "thought this [i.e., hourly] was how all financial planners worked...until they tried to find one." Without prior experience working with a financial services professional, many clients presume that financial consultants structure their services much like the majority of other consultants in the country. But, in reality, project- or hourly based, fee-only financial advisors are very few and far between.

CONSUMERS ARE EAGER FOR ADVICE

Recently, my office received a phone call from a frustrated consumer. She had visited NAPFA's web site and obtained the names of several fee-only planners in her area. She began calling these advisors to inquire about establishing a working relationship. By the time she called my office, she was hopping mad, and very sad.

As the details unfurled, I learned that every other fee-only advisor she'd called so far had turned her away. "Won't you please work with me," she almost begged. "I know I only have $480,000 and most of it is tied up in my 401(k), but I really need the help."

Stories like this tug at my heart, and they are not at all uncommon. We get them all the time, and are happy to assist these callers. The fact that the other planners she'd called had not only turned her away, but had turned her away empty-handed without even a referral to someone who could help her on her own terms, only underscores the fact that there is much work to be done to spread the word (both to consumers and to other advisors).

The message is this: There are a growing number of competent, objective advisors who will work with Middle Market and do-it-yourself clients. We want these average Americans. They are our ideal clients. Send them our way. We will help them!

On the other hand, not all my clients have been turned away from asset management firms. In fact, not all of my clients are young, middle income, and/or struggling. And I sometimes receive inquiries from prospective clients who have been working with an advisor on an assets under management basis. They are curious to explore how we might work together. Until they read about my fee-only, hourly practice in the popular consumer press or hear about me from a colleague, they believe that they are relatively happy with the retainer-based relationship they have with their current investment advisor or financial planner.

But when Jonathan Clements goes on record in the *Wall Street Journal* saying that "most planners cost too much" due to potentially unnecessary and/or high asset management fees, consumers take note.[9] And when Linda Stern says in *Newsweek* that "no-commission advice is a good idea, but it's possible to overpay a fee, too. If all you are getting is asset allocation, [that's] pretty darned pricey," consumers may rethink previous decisions.[10]

Just this week, a gentleman whom I'd known and worked with before (in my old incarnation as an advisor to the affluent) called to say he'd read the Clements article (quoted above) in the *Wall Street Journal*. He referred to both of my quotes and to Mr. Clements' thoughts regarding the benefits of working with an hourly, as-needed advisor. He shared a bit of information about his personal financial situation, and recapped the assets under management agreement he had in place at a local wealth management firm.

The Clements article had sparked his interest!

After several years of ongoing management, he wondered if the fees he was paying were still a good value. We could calculate the approximate amount of time needed to monitor and review his holdings and maintain his portfolio's balance. He admitted that he enjoyed his personal interactions with the advisor, but didn't care about the newsletters, quarterly reports and other "value-added services" that were being offered. While I was hesitant to sell him on my services, or convince him right then and there that he'd be better off utilizing an hourly, as-needed approach, he pressed me for an initial consultation. We agreed to meet to further review his needs and determine if periodic check-ups under the hourly, as-needed service model might better suit him. Frankly, I could tell from the initial conversation that I'd be able to provide the services he needed and deemed important — while substantially reducing the fees he had been paying on retainer.

SUCCESSFUL, AND STILL VALUE-ORIENTED

Consumers who engage my services on an hourly, as-needed basis after paying asset management fees are thrilled with the savings and the value. They tell their friends. They don't quibble over their bills or challenge my $180-an-hour rate. In spite of being able to pay asset management fees and meet the account minimums imposed by other firms, these consumers are still value-oriented. And compared to an ongoing retainer-based service, the fees they'll pay to me for my periodically scheduled services seem more than reasonable to them.

While they may be highly successful individuals, they still hold working-class values. They are either "Millionaires Next Door" or "Millionaires-in-the-Making." Why should they pay for more help and supervision than they need and want to simply because they can afford to pay for it?

DEBUNKING THE MYTHS

In this chapter, I've highlighted a number of opportunities and benefits in working with the Middle Market. However, there are a lot of naysayers out there. I'd like to spend some time sharing my responses to the primary criticisms I hear about serving this market.

1. **"You Can't Make a Living."**

First, let's define what "a living" is. My billing rate is $3 per minute, which is not unlike the rate of many consultants from other professions. Why is it that an attorney charging the same rate per hour can make a living, but financial planners cannot? We *can* make a living working with the Middle Market if our service model enables us to be compensated for all of our work, and we can work efficiently enough to meet our billable hours objective.

My personal objective is to bill out 50% of the time I allocate to financial planning work. I find that this objective requires concentration and discipline, but it's doable. I also have two CERTIFIED FINANCIAL PLANNER® practitioners on staff now, and I receive a portion of their billings. Although overhead generally runs about 40%, mine stays under 33%. You do the math and determine if this looks like a professional living to you.

2. **"Clients Won't Pay For It."**

Some people won't, that's a fact. But there are plenty of people who will. Middle Market practitioners offering their services for a fee report that consumers do indeed pay for advice. In fact, those practitioners are thriving! Middle Market consumers may be very conscious of *how much* they pay, but do *not* deny the fact that they have to pay. They recognize that there is no "free lunch," and they're willing to pay a professional advisor for expertise and objectivity.

3. **"We Won't be Able to be Compensated for the Value We Provide."**

Frequently, the most valuable services planners provide to clients are intangible. We confirm whether clients are on track to achieve their objectives and we validate and improve upon their strategies and approaches. We help make whatever adjustments are necessary along the way. How can we put a dollar figure on the intangible values we provide?

I use the example of a visit to the doctor's office. Should one pay more for an office visit that reveals a life threatening illness? If so, how do you place a value on it? Of what value is an office visit to a patient who discovers they don't have a life threatening illness, when they couldn't sleep for days worrying they might have something seriously wrong with them?

One of my favorite personalities in our industry advocates value-based pricing. I think the concept has great merit; however, in my opinion determining the appropriate value for the broad range of services we provide is nearly impossible. We can adjust the fee we charge for a specific project, based on complexity as well as time involved. But, as I mentioned earlier, it's nearly impossible to put a dollar figure on many of the intangible services we provide.

I charge for my time and energy — that's easy to communicate and it's easy to understand. (See Figure 4.1 at the end of this chapter for a copy of my "Client Service Agreement – Hourly Engagement" form.) And I feel that it's the most equitable way for the client to compensate the advisor. Advisors must feel they are being adequately compensated for the work they do. I like hourly. It works for me.

4. **"IMPLEMENTATION WON'T GET DONE."**

The most enjoyable part of my job is working *with* clients and providing *advice*. The thing I least liked about some of my previous roles in financial planning was all the paperwork (filling out forms, transferring money, etc.).

Now I provide specific advice and recommendations, as well as step-by-step instructions so that the clients can implement those recommendations on their own. In rare circumstances, we'll assist special needs clients with certain stages of the implementation process (such as an elderly client who needs assistance in securing a bond portfolio, transferring or retitling assets; or clients who are unable or unwilling to complete the implementation steps themselves).

An important key to success for hourly as-needed practitioners is to increase the percentage of billable hours. You can't bill a client accurately if you don't properly estimate the time involved when you give them your fee quote. Like many other planners I speak with, I also tend to underestimate the amount of time it takes to carry out various implementation steps (primarily because there are so many variables involved). However, if I transfer the implementation responsibility to the client, while continuing to serve as their guide or coach, I can continue to do what I do best — provide advice and coaching — and I can bill for it. This drastically reduces my fee to the client, and it allows me to focus on the parts of my job that I love.

Virtually all of my recommendations are implemented — by the clients themselves. Part of the reason for this high success rate is my approach. When clients come to me, they are expecting me to supply them with advice, guidance and clear instructions on how to implement my recommendations. They know going into the relationship that they will be responsible for carrying out their plan.

The majority of my clients are validators or do-it-yourselfers (see Chapter 1), and they've never worked with another advisor (or at least no one they considered their trusted advisor). They've managed their personal finances on their own in the past, but now feel it's appropriate (or necessary) to have a professional occasionally review their situation.

5. **"Don't You Worry About Liability Exposure?"**

Because I limit the scope of my engagements to specific issues or tasks, and then communicate these limitations in writing to the client, I feel that I am exposed to fewer liability concerns than some planners who communicate that their services are comprehensive. Planners themselves define the term "comprehensive" differently — so imagine how the legal profession and disgruntled clients (or clients' children) will define our "comprehensive" responsibilities.

6. **"Developing a Practice to Serve the Middle Market is Not Building a Business You Can Sell."**

Many financial planners want to operate a practice, not build a business. Building a business requires many additional things. To build a business, one must first build a practice, then streamline and systematize the processes, and then train staff to follow the same procedures and produce the same results. Building a business involves managing and supervising people. Many financial planning practitioners are excellent technicians; they may even be pretty good entrepreneurs, but they can be lousy managers. I discovered that I am not a good manager, but I have surrounded myself with self-directed professionals who are helping me build a business.

Most purchases of financial planning firms are for the assets under management or some other type of annual, renewable income. Those who do not have contractual, renewable income may be able to transfer their client base to another advisor or newer planners they mentor. There is income potential for this type of service model if the transition is well planned and well executed.

In this chapter, we explored the primary reasons why I feel practitioners should consider catering to the Middle Market. In Chapter 5, I'll offer tips and insights on the financial planning issues that matter most and that are common to most middle Americans. And in Chapter 6, we'll discuss effective marketing tactics and communications strategies for the "All-American Planner."

Figure 4.1

GARRETT FINANCIAL PLANNING, INC.
Client Service Agreement - Hourly Engagement

Please review this Agreement carefully as it sets forth the understanding between you ("Client") _____ and Garrett Financial Planning, Inc. ("GFP") regarding the services GFP will provide you. If you have any questions about the content of this Agreement we should discuss them before you sign this Agreement.

1. **INITIAL SERVICES.** GFP will provide consultations addressing the specific issue or issues you request as indicated below. GFP will provide you with a detailed financial analysis and recommendations to guide you toward the achievement of your objectives. GFP will limit its analysis to the specific areas indicated below. You understand that information regarding specific issues not revealed to or analyzed by GFP may have a direct impact on the suitability or accuracy of specific recommendations given.

2. **SPECIFIC SERVICES REQUESTED.** Please initial below to indicate the specific services you are requesting from GFP:

    ___ Cash flow analysis   ___ Retirement capital needs
                                              analysis
    ___ Current portfolio review or analysis   ___ Insurance review
    ___ Portfolio allocation and investment   ___ College education funding
        recommendations
    ___ Estate plan review   ___ Income tax planning

    Other services:

    ___ _____ ___ _____

    ___ _____ ___ _____

    Estimated Fee Range for Services:_____

3. **FUTURE SERVICES.** In addition to the specific services requested pursuant to this Agreement, GFP may provide you with financial advisory services in the future upon specific request from you. The scope of such services will be determined at the time such services are requested. Such additional services will be subject to the provisions of this Agreement, including the provisions relating to payment of fees and the limitations on GFP's duties and liabilities.

Figure 4.1 (Cont'd)

4. **FEES.** GFP's fees for advisory services, including future services, will be based primarily on the amount of time expended on your behalf and on the billing rate for each consultant devoting time to this matter. GFP's billing rates are currently $180 per hour for Lead Certified Financial Planners™, $150 for Staff Certified Financial Planners™, and $60 per hour for Paraplanners. These billing rates are subject to change upon written notice to you.

5. **PAYMENT OF FEES.** You agree to submit the lesser of $500 or one-half of estimated fee range (as indicated in paragraph 2, above) upon signing of this Agreement. The balance of actual fees for initial services provided will be due and payable to GFP immediately upon presentation of recommendations to you. GFP will invoice you for the amount of fees for any future services performed. Payment of such invoices shall be made within twenty (20) days of the date of the invoice.

6. **CLIENT REPRESENTATIONS.** You represent to GFP the following and understand and agree that GFP is relying on these representations as an inducement to enter into this Agreement:

    -   You agree that you will provide GFP with the necessary information to provide the agreed upon services.

    -   You understand that the responsibility for financial decisions is yours and that you are under no obligation to follow, either wholly or in part, any recommendation or suggestion provided by GFP.

    -   You understand that GFP obtains information from a wide variety of publicly available sources and cannot guarantee the accuracy of the information or success of the advice which it may provide. The information and recommendations developed by GFP are based on the professional judgment of GFP and the information you provide to GFP. You agree that GFP will not be liable for errors of fact or judgment as long as it acts in good faith; provided, however, that securities laws impose liabilities under certain circumstances on persons who act in good faith, and nothing in this Agreement shall in any way limit or waive any rights you may have under federal or state securities laws.

    -   You understand and agree that due to the limited nature of this engagement GFP is under no obligation to contact you to recommend changes to your financial plan or any of the recommendations and advice provided under this Agreement in the future.

Figure 4.1 (Cont'd)

- You understand that all investments involve risks and that some investment decisions will result in losses. You understand that GFP cannot guarantee that your investment objectives will be achieved.

- You understand and agree that, except as otherwise provided herein, GFP will not be liable for any loss incurred as a result of the services provided to you by GFP.

- You understand and agree that GFP performs services for other clients and may make recommendations to those clients that differ from the recommendations made to you. You agree that GFP does not have any obligation to recommend for purchase or sale any security or other asset it may recommend to any other client.

7. **CONFIDENTIALITY OF INFORMATION.** GFP will regard any information provided by you as confidential.

8. **TERMINATION.** This Agreement may be terminated at any time upon written notice to either GFP or you. If this Agreement is terminated by either party all fees due at time of termination will be due and payable by you immediately. GFP will immediately refund any unearned, prepaid fees.

9. **IMPLEMENTATION OF INVESTMENTS.** At your direction, GFP will assist with the implementation of investment and other recommendations. GFP will not initiate a transaction in any investment account without prior approval of Client.

10. **MULTIPLE CLIENTS.** In the event Client is more than one individual, GFP is authorized to accept the direction of either party and such direction will be binding on all parties.

11. **COMMISSIONS.** The Client understands GFP will not receive commissions on transactions that may result from the implementation of the Client's financial plan.

12. **ASSIGNMENT.** GFP will not assign the Agreement to any other party without your written consent.

13. **GOVERNING LAW.** This Agreement shall be governed by the laws of the State of Kansas.

Figure 4.1 (Cont'd)

CLIENT HEREBY ACKNOWLEDGES RECEIPT OF GARRETT FINANCIAL PLAN-
NING'S FORM ADV PART II ON _____.

ACCEPTED this ____ of _____, _____   Client _____

     (day)   (month)   (year)

                                               Client _____

_____

Signature on behalf of Garrett Financial Planning, Inc.

ENDNOTES

1. Lewis Braham, "Online Advice: Remote – and Reassuring," *BW Online* (May 28, 2001);http://www.businessweek.com/magazine/content/01_22/b3734024.htm.

2. Stanley and Danko, *The Millionaire Next Door*, p. 4 (Simon & Schuster, 1996).

3. Jonathan Clements, "Some Advice Worth Paying For: Most Planners Cost Too Much," *Wall Street Journal*, p. D1 (August 7, 2002).

4. Karen Hansen Weese, "Mixed Messages," *Investment Advisor* (November 3, 2001) at http://www.investmentadvisor.com.

5. Id.

6. Id.

7. Id.

8. M.P. Dunleavey, MSN MoneyCentral, "*You're Never too Poor to Plan* " (January 14, 2002), at: http://moneycentral.msn.com/articles/family/basics/8558.asp.

9. Jonathan Clements, "Some Advice Worth Paying For: Most Planners Cost Too Much," *Wall Street Journal*, p. D1 (August 7, 2002)

10. Linda Stern, "It's Time for a Checkup," *Newsweek*, p. 67 (April 1, 2002).

Chapter 5

FINANCIAL PLANNING BASICS FOR THE MIDDLE INCOME CLIENT

A MARKET IS NEVER SATURATED WITH A GOOD PRODUCT, BUT IT IS VERY QUICKLY SATURATED WITH A BAD ONE.

–Henry Ford

Validators and do-it-yourselfers may have sufficient assets to invest in the extensive analysis and advice available from qualified financial advisors; however, most who characterize themselves as beginners, lower-middle and middle income individuals are not likely to need – or choose to pay for – the full range of analysis and advice provided by many experienced comprehensive financial planners. Therefore, *determining the appropriate level of services for a middle market client is one of the greatest challenges* facing practitioners who wish to serve this market segment.

Those of us who have completed course work and examinations to receive a certification, professional designation, or advanced degree in financial planning have been exposed to an enormous knowledge base. The CFP® Board of Standards has outlined the subject matter and procedures to be followed by CFP® practitioners in the production of financial plans. The subject matter is extremely comprehensive and the procedures are equally thorough. The six-step financial planning process endorsed by the CFP® Board of Standards (see Chapter One) includes the implementation and monitoring of financial plans by the advisor.

I agree that a practitioner should embrace a comprehensive approach to financial planning, assist with implementation (even if it's only coaching), and help clients monitor the success of their financial plan. But I don't believe that most Americans need to outsource the implementation and ongoing supervision of their personal finances to a professional advisor. Also, most average Americans do not need advice and services in all areas of financial planning. They do, however, need access to competent advisors who are trained and experienced in all areas of financial planning.

In my opinion, it is our job as advisors to:

- help clients determine what their needs are;

- assess what services are required at any given time; and

- decide how best to allocate resources to enable them to accomplish their objectives.

Middle America doesn't need, and can't afford, to hire us to perform every analysis that we're capable of performing. I assert that our responsibility is to quickly diagnose the situation and provide advice and solutions to address the current and most important needs now.

We must remember that financial planning is *a process*. Each and every area of a person's financial life need not be addressed during the first engagement. The development of a financial plan, as well as the advisory relationship, can and should evolve over time.

The owner of one of the wealth management firms I worked for impressed upon his staff to "do the doable." I apply this mantra on a daily basis when working with clients and prospective clients. I must be able to determine what they're willing to accept with regard to the services I recommend, the recommendations I may provide, and the fee that

I will charge. Then I attempt to "do the doable" by convincing the client to move ahead to address their most pressing needs and concerns *now*.

I'd much rather have a series of limited engagements with a client over time, eventually culminating in a comprehensive financial plan, than no engagement at all. This, of course, also serves the client's best interests. While a typical middle income or validator client may be apt to turn away from a more complete analysis and/or comprehensive plan, he may be more willing to take a series of steps toward the completion of a financial plan that will be worked out over time.

To work effectively with the Middle Market, it is imperative that planners gain skills to enable us to quickly hone in on a client's most critical financial planning issues, and determine how best to allocate their limited resources to address these issues.

In this chapter, we will focus on specific financial planning topics and commonly used strategies and tips I recommend for those practitioners working with middle income clients.

CASH FLOW

Determining a client's cash flow needs can be an extremely time consuming and painful exercise. We've all heard of many different strategies used in determining where money goes. Some advisors ask their clients to pour over months worth of check registers and credit card statements, categorize all expenditures, and provide them with an historical average monthly budget. While this exercise may be very enlightening to some clients, it also can be a deal breaker.

I've found that determining cash outflow is usually one of the most time-consuming and agonizing parts of the homework I could assign to a new client. To accurately gauge where their money has gone, the clients must be extremely committed to the process and have time to fulfill your request. I find that most clients come to me seeking answers, not homework assignments. In fact, if a prospective client determines that the work involved on their part is too significant, they may decide to just "skip all that" and cancel the engagement.

Therefore, we must find ways to ascertain a client's cash flow needs without jeopardizing the engagement. We must "do the doable."

Too often, I have discovered that "budgets" provided to me for my analysis are, in reality, the "best guesstimates" of what clients think their cash flow needs are. They provide listings containing every imaginable expenditure. In their attempt to be *thorough*, we discover that they "say" they plan to spend more than they even make. Individuals can't spend more then they take in unless they are depleting assets or going into debt. Clients have also provided me with "budgets" that implied they had regular surplus income, only to discover during the presentation of my analysis that they didn't have any surplus at all. Most Americans, by nature, spend whatever surplus we have. If we have no debts to pay or investments we know we must make, it all goes toward basic living expenses and/or things we want or think we need.

I determine the cash flow needs much more quickly and easily – and I feel, more accurately, too – than usually occurs using the conventional techniques. If I'm working with a wage earner, I start with the net income illustrated on their paycheck stub. I also need to know their liability payments, current investment contributions, insurance premiums and itemized deductions. This information can be readily obtained from my Confidential Questionnaire (which prospective clients complete prior to our initial meeting; see Figure 5.1), paycheck stubs, tax returns, investment account statements and insurance declaration statements. This is data we generally request for all new client engagements. Next, I subtract the current liability payments, insurance premiums and investments from the client's net pay to determine their basic living expenses. I presume that the clients are spending their net paychecks unless I have proof that they are saving part of this money or they are regularly going into debt.

Figure 5.1

Date of Completion:_____

GARRETT FINANCIAL PLANNING, INC.
CONFIDENTIAL QUESTIONNAIRE

CLIENT NAME (1): _____	CLIENT NAME (2): _____
Home Address: _____	Home Address: _____
City, State, Zip: _____	City, State, Zip: _____
Home Phone: _____	Home Phone: _____
Work Phone: _____	Work Phone: _____
Fax: (Home or Work) _____	Fax: (Home or Work) _____
E-mail: _____	E-mail: _____
Social Security #: _____	Social Security #: _____
Birthdate: _____	Birthdate: _____

Primary Contact Person during business hours?_____

Contact me by (circle one)
E-mail   or   Phone

FAMILY MEMBERS (PLEASE LIST CHILDREN AND OTHER DEPENDANTS.)

Name	Relationship	Date of Birth	Dependent	Resides? (City & State)
_____	_____	__/__/__	Y N	_____
_____	_____	__/__/__	Y N	_____
_____	_____	__/__/__	Y N	_____
_____	_____	__/__/__	Y N	_____

CLIENT EMPLOYER (1):	CLIENT EMPLOYER (2):
Title/Job: _____	Title/Job: _____
Number of years with this employer? _____	Number of years with this employer? _____
Anticipated employment changes? _____	Anticipated employment changes? _____
When do you plan to retire? _____	When do you plan to retire? _____
Salary: _____	Salary: _____
Self Employment Income: _____	Self Employment Income: _____
Bonus/Commissions: _____	Bonus/Commissions: _____
Other Earned Income: _____	Other Earned Income: _____
TOTAL (Current Yr) = _____	**TOTAL (Current Yr) =** _____

Figure 5.1 (Cont'd)

Who prepares your tax return?

Name _____

☐ Self
☐ Paid Preparer

Address _____

Phone (___) _____-_____

Fax   (___) _____-_____

Do you have estate planning documents?
When and in what state were they drafted?

Wills	Y N	_____
Living Trusts	Y N	_____
Power of Attorney	Y N	_____
Living Will	Y N	_____
Other Documents	Y N	_____

How were your current investment assets selected? _____
_____
_____

INDICATE WHICH OF THE FOLLOWING STATEMENTS SUMMARIZE YOUR ATTITUDES OR BELIEFS USING A SCALE OF 1-5.
(1 being most true and 5 least true)

_____ I would rather work longer than reduce my standard of living in retirement.
_____ I feel that I/we can reduce our current living expenses to save more for the future if needed.
_____ I am more concerned about protecting my assets than about growth.
_____ I prefer the ease of mutual funds over individual securities.
_____ I am comfortable with investments that promise slow, long-term appreciation and growth.
_____ I don't brood over bad investment decisions I've made.
_____ I feel comfortable with aggressive growth investments.
_____ I don't like surprises.
_____ I am optimistic about my financial future.
_____ My immediate concern is for income rather than growth opportunities.
_____ I am a risk taker.
_____ I make investment decisions comfortably and quickly.
_____ I like predictability and routine in my daily life.
_____ I usually pick the tried and true, the slow, safe but sure investments.
_____ I need to focus my investment efforts on building cash reserves.
_____ I prefer predictable, steady return on my investments, even if the return is low.

RATE YOUR WORKING RELATIONSHIPS WITH EACH OF THE FOLLOWING ADVISORS THAT APPLY:

Adviser	Dissatisfied		Satisfaction Rating	Very Satisfied		Not Applicable
Financial Planner	1	2	3	4	5	X
Broker	1	2	3	4	5	X
Broker	1	2	3	4	5	X
Accountant	1	2	3	4	5	X
Tax Preparer	1	2	3	4	5	X
Attorney	1	2	3	4	5	X
Insurance Agent	1	2	3	4	5	X
Insurance Agent	1	2	3	4	5	X

Figure 5.1 (Cont'd)

	CLIENT (1)			**CLIENT (2)**		
INSURANCE						
	Coverage/Cost	Group	Individual	Coverage/Cost	Group	Individual
Health	_____	❑	❑	_____	❑	❑
Disability	_____	❑	❑	_____	❑	❑
Disability	_____	❑	❑	_____	❑	❑
Life	_____	❑	❑	_____	❑	❑
Life	_____	❑	❑	_____	❑	❑
Life	_____	❑	❑	_____	❑	❑
Homeowners	_____	❑	❑	_____	❑	❑
Auto	_____	❑	❑	_____	❑	❑
Auto	_____	❑	❑	_____	❑	❑
Umbrella Liability	_____	❑	❑	_____	❑	❑
Professional Liability	_____	❑	❑	_____	❑	❑
Long Term Care	_____	❑	❑	_____	❑	❑

Have you ever been turned down for Insurance?   ❑ Yes   ❑ No

ASSETS
(If you have this information in a format of your own design please feel free to omit this section. Please attach necessary documentation.)

Bank Accounts

Bank Name	Checking [C], Savings [S], or Money [MM]	Ownership	Avg. Balance
_____	_____	_____	$_____
_____	_____	_____	$_____
_____	_____	_____	$_____

CD's

Where Held?	Interest Rate	Maturity Date	Ownership	Apx. Value
_____	_____%	_____	_____	$_____
_____	_____%	_____	_____	$_____
_____	_____%	_____	_____	$_____

Attach a copy of your most current brokerage, mutual fund and retirement statements.

Please list below and estimate a value for any other investment assets not appearing on the list above or the statements provided:
_____
_____
_____

PERSONAL PROPERTY

	Estimated Value
Primary Residence	_____
Furnishings (Liquidation Value)	_____
Vehicle _____	_____
Vehicle _____	_____
Other _____	_____
Other _____	_____

Figure 5.1 (Cont'd)

LIABILITIES

	Average	
Credit Cards	Interest Rate*	Monthly Payment	Current Balance
_____	_____%	$_____	$_____
_____	_____%	$_____	$_____
_____	_____%	$_____	$_____
_____	_____%	$_____	$_____

*If not paid in full each month

Debts (Residence, Auto, Business, School)	Term	Interest Rate	Payment	Current Balance	Original Balance
_____	_____	_____%	$_____	$_____	$_____
_____	_____	_____%	$_____	$_____	$_____
_____	_____	_____%	$_____	$_____	$_____
_____	_____	_____%	$_____	$_____	$_____

Have you received a copy of your credit report recently?   **Yes**   **No**

Please comment on the advice you seek.

_____

_____

_____

_____

_____

_____

_____

_____

_____

_____

THESE ITEMS MAY BE NEEDED, SHOULD YOU ENGAGE OUR SERVICES:

Prior Year Tax Return	Paycheck Stubs
Brokerage Account Statements	Mutual Fund Account Statements
Trust Account Statements	Employee Benefits Booklet
Retirement Plan Account Statements	Legal Documents
Loan Documents	Insurance Policies

If you will be coming to our office for your financial consultation, please bring this completed form with you.
If we will be teleconferencing with you, please (1) keep a copy of your completed form,
(2) fax or mail a copy to us at the following address:
Garrett Financial Planning, Inc. • 12700 Johnson Drive • Shawnee, KS. 66216-1643
Phone: (913) 268-1500 • Fax: (913) 268-6195
Email: info@gfponline.com
Visit us on the web at **www.GarrettFinancialPlanning.com**

This approach eliminates a significant amount of the client's homework and increases our likelihood of receiving requested data in a timely manner.

For clients with variable income, we approach the question of cash flow needs in a similar fashion. How much income have they netted this year? Have they increased or decreased net worth over this time period? If they earned it and didn't save it, then they spent it. And if their balance sheet reveals that they increased liabilities or decreased assets, then they actually spent more than they made.

We must know our clients' current cash flow needs so that we can determine whether they're on track to sustain their current standard of living in retirement. I calculate whether clients can continue to spend and save as they currently are spending. If they can't, I recommend they begin an automatic investment plan that will help them achieve their stated retirement goals. Occasionally, the additional savings requirement will be (or at least appear to be) difficult to meet, so clients must adjust their original objectives (e.g., retirement age), or focus on their current expenditures. If we set up an automatic investment plan to save the additional dollars but they can't make ends meet, I encourage them to begin tracking and monitoring their expenditures going forward. I provide them with several copies of our Cash Flow Questionnaire worksheet to use (see Figure 5.2 and the CD-ROM).

Figure 5.2

The Garrett Planning Network, Inc.

CASH FLOW QUESTIONNAIRE

ITEM	MONTHLY	ANNUAL
HOUSING		
House payment	_____	_____
Rent payment	_____	_____
Lease payment (not mortgage)	_____	_____
Property improvements	_____	_____
Home association dues	_____	_____
Household incidentals (supplies)	_____	_____
Household furnishings	_____	_____
Other: _____	_____	_____
Other: _____	_____	_____
Subtotal:	_____	_____
FOOD		
Groceries	_____	_____
Dining out	_____	_____
Other: _____	_____	_____
Other: _____	_____	_____
Subtotal:	_____	_____
CLOTHING		
Clothing	_____	_____
Dry cleaning	_____	_____
Other: _____	_____	_____
Other: _____	_____	_____
Subtotal:	_____	_____
PERSONAL CARE		
(Hair styling, etc.)	_____	_____
Other: _____	_____	_____
Subtotal:	_____	_____

Figure 5.2 (Cont'd)

ITEM	MONTHLY	ANNUAL
AUTOMOBILE		
Monthly payment	_____	_____
Operating expenses (gas, oil, etc.)	_____	_____
Maintenance	_____	_____
Lease payment	_____	_____
Other: _____	_____	_____
Subtotal:	_____	_____
PROPERTY TAX		
Automobile	_____	_____
House	_____	_____
Boat	_____	_____
Trailer	_____	_____
Other: _____	_____	_____
Subtotal:	_____	_____
UTILITIES		
Telephone	_____	_____
Cellular Phone	_____	_____
Water	_____	_____
Electric	_____	_____
Gas	_____	_____
Trash removal	_____	_____
Cable	_____	_____
Other: _____	_____	_____
Other: _____	_____	_____
Subtotal:	_____	_____
ENTERTAINMENT		
Books	_____	_____
Newspaper	_____	_____
Movies (theatre, video, plays, etc.)	_____	_____
Club dues (golf, music, etc.)	_____	_____
Other: _____	_____	_____
Other: _____	_____	_____
Subtotal:	_____	_____
PROFESSIONAL EXPENSES		
Travel	_____	_____
Vehicle rental	_____	_____
Parking	_____	_____
Lodging	_____	_____
Meals	_____	_____
Entertainment	_____	_____
Other: _____	_____	_____
Other: _____	_____	_____
Subtotal:	_____	_____

Figure 5.2 (Cont'd)

ITEM	MONTHLY	ANNUAL
ALIMONY (PAID)		
Subtotal:	_____	_____
CHILD SUPPORT (PAID)		
Subtotal:	_____	_____
CHILD CARE		
Daycare	_____	_____
Domestic help (babysitter)	_____	_____
Other: _____	_____	_____
Subtotal:	_____	_____
GIFTS		
Birthdays	_____	_____
Christmas	_____	_____
Anniversaries	_____	_____
Other: _____	_____	_____
Other: _____	_____	_____
Subtotal:	_____	_____
CHARITABLE CONTRIBUTIONS		
(Churches, schools, etc.)	_____	_____
Other: _____	_____	_____
Other: _____	_____	_____
Subtotal:	_____	_____
MEDICAL EXPENSES		
Doctor visit co-pay	_____	_____
Prescription co-pay	_____	_____
Dental care	_____	_____
Vision care	_____	_____
Other: _____	_____	_____
Subtotal:	_____	_____
INSURANCE		
Health	_____	_____
Automobile	_____	_____
Homeowners	_____	_____
Renters	_____	_____
Life	_____	_____
Umbrella liability	_____	_____
Professional liability	_____	_____
Other: _____	_____	_____
Other: _____	_____	_____
Subtotal:	_____	_____

Figure 5.2 (Cont'd)

ITEM	MONTHLY	ANNUAL
CREDIT CARDS		
Credit card #1: _____	_____	_____
Credit card #2: _____	_____	_____
Credit card #3: _____	_____	_____
Credit card #4: _____	_____	_____
Credit card #5: _____	_____	_____
Credit card #6: _____	_____	_____
Other: _____	_____	_____
Other: _____	_____	_____
Subtotal:	_____	_____

NOTES:

_____

_____

_____

_____

_____

_____

_____

_____

_____

_____

_____

_____

_____

_____

_____

_____

_____

_____

_____

_____

_____

_____

_____

_____

_____

_____

In other words, planners must *begin* with the *end* in mind. Clients engage our services to answer the question, "when can I retire" or "how much do I need to save now so that I can to retire when I want to?" Presuming that clients are spending all of their income that isn't being saved, we "solve for" whether they can afford to continue their same spending patterns. This is a quick and easy way to answer the question, "how much can I afford to spend?"

Americans generally spend whatever we think we can afford to. As financial planners, one of our primary responsibilities is to empower and motivate our clients to do what they have asked us to help them do. Clients want to retire someday, take care of their loved ones and enjoy their lives. Therefore, we must tell them how much they can spend and still achieve their objectives, now and in the future. When a client knows how much they *can* spend, and they *know* the ramifications should they go overboard, then they will determine that this is how much they *need* to spend.

Effective money management takes a significant amount of discipline. However, budgeting is a very simple concept. Rather than burden your clients with having them determine how much they are spending, tell them how much they can afford to spend.

Of course, if I'm working with a client who diligently tracks their expenditures, I will start with their numbers. Frequently, however, the result is the same – it appears that they are spending more then they make or, most commonly, they have surplus cash flow. When asked about surplus cash flow, we discover that this money never shows up on the balance sheet. It is not used to pay down debt or saved for the long-term. Instead, it is spent.

Preparing for Cash Flow Shortfalls

I am often asked, "How much should I keep in cash reserves?" There is no single answer that is appropriate for everyone. I don't like most of the general guidelines that are espoused. The concept of having on hand "X" months' of basic living expenses is undeniably essential, but how one funds those living expenses, and how many months of expenses are funded varies according to the individual. A client who's been employed by the federal government for the past 20 years may need significantly less reserves than an individual who is new to a job and who is paid 100% commissions. Regardless of whether the individual *needs* a certain amount of cash reserves, they may not be *comfortable* with that amount.

Also, many avenues may exist to help fund this cash flow need in the event of an emergency. Many middle Americans receive gifts or loans from family members, borrow money on a home equity line of credit or from their 401(k) plan, or liquidate investments when an emergency or unplanned opportunity arises. How much money can your client access in these events? How much are they willing to prepare for? They must have cash reserves to cover those potential emergencies or unforeseen opportunities if they don't have access to other resources.

I recommend that all clients with at least 20% equity in their homes secure a home equity line of credit (if they don't have one already) because there is generally no time to apply for a line of credit in the event of an emergency or an unplanned opportunity. Many emergencies are caused by temporary lapses in employment, and obtaining credit without an income can be difficult if not impossible to do.

To limit the number of unplanned expenditures, planners must explore the cash flow needs and desires of our clients during the financial planning process. Certain events can, and will occur; therefore, money should be allocated for these predictable expenses. We must account for periodic maintenance and repairs to houses, cars and other personal property. In addition, we must consider and plan for health care costs for clients and their families. If clients want to fulfill certain financial objectives (e.g., paying for a wedding or a family vacation), we should plan for those expenditures as well. Since we can estimate the costs and timing of these predictable expenditures, clients can begin an automatic savings plan to accumulate sufficient resources for each type of expense.

For example, clients in the accumulation stage typically replace their vehicles every seven years at a net trade-in cost of $25,000.

Therefore, we would build into their budget an "auto escrow" amount. The client should set aside $250.00 per month, assuming they get a 5% return on their money, to fund the replacement of vehicles at this cost and frequency (see the Auto Escrow worksheet in Figure 5.3 and on the CD-ROM).

Costs related to the maintenance, repair or replacement of a vehicle continue as long as a car is driven; thus, we must include a projection of these costs in our cash flow analyses. Regardless of whether the "auto escrow" amount is used to repair a vehicle, save for the purchase of the next automobile, or make a current lease or loan payment, this monthly expense should be built into our budgets. When we plan for the ongoing expense of operating, maintaining and replacing vehicles, we minimize or eliminate the impact of one of the primary "unplanned" cash flow emergencies that affect many Americans.

These are the strategies I follow to help clients resolve spending problems. First, I begin by determining liability payments and other required expenses. Then, I subtract this amount from the clients' net income to determine discretionary income. From there, I talk clients through the process of allocating their remaining funds where they can provide the highest value.

Then, I briefly talk them through the principles espoused by the authors of *Your Money or Your Life: Transforming Your Relationship with Money*.[1] I provide them with a one page written copy of these fundamental money management principles. I also keep several copies of this book on hand and give a copy to any client with cash flow problems who indicates a willingness to try the money management principles. Other books I sometimes recommend include:

- *Affluenza: The All-Consuming Epidemic*, by John De Graaf, David Wann and Thomas H. Naylor.[2]

- *Getting a Life: Stategies for Simple Living*, by Jacqueline Blix and David Heitmiller.[3]

Figure 5.3

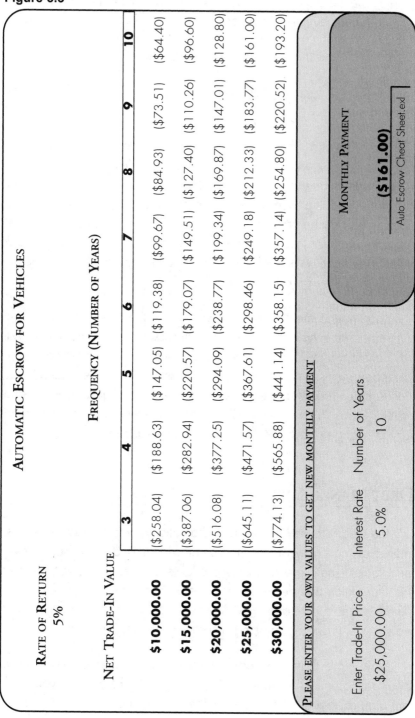

Automatic Escrow for Vehicles

Rate of Return
5%

Frequency (Number of Years)

Net Trade-In Value

	3	4	5	6	7	8	9	10
$10,000.00	($258.04)	($188.63)	($147.05)	($119.38)	($99.67)	($84.93)	($73.51)	($64.40)
$15,000.00	($387.06)	($282.94)	($220.57)	($179.07)	($149.51)	($127.40)	($110.26)	($96.60)
$20,000.00	($516.08)	($377.25)	($294.09)	($238.77)	($199.34)	($169.87)	($147.01)	($128.80)
$25,000.00	($645.11)	($471.57)	($367.61)	($298.46)	($249.18)	($212.33)	($183.77)	($161.00)
$30,000.00	($774.13)	($565.88)	($441.14)	($358.15)	($357.14)	($254.80)	($220.52)	($193.20)

PLEASE ENTER YOUR OWN VALUES TO GET NEW MONTHLY PAYMENT

Enter Trade-In Price	Interest Rate	Number of Years
$25,000.00	5.0%	10

Monthly Payment

($161.00)

Auto Escrow Cheat Sheet.exl

- *The Overspent American: Why We Want What We Don't Need*, by Juliet B. Schor.[4]

- *The Richest Man in Babylon*, by George S. Clason.[5]

For a list of my "Recommended Personal Finance Books for Clients," see Appendix B.

The client and I then schedule our next meeting, which I generally set for four to six weeks into the future. I want clients to have enough time to work through the basic principles we discussed at our first meeting, while keeping them accountable for what they say they want to accomplish between meetings. I don't do any work behind the scenes. All of my work for these clients is done with them. Our meetings usually last one hour. We book the next appointment, clarify their assignment(s), and they pay on their way out.

I continue to meet every few weeks until the client begins to consistently achieve their objectives for each session. Over time, clients will have either gained control over their cash flow, or they stop coming in for appointments. Unfortunately, the success rate I've experienced is less than satisfying. It takes people a long time to change old habits and belief systems. Many clients will not invest the time and energy necessary to change. However, those that do make it all worthwhile.

DEBT MANAGEMENT

The credit industry has evolved dramatically over the last few years. Individuals can now obtain their credit reports and credit scores over the Internet. There are resources available to help individuals interpret this information and determine how credit scores can hurt or help them. I like www.nolo.com and www.Myvesta.org for their resources on debt management, and establishing, improving and repairing credit.

Now more than ever, adults must maintain good credit because credit ratings affect so many areas of our lives. Frequently, you can't rent a car or book a hotel room without a credit card. Insurance companies, lenders and many employers use credit scores in making their underwriting, lending and hiring decisions. People who have poor credit will pay higher insurance premiums and loan rates (presuming they can get insurance coverage or borrow money in the first place). These additional costs further impair their abilities to maintain good credit. If we have poor credit, we may miss out on a job promotion or not get the job in the first place. Having bad credit can cost clients in more ways than they realize. It takes only one moment of compulsive spending in front of a timeshare salesman, or one missing paycheck, to negatively impact one's credit and financial plans. However, it can take months or years to recover.

When counseling clients on debt management issues, I stress that paying off debts and improving our credit takes time and discipline, but the rewards are worth it. For a period of time, they must be brutally honest with themselves, and with me, about how they spend their money. They must track where every penny is spent for the near future. Planners must raise their clients' consciousness about their spending habits.

I also provide the following types of informational sheets, which we at my firm call "One-Sheets" to help explain certain topics and assist in the implementation of our recommendations. Figures 5.4, 5.5, 5.6, and 5.7 are quick resource sheets that we place behind the Appendix tab in the client's plan binder. I'll share other examples of our "One-Sheets" throughout this chapter and on the accompanying CD.

Figure 5.4

How can I get a copy of my credit report?

There are three major credit bureaus – Equifax, Trans Union and Experian. It's best to order your report from all three. The federal Fair Credit Reporting Act (FCRA) entitles you to a copy of your credit report, and you can get one for free if:

- you've been denied credit because of information in your credit report and you request a copy within 60 days of being denied credit;
- you're unemployed and looking for work;
- you receive public assistance; or
- you believe your file contains errors due to fraud.

In addition, you can get one free copy a year if you live in Colorado, Georgia, Maryland, Massachusetts, New Jersey or Vermont.

The law says that if you don't qualify for a free report, you should pay no more than $8.50 to obtain a report from Equifax (P.O. Box 740241, Atlanta, GA 30374, 800-685-1111, http://www.equifax.com), Trans Union (P.O. Box 1000, Chester, PA 19022, 800-888-4213, http://www.tuc.com) or Experian (P.O. Box 2002, Allen, TX 75013, 888-397-3742, http://www.experian.com).

Provide the following information:

- your full name (including generations such as Jr., Sr., III)
- your birth date
- your Social Security number
- your spouse's name (if applicable)
- your telephone number, and
- your current address and addresses for the previous five years.

Reprinted with permission from the publishers, Nolo, Copyright © 2002, http://www.nolo.com.

Figure 5.5

WHAT SHOULD I DO IF I FIND MISTAKES IN MY CREDIT REPORT?

As you read through your report, make a list of everything out-of-date. The credit bureaus should remove this information from your credit report:

- Lawsuits, paid tax liens, accounts sent out for collection, criminal records (except criminal convictions, which may be reported indefinitely), late payments and any other adverse information older than seven years.
- Bankruptcies older than ten years from the discharge or dismissal. Credit bureaus often list Chapter 13 bankruptcies for only seven years, but they can stay for ten.
- Credit inquiries (requests by companies for a copy of your report) older than two years.

Next, look for incorrect or misleading information, such as:

- Incorrect or incomplete name, address, phone number, Social Security number or employment information
- Bankruptcies not identified by their specific chapter number
- Accounts not yours or lawsuits in which you were not involved
- Incorrect account histories – such as late payments when you paid on time
- Closed accounts listed as open – it may look as if you have too much open credit, and
- Any account you closed that doesn't say "closed by consumer."

After reviewing your report, complete the "request for reinvestigation" form the credit bureau sent you or send a letter listing each incorrect item and explain exactly what is wrong. Once the credit bureau receives your request, it must investigate the items you dispute and contact you within 30 days. Some states require bureaus to complete reinvestigations more quickly. If you don't hear back within 30 days, send a follow-up letter. If you let them know that you're trying to obtain a mortgage or car loan, they can do a rush investigation.

If you are right, or if the creditor who provided the information can no longer verify it, the credit bureau must remove the information from your report. Often credit bureaus will remove an item on request without an investigation if rechecking the item is more bother than it's worth.

If the credit bureau insists that the information is correct, call the bureau to discuss the problem:

- Experian: 888-397-3742
- Trans Union: 800-888-4213
- Equifax: 800-685-1111

If you don't get anywhere with the credit bureau, directly contact the creditor and ask that the information be removed. Write to the customer service department, vice president of marketing and president or CEO. If the information was reported by a collection agency, send the agency a copy of your letter, too. Creditors are forbidden by law to report information they know is incorrect.

If you feel a credit bureau is wrongfully including information in your report, or you want to explain a particular entry, you have the right to put a brief statement in your report. The credit bureau must give a copy of your statement – or a summary – to anyone who requests your report. Be clear and concise; use the fewest words possible.

Reprinted with permission from the publishers, Nolo, Copyright © 2002, http://www.nolo.com.

Figure 5.6

WHAT CAN I DO TO REBUILD MY CREDIT?

After you've cleaned up your credit report, the key to rebuilding credit is to get positive information into your record. Here are two suggestions:

- If your credit report is missing accounts you pay on time, send the credit bureaus a recent account statement and copies of canceled checks showing your payment history. Ask that these be added to your report. The credit bureau doesn't have to, but often will.

- Creditors like to see evidence of stability, so if any of the following information is not in your report, send it to the bureaus and ask that it be added: your current employment, your previous employment (especially if you've been at your current job fewer than two years), your current residence, your telephone number (especially if it's unlisted), your date of birth and your checking account number. Again, the credit bureau doesn't have to add these, but often will.

Reprinted with permission from the publishers, Nolo, Copyright © 2002, http://www.nolo.com.

Figure 5.7

I'VE BEEN TOLD THAT I NEED TO USE CREDIT TO REBUILD MY CREDIT. IS THIS TRUE?

Yes. The one type of positive information creditors like to see in credit reports is credit payment history. If you have a credit card, use it every month. Make small purchases and pay them off to avoid interest charges. If you don't have a credit card, apply for one. If your application is rejected, try to find a cosigner or apply for a secured card – where you deposit some money into a savings account and then get a credit card with a line of credit around the amount you deposited.

But a word of caution: It won't do you any good in the long-run to apply for credit before you're back on your feet financially. You'll just end up with high cost credit that will put you back in the hole again. Even if you can get a card earlier, wait until you are ready to start using credit again.

Reprinted with permission from the publishers, Nolo, Copyright © 2002, http://www.nolo.com.

Once the clients have had the opportunity to receive a copy of their credit report and file a letter with the credit bureau disputing any inaccuracies, we meet again to establish a debt reduction plan.

I use Quicken's Debt Reduction Planner to produce a suggested repayment schedule. We require that clients bring current copies of all liability statements and their credit report to the meeting. During the meeting, we review the repayment schedule and mutually determine a plan of action that the clients themselves will implement prior to our next meeting. We schedule the next meeting two to three months in advance. Clients are asked to bring their most current liability statements and any documents used to track expenditures. We continue to meet on this frequency until period objectives are met. We then schedule a follow-up "accountability meeting" for six months in the future. These accountability meetings may continue for quite a while. My role is to serve as accountability coach and see that clients stay on task. The clients do all the work. My only billable time is that spent directly in front of the client.

Strategies for Handling Credit Problems

There are many community and private credit counseling providers available today. Occasionally, I receive inquiries from people who would be better served by groups such as Consumer Credit Counseling Services (CCCS) or www.Myvesta.org. If I don't feel that I can effectively and affordably assist prospective clients, I refer them to our local CCCS office or to www.Myvesta.org.

When I first re-directed my practice to work on an hourly, as-needed basis with clients, I anticipated a lot of cash flow problems. Fortunately, the overwhelming majority of my clients have positive cash flow, and I'm not doing much debt management planning. Nevertheless, effective debt management is a common problem for middle Americans. Practitioners who decide to offer these services will find it frustrating, yet very rewarding. It is a much-needed service and, when successful, literally changes peoples lives.

Figure 5.8

HELPING YOUNG ADULTS AVOID FINANCIAL PITFALLS
03/05/2002

According to Holden Lewis, a writer for www.bankrate.com, today's young adults should be called "Generation D" — for debt. He says 80% of today's young people are financially ignorant and that few institutions teach financial literacy to youths.

Consider:

1. Most high school graduates don't know how to balance a checkbook. They are more likely to know how to calculate the volume of a sphere than how to calculate how long it takes to pay off a $500 credit card balance at 21 percent interest, he says.

2. According to the American Savings Education Council, one-fifth of students ages 16 to 22 say they have taken a personal finance course at school. That leaves four-fifths who haven't taken such a course.

3. A GE Center for Financial Learning survey revealed that 41% of teenagers don't have or don't know if they have a savings account and 10% of teenagers carry a monthly credit card balance of $1,000 or more.

4. A study by Nellie Mae states that 78% of undergrads in 2000 had credit cards; the average balance: $2800.

5. A recent Harris poll (July 2001) found that nearly half of college seniors feel that they are not knowledgeable about investing and financial planning. They also feel they lack knowledge about basic financial tools.

6. These financially irresponsible teenagers and recent college grads enter the work force as financially unprepared adults.

7. Oppenheimer Funds and Third Millennium sponsored a study that found that half of single women aged 21-34 believe that at this time of their lives money is for spending, not saving.

8. Young single women (21-34) are more likely to accumulate 30 pairs of shoes over $30,000 in their retirement fund.

9. More and more young adults are filing for bankruptcy before age 30. A study by Elizabeth Warren, a law professor at Harvard Law, estimates that 120,000 people age 25 and under filed for personal bankruptcy in 2000. That's up from about 80,000 people in that age range who filed for bankruptcy in 1991.

This excerpt is from an article written by Marie Swift, Director of Corporate Communications for the Garrett Planning Network, Inc., as published on www.GarrettPlanningNetwork.com. The text of the full article can be found on the CD-ROM for this book.

RISK MANAGEMENT

Life Insurance

Virtually every middle American has inadequate life insurance coverage. Most middle Americans also have limited budgets. We utilize low-cost, high-quality term life insurance with most clients because (1) they need a lot of pure life insurance protection, and (2) they also have tax advantages investment strategies available to them that are not fully being utilized.

SRI Consulting released a survey in 1999 revealing that some 73% of U.S. households have life insurance coverage. Eighty percent of those households only have coverage provided through their employer or another group plan.[6] The survey revealed a decline in the number of cash value life insurance policies. Americans are replacing their cash-value policies with term insurance. One of the facts affecting this trend is the availability of attractive, tax-deferred investment options.

When reviewing clients' overall objectives, I find that they generally need to (1) save more for retirement and (2) buy more life insurance. But the fact that they have limited resources (and lots of other requirements for their money) cannot be overlooked either. While preparing the retirement capital needs analysis, we also determine the appropriate amount of life insurance coverage needed.

Next I discuss the assumptions that went into the calculation of additional life insurance needs with the clients. The default assumption is that nothing changes the current plan. If the couple is planning to retire at a certain age and lifestyle, provide a college education for their kids, and build their dream home in five years, we assume nothing would change if one of them were to die prematurely. We also assume that nothing changes regarding the employment status or earning potential of the survivor.

But, are these things likely to change? When working with young couples, we discuss what life might be like if one of them weren't around. Other possible questions include: What would be the likelihood of a "stay-at-home" parent continuing to have no earned income? Would the survivor stay in their current home? Would they want the mortgage paid off at the death of either party?

If the clients can afford it, we generally conclude that they should obtain sufficient insurance to provide for the life they are planning together, even if one dies prematurely. However, in the event that clients must weigh the options and choose between fully insuring their surviving family or providing for their future should they live, a compromise must be reached.

Some couples I've worked with have determined that they are comfortable taking certain risks and have elected to provide just enough life insurance to support the survivor for twenty years and provide for their kids' college educations.

However, a lot of things can happen in twenty years. What if the clients live to a ripe old age? We must plan for the possibility of premature death, but balance that consideration with our plans for living. Middle Americans need our help in determining and achieving the appropriate balance.

I currently use MoneyTree Software's EasyMoney module for the life insurance needs analysis. Once the coverage requirement is determined, we consider the appropriate type of coverage, and then have the client either contact the company directly, or have one of a select group of insurance specialists implement our recommendations.

Tip: Many good consumer publications on all types of insurance can be found at http://www.insurance.wa.gov/readonlin.htm.

Disability Income Protection

In addition to inadequate life insurance coverage, most middle Americans also have limited or no income protection in the event of long-term disability. The majority of our clients have long-term disability coverage through their employers; however, this coverage rarely exceeds 67% of pre-tax earnings. Most middle Americans can't comfortably absorb that drastic a change in their lifestyles, but unfortunately that is what most would have to do.

A long-term disability could not only affect the client's current situation, it could also dramatically affect their lifestyle when the benefit expires at age 65, primarily because they won't have received sufficient income to save as aggressively as they should for retirement.

Obtaining additional coverage by purchasing a personal policy may not eliminate the long-term cash flow problem either. Thus, regardless of how much insurance clients may have, long-term disability can severely impact their financial plans.

Planners must discuss the risks clients face currently, the option of self-insuring or purchasing additional coverage, and the impact each may have on their lifestyle. Disability insurance is not cheap, but the impact of the lack of adequate coverage may not be tolerable.

Figure 5.9

DISABILITY INSURANCE POLICY CHECKLIST

Date:_____

	YES	NO
1. Does my company have a Comdex rating of at least 80?	____	____
2. Is my policy non-cancelable?	____	____
3. Are the premiums guaranteed?	____	____
4. Does the definition of total disability protect me in my occupation?	____	____
5. Are part-time and full-time return-to-work income replacement benefits included and payable to age 65?	____	____
6. Can I receive benefits without being totally disabled first?	____	____
7. Does my policy use the "earned and received" method of accounting during my residual (partial) disability?	____	____
8. Can my earnings loss be averaged to generate a greater benefit?	____	____
9. When I am on claim, are my policy benefits adjusted for inflation?	____	____
10. Can I increase my monthly benefits even if I am uninsurable?	____	____
11. Can these increases be made (and are they payable) during an existing claim?	____	____
12. Does my policy pay benefits for my lifetime if totally disabled?	____	____
13. Do I have a policy (Business Overhead Expense Disability Plan) to cover my business expenses if I am disabled?	____	____
14. Do I have a policy (Reducing Term Disability Plan) to cover my business loan payments?	____	____
15. Do I have maximum benefits based on my current income and fixed business expenses?	____	____

Note: It is advisable to review your disability insurance policies once a year with a qualified specialist.

Figure 5.9 (Cont'd)

DISABILITY INSURANCE ANNUAL PREMIUMS
(Per $1,000 of Monthly Benefit)

PLAN DESIGN: 90-Day Elimination Period
$1,000 per month benefit
Benefit Period "To Age 65"
Benefit Update Rider
Cost of Living Adjustment Rider
Residual Benefit Rider

5A OCCUPATION CLASS

This class includes persons in professional, managerial, and technical occupations within select business and professional sectors of the economy. These occupations require extensive education, training, and experience. All work is performed in an office setting with less than 20% of the person's time spent out of the office and no direct supervision of persons with manual duties.

Age	Male	Female
30	$370	$540
35	$420	$640
40	$550	$780
45	$670	$900
50	$840	$1,070

4A OCCUPATION CLASS

This class consists primarily of those professional, managerial, and technical occupations which are not generally eligible for our most favorable classes. Work may involve more than 20% of the person's time being spent outside of the establishment. Occupational duties involve no direct supervision of persons with manual duties.

Age	Male	Female
30	$390	$620
35	$450	$670
40	$580	$820
45	$710	$950
50	$900	$1,120

Figure 5.9 (Cont'd)

3A OCCUPATION CLASS

This class is made up of social service, clerical, medical support, and select commissioned sales occupations in which stability and potential high earnings qualify individuals for long-term benefits. It also includes those medical and dental occupations that have demonstrated less favorable experience than class 4. Work is performed in a hospital, office, or retail setting and involves only light manual duties. Occupations that meet the criteria of class 3 may be rated as class 4 if the individual has had personal earned income of at least $50,000 in each of the three years prior to application.

Age	Male	Female
30	$450	$750
35	$500	$800
40	$650	$970
45	$780	$1,100
50	$1,000	$1,300

Females can receive up to a 30% premium discount if insurance is employer-sponsored. Premiums shown are not discounted.

Reprinted with permission of John Ryan, Ryan Insurance Strategy Consultants, 8301 E. Prentice Ave., Suite 310, Greenwood Village, CO 80111.

Medical Insurance and Long-Term Care Insurance

The 2001 U.S. Census revealed that the majority of middle Americans have health insurance.[7]

CITIZENS COVERED BY HEALTH INSURANCE

Household Income	Total	Private	Medicaid	Not Covered
$50,000 - $74,999	88.2%	83.1%	3.6%	11.8%
$75,000 and higher	91.7%	88.4%	2.1%	8.3%

In many cases, employers pay all or part of the cost of a full-time employee's health insurance. Employees may also be able to obtain health insurance for their spouses and children through their employer's plan. Frequently, when I work with married couples both spouses have employer-provided health insurance available. We must then consider which spouse's plan is best for the family's coverage, from a quality, flexibility and cost standpoint.

Ineligible employees and individuals without employer-sponsored health insurance may be able to obtain group coverage through a professional organization, alumni association or labor union. High-risk individuals may have access to a high-risk pool available through their state.

Individual policies are more expensive than group coverage, but the coverage can be tailored to fit specific needs. Most individual plans offer options including Health Maintenance Organizations (HMOs), Preferred Provider Organizations (PPOs), point-of-service plans and traditional fee-for-service plans. Individual policies must be compared carefully because premiums and benefits can vary widely.

Clients engage us to provide advice regarding employer-provided health insurance plans. If individual coverage is needed, planners must coach clients on the benefits to look for in a policy and refer them directly to a qualified, independent insurance specialist to secure coverage.

Some employers provide health insurance benefits to their retirees. However, these benefits are generally not guaranteed. Care must be exercised when planning for long-term retirement income needs; health insurance for retirees can easily run $200 per month or more.

The USAA Educational Foundation provides an informational piece on comparing health insurance plans (see www.usaaed foundation.org.) and useful health insurance shopping tips. They discuss employer-sponsored group plans and individual plans.

Long–Term Care Insurance

Long-term care insurance provides coverage for medical care and assistance in a nursing facility or in the home or a community environment. Determining whether long-term care insurance should be purchased depends on many factors, primarily age, health status, income and assets, and need for security.

It's difficult to know if, when, and for how long one may need long-term care. USAA Educational Foundation provides guidelines regarding who should, and should not, purchase long-term care insurance. See www.usedfoundation.org.

The majority of Americans should consider obtaining long-term care insurance at some point. The USAA Education Foundation guidelines (at www.usaafoundation.org) illustrate that if you don't have enough income and assets to purchase the insurance, you shouldn't. At the time assets are nearly depleted Medicaid will provide assistance. But, there are also occasions when clients are self-insured or choose to take on the risk of paying for long-term health care and assistance. Often, clients are reluctant to seriously discuss long-term care needs. They are convinced that they and their loved ones will not end up in a nursing home. Clients may actually avoid or limit the amount of time they spend in a nursing home if they have insurance with home health care benefits. Thus, education is the key.

We provide clients who should consider long-term care insurance with a copy of the National Association of Insurance Commissioner's *Shopper's Guide to Long-Term Care Insurance*.[8] The Guide thoroughly covers all the major issues a client should consider when shopping for long-term care insurance. We also provide clients with contact information on long-term care insurance specialists to assist with selection and implementation.

Clients should consider buying long-term care insurance if there is a family history of chronic illness or need for long-term health care. We also must consider who could provide care in the event of a long-term need. I have asked the petite spouse of a husky client, "if he broke his hip, you'd be able to care for him, but could you lift him?"

Once clients conclude that long-term care insurance may be appropriate for them, they ask, "when should we buy it?" "The day before you actually need it," I respond. I then explain the trade-offs we must make. Generally, I recommend that clients who should own long-term care insurance purchase it between 60 and 65 years of age. Of course there are times when I recommend coverage for much younger clients. However, most clients I work with choose to take the risk of waiting a few years before buying coverage, so they can continue to save aggressively for retirement.

I strongly encourage clients to get quotes on policies with 4 or 5 years and lifetime coverage, cost of living adjustments, home health care benefits, and a waiting period of six months to a year. The daily benefit and the benefit period are adjusted until the clients and the insurance specialist arrive at the type of insurance protection the client is willing to pay for. Occasionally clients will discuss the policy quotes they receive with me before they buy a policy.

Property and Casualty Insurance

We provide advice to clients regarding their auto, homeowners and liability insurance coverages. The most important thing I concern myself with is whether the coverage is appropriate, adequate and reasonably competitive. We frequently find that liability coverages should be increased, deductibles should be increased, and riders need to be added to their policies.

We ask clients to provide us with a copy of their most current insurance declaration pages. These reports provide us with the majority of the information we need to determine whether the coverage is appropriate and adequate, and assess its competitiveness.

I have established relationships with property and casualty insurance specialists. Some of these specialists represent many of the top property-casualty companies in the country. Others represent only one company, which happens to be extremely competitive in the areas of auto and homeowners insurance.

Consumers should periodically obtain quotes from other insurance companies to make certain that they have appropriate and competitive insurance protection. However, many consumers do not know what they should be looking for in a policy and what they should be prepared to pay. Frequently Middle Market consumers can save $100 to $300 a year simply by shopping around. I do not advocate that a consumer with an established history with their property and casualty insurance providers change companies merely to save a few dollars. I feel that obtaining appropriate and adequate protection with one insurance company and staying with that insurance company for many years much better serves consumers. Claims paying ability and customer service are the most important considerations.

There have been dramatic changes in the property and casualty insurance industry in recent years. For example, I recently purchased a home and went shopping for homeowners as well as replacement coverage for my car. In my search I learned that State Farm discontinued writing coverage on homes in my area. I also discovered that Allstate only insures homes up to 30 years old. My house is 73 years old. I talked with another carrier who wouldn't provide coverage because I didn't have homeowners coverage immediately before I purchased my new home. Another company whom I really wanted to use turned me down because of some old wiring still in my home. They are an outstanding company, with the best premium rates and coverages around, and their underwriting requirements reflect why that they are able to offer such competitive rates. They only take preferred risks.

We live in a part of the country that is known for hailstorms. I know, you probably think of Kansas as Tornado Alley. But hail, wind, and ice storms damage significantly more property each year then do tornados. In working with my property and casualty insurance specialists, I learned that most companies depreciate roofs. However a few companies still offer full replacement value. In an area such as ours, having full replacement coverage for the roof can mean the difference between being adequately insured and opening yourself up to a cash flow emergency.

When we are engaged to help our clients shop for proper coverage, we fax the declarations pages to a couple of our insurance specialists. Generally within 48 hours we receive suggestions for improvements, as well as quotes from their top providers. It is not at all uncommon for our P & C specialists to recommend that clients not change their current coverage, or change their coverage, but stay with their current carrier.

The specialists we work with know that to continue to receive opportunities to replace or add coverages for our clients, they must provide us with objective feedback regarding the client's current coverage. It takes time to develop a trusting relationship with the various specialists with whom we work. However, once these relationships have been developed, these specialists can serve an extremely valuable role to the general practitioner serving the Middle Market consumer, and the consumers themselves.

As general practitioners we cannot be specialists in all areas of the financial planning process. Middle Market consumers cannot afford to hire experts in every area. Nor can they afford to go without competent advice. By strategically aligning ourselves with allied professionals as we do, our clients receive quality, affordable advice in areas outside of our scope of expertise.

Occasionally clients have other types of property and casualty insurance or insurance needs. We refer these clients directly to their property and casualty insurance specialist, or one of the specialists we work with, to review and update these coverages.

Tips for purchasing homeowners insurance and auto insurance are listed in Figure 5.10.

Figure 5.10

HOMEOWNERS INSURANCE BUYING TIPS

BASIC COVERAGES:

COVERAGE FOR THE STRUCTURE OF YOUR HOME – pays to repair or rebuild your home if it is damaged or destroyed by fire, hurricane, wind, hail, lightning or other disaster listed in your policy. Separate coverage must be obtained for flood and earthquake protection.

Be sure to obtain "full replacement cost" coverage for your home. Note: you do not need to insure the land, only the physical structures and contents.

Most policies also cover "detached" structures, (i.e., garage or shed) up to 10% of the coverage on the structure. Additional coverage can be purchased.

COVERAGE FOR YOUR PERSONAL PROPERTY – pays to replace the contents of your home if items are stolen, damaged or destroyed by a covered risk. Most policies cover up to 70% of the amount of your coverage on the structure.

If you have specialty items (jewelry, electronics, antiques) or collectibles (stamps, coins, figurines) you may need a separate "Rider" for those items. Consult with your homeowners' insurance agent to confirm that your coverage is adequate.

Consider videotaping and/or completing a detailed inventory listing of the contents of your home. Keep this documentation off premises, such as in a safe deposit box.

LIABILITY PROTECTION – covers you against lawsuits for bodily injury or property damage that you, family members or your pets cause to other people.

Liability limits generally start at $100,000. We recommend at least $300,000 of liability protection.

You can purchase an umbrella liability policy, which provides coverage above and beyond your auto and homeowners liability protection. This coverage costs about $150 to $250 per year for a $1,000,000 policy.

Figure 5.10 (Cont'd)

WAYS TO REDUCE COSTS OF HOMEOWNERS INSURANCE:

SHOP AROUND for competitive quotes.   www.insure.com
                                             www.quicken.com/insurance

Check the financial health of insurance companies with rating companies such as A.M. Best (www.ambest.com) and Standard & Poor's (www.standardandpoors.com/ratings)

INCREASE YOUR DEDUCTIBLES – We recommend deductibles of at least $500. If you can afford to raise it to $1,000, you may save as much as 25% according to the Insurance Information Institute.

PURCHASE AUTO, HOMEOWNERS AND UMBRELLA LIABILITY COVERAGES THROUGH SAME COMPANY

INQUIRE ABOUT DISCOUNTS

For more tips on homeowners insurance visit www.iii.org/individuals/homei.
Adapted with permission from the Insurance Information Institute.

Figure 5.10 (Cont'd)

AUTO INSURANCE BUYING TIPS

BASIC COVERAGES:

COLLISION – pays for damage to your car resulting from a collision or accident.

COMPREHENSIVE – coverage for most everything other than collision or accident, such as wind or hail damage, broken windshield, and theft.

BODILY INJURY LIABILITY – covers you and any other designated driver if you cause injury to another person.

The Insurance Information Institute recommends that you have $100,000 of bodily injury protection per person and $300,000 per accident.

PROPERTY DAMAGE LIABILITY – covers damages that you may cause to someone else's property, i.e., vehicle, fence, landscape, etc.

MEDICAL PAYMENTS OR PERSONAL INJURY PROTECTION (PIP) – pays for medical payments and possibly lost wages of someone injured in an auto accident.

UNINSURED AND UNDERINSURED MOTORIST COVERAGE – reimburses you if accident is caused by an uninsured or underinsured driver.

WAYS TO REDUCE COSTS OF AUTO INSURANCE:

SHOP AROUND for competitive quotes.　　　　www.insure.com
　　　　　　　　　　　　　　　　　　　　　www.quicken.com/insurance

INCREASE YOUR DEDUCTIBLES for Collision and Comprehensive coverages.

According to the Insurance Information Institute increasing your deductible from $200 to $500 could reduce your collision and comprehensive coverage cost by 15% to 30%. Going to a $1,000 deductible can save you 40% or more.

MAINTAIN A CLEAN DRIVING RECORD

PURCHASE AUTO AND HOME OWNERS COVERAGE THROUGH SAME COMPANY

INQUIRE ABOUT DISCOUNTS

For more tips on auto insurance visit www.iii.org/individuals/auto.
Adapted with permission from the Insurance Information Institute.

FUNDAMENTAL FINANCIAL PLANNING OBJECTIVES

Home Ownership

Owning a home is truly part of the American dream. According to the U.S. Census Bureau, over 70% of married couples age 30 or older own their own home.[9] As ages increase, the percentage of home ownership increases. These statistics have increased over the years as more liberal lending policies have been introduced. It is now possible to purchase a home with as little as 3% down — and sometimes zero down.

There are many advantages and disadvantages to owning your own home. Advantages include: pride of ownership; building equity in a place of your own; ability to deduct mortgage interest and real estate taxes on your federal and state income tax returns; and building long-term security.

There are also disadvantages that must be acknowledged. Owning a home is a big responsibility. When the furnace goes out or the lawn needs mowing, you have to take care of it or hire someone and pay him or her to do things you can't or don't want to do. Some middle Americans are better off renting. Yes, their rents can go up year after year, but so can real estate taxes and maintenance expenses. Renting has its benefits. It is simple and you won't get whacked with unexpected expenses relating to the maintenance of the property. However, you'll never stop paying rent. With home ownership, eventually the mortgage will be paid off and your only expenses that continue indefinitely are real estate taxes, homeowners insurance and maintenance. Generally, these expenses are significantly less then rent. Plus, you have a fully paid for, appreciating asset (hopefully).

At some point, homeowners may decide to sell their homes and seek out low maintenance housing alternatives. We are seeing more and more clients these days looking to purchase a home, which they plan to stay in throughout retirement. Generally, these clients want a ranch-style home or patio home, with all of their essential services on the main floor. They want a small yard or one with outside maintenance provided. They want a newer home, with only minor maintenance needed for the foreseeable future. Many of these clients are desiring to downsize their current residence for one that is more appropriate for their retirement needs; however, the cost of the new residence is often many times equal to or greater than the home in which they currently live. The costs for maintenance and utilities may go down, but the additional cost of higher real estate taxes and homeowner's association dues must be factored into our planning discussions.

Helping clients achieve their financial planning dreams is what I enjoy most about my job. Purchasing a home for many middle Americans is their single biggest financial decision and, often times, their most significant near term goal. In a relatively short period of time, we can help clients determine what is the right price range, how they should fund the down payment, what type of mortgage is right for them, and where they can find competitive interest rates.

If this project is part of a more comprehensive financial plan, the answer to what is "affordable" will be more scientifically derived. As planners working with the Middle Market we may be asked to address this issue in relative isolation. In that event, we must start with the client's current budget, including housing costs. We then make adjustments for the income tax benefits of owning a home and the additional costs that come with home ownership to determine the affordable price range.

With the information provided on our Confidential Questionnaire (see Figure 5.1) and additional data gathering, we are able to provide input as to where they should obtain the down payment and what type of mortgage is appropriate.

We check www.BankRate.com for indications of current interest rates and then call local, competitive mortgage companies to get current rate quotes for the client. Or you can use www.BankRate.com's feature, which provides an option to get quotes from lenders in your area. Check out this service and compare it with the quotes you obtain from lenders who are known for being very competitive in your area.

Occasionally, clients or lenders fax us copies of "Good Faith Estimate" forms for our review and feedback. The interest rate is a critical factor and many lenders will quote the same rate. The "Good Faith Estimate" will provide you with the details of other costs involved. Lenders can vary greatly on their costs.

Do your due diligence thoroughly the first time and you'll arrive at a good list of competitive lenders you can call for quotes when a client needs a first or second mortgage. These lenders can also provide you with information on any available "First Time" homebuyers programs. Try www.AskJeeves.com and type in "first time home buyers programs." You'll find a lot of information about state sponsored programs, as well as other tips.

This process generally takes two to four hours. Most of this time is spent in front of the client.

As I mentioned above, there are tax advantages to owning your own home. However, I too frequently hear, "I think we should buy a bigger house because we need the tax breaks." Clients need our guidance to help them determine how many of these "tax breaks" they can afford. Remember, just because interest on a mortgage is tax deductible, one still has to pay the mortgage. The mortgage may cost only 5% after adjusting for the tax benefits, but it still costs 5% a year on the total amount borrowed.

One of the other things planners often fail to consider is the actual value of the mortgage deduction. To truly evaluate the tax benefits, we also must consider the automatic standard deduction we would receive if we didn't itemize. For many middle Americans, the total of their itemized deductions is not significantly greater than their standard deduction. Therefore, we may be overestimating the value of the tax benefits of owning a home.

Let's consider the simple comparison in the following example. Suppose the clients pay $700 per month now on rent and they want to find out how much house is "affordable." An $80,000 mortgage at

7% for 30 years would result in a principal and interest payment of $532 per month. The total payment, including real estate taxes and insurance would be approximately, $690/month (at least in the Kansas City market). This is before factoring in the tax savings. On the surface, it looks like an $80,000 mortgage, with the additional maintenance expenses associated with home ownership may come out pretty even to the client's current rent.

I use www.FinanCenter.com for these types of calculations. They have an incredible variety of calculators on this site and the reports and graphs are very well done.

Clients often ask me whether they should accelerate the repayment schedule on their mortgage, or pay off their mortgage entirely. I used to nearly always recommend that they do the "right" thing financially. However, over time I've come to realize that the psychological reasons clients may have for wanting to pay off their mortgage are far more important. I tell them that there are two answers to that question. One is financial and the other is psychological, and sometimes the two don't always agree. We must keep in mind that security is one of the primary motivators of our clients. Owning your home, free and clear, provides clients with possibly the greatest feeling of financial security they will ever have.

Other clients may want to accelerate their mortgage payments so they can eliminate the need for private mortgage insurance (PMI). Typically, if a borrower has less then a 20% down payment they must pay PMI. This additional expense might be about $60/month on an $80,000 mortgage. However, you may now request that your mortgage company remove the PMI once you have at least 20% equity. This equity can be obtained by appreciation and/or by paying down the mortgage. We provide clients with a "One-Sheet" on how to eliminate the PMI (see Figure 5.11) and coach them on the process.

Figure 5.11

> ### CANCELLATION OF PRIVATE MORTGAGE INSURANCE (PMI)
>
> Only your lender knows for sure if you can cancel your PMI. Many lenders have specific requirements for canceling. If your loan closed on or after July 29, 1999 the Homeowners Protection Act (HPA) requires your lender to cancel PMI at your request when your mortgage balance reaches 80% of your home's original value. Or, your mortgage insurance will cancel automatically by your lender when it reaches 78%. Please call your lender directly for details.

As I mentioned in the section on debt management (above), I strongly encourage all clients with at least 20% equity to have a home equity line of credit for emergency purposes. Even if a client doesn't have a first mortgage any longer, it may be necessary for them to access the equity in their home on short notice.

Over the last few years I've worked with a lot of clients who needed to refinance their mortgages. General guidelines state that if you can reduce your interest rate by 2% you should refinance. However, there have been many occasions where the reduction in interest rate was much less than that, but due to certain circumstances, it made sense to refinance. For instance, if the homeowner plans on staying in the house forever, a very small reduction in interest rates, presuming the upfront costs are reasonable, may be worthwhile. However, in my experience, clients generally need to stay in their home for at least 3 years to come out ahead on a refinancing. There is a calculator at www.FinanCenter.com that can assist you in determining how long it takes to be "in the money" after refinancing. You'll need the information from the "Good Faith Estimate" to complete this calculation.

The equity buildup in one's home may also be accessed for retirement income. In some circumstances, using a reverse mortgage can be a very appropriate financial planning strategy. The clients must be at least 62 years of age and typically have a least 70% equity in their home. For more information visit AARP's guide to reverse mortgages at www.aarp.org/revmort. We provide a copy of this guide to clients who may benefit from a reverse mortgage.

College Funding

The most important financial goals to middle Americans tend to be:

- Owning their own home

- Educating their kids

- Retiring comfortably

College funding is almost always a priority for my clients with children. Parents want to pay the lion's share of the costs to send their children to the college(s) of their choice. Yet, most of my clients had to pay part or all of their own way through college. Tuition is five to ten times the amount it was when my clients were in college. Fortunately, required room and board has not increased that dramatically.

The standard of living for college students is much greater now than it was when their parents were in school. The parent's (my) generation drove old, fully paid for cars – if we had one. Two pairs of good jeans was a wardrobe. We didn't have cell phones, computers, Palm Pilots and three pairs of Nikes. We didn't eat out much, and when we did it was on the cheap. Cooking to a college student meant "mac and cheese" out of a box, 3 for $1.

But the generation heading off to college has had it pretty good as young, middle Americans. Their standard of living may drop dramatically when they move away from home. Parents don't want to see their kids have to struggle. They often desire to provide more financial support to their college students than they can afford. Helping our clients to balance priorities is one of our most important jobs as financial planners.

Quicken (www.quicken.com) has a wonderful tool that allows you to quickly find the current tuition rates and room and board for any college in the country. I find it valuable to have costs for our local colleges and universities readily available.

Most clients that hire me for college-funding advice also engage me to provide retirement projections. Thus, we know what assets and discretionary income they have to accomplish both goals. Generally, some compromise must be achieved. Clients will either have to tighten their budget, or make other adjustments, such as working longer. They may have to forgo their plan to retire at 60 if they want to send junior to the art institute.

Most clients are willing to adjust their retirement objectives — but only so far. If they can retire at 65 and still be able to send junior to the art institute, they want our help to make it happen. However, if our analysis reveals that they would have to work 15 years longer than they had hoped to, the shortfall is coming out of the kid's college education fund.

I rarely meet parents that will forego their retirement to make sure they pay for their kids' college educations. But it does happen. I have worked with families who would do anything to make sure they could send their children to any institution they wanted to go. Education of their children is the primary goal of these clients.

It is my belief that if a person wants to go to college, they can and should go. There are lots of options to help them achieve that goal. But parents may not have the option of working forever.

The *cost* of a college education varies greatly depending on the institution selected, the financial assistance available, and the student's lifestyle. The tuition to attend the community junior college is often a fraction of the price to attend the state university. In-state tuition is significantly cheaper than out-of-state tuition.

If the student attends his first two years at junior college, then transfers to the university of his choice, mom and dad could save a lot of money, and the diploma still says "My-Choice-U." What negative impact would attending junior college for two years and then graduating from the state/private university have on the child's career or life ambitions? We need to help our clients determine the financial impact of these decisions.

This is the art of what we do. We must help the client achieve appropriate balance for themselves without letting our personal judgments interfere. We are advisors and there is a fine line between providing advice and making judgments. It's their life, and we are hired to help them plan for their life *financially*.

At the rate technology and distance learning programs are advancing, and traditional college tuitions increasing, in the future we may be seeing a lot of students attend "virtual" college classes.

The cost of sending a child to college can be a difficult thing to estimate. We must project the type of institution they will attend, how many years they should plan for, how much college costs may inflate and the cost of room and board. Unless they can easily fund both their retirement and education objectives (which makes trying to achieve a balance a moot point), we generally run two scenarios. We start by getting input from the clients regarding (1) the minimum goals they want to accomplish, and (2) their optimum goals. The first projection will show how their retirement plans will be impacted if they are funding for the minimal level of college support. The second scenario will reveal the impact of the full funding objective. With that information, we can assist the client in making the best decisions for them.

There are many excellent college-funding calculators on the web. I recommend www.Quicken.com and www.FinanCenter.com. As I mentioned earlier, we use MoneyTree's EasyMoney as our primary financial planning software. EasyMoney has a quality education-funding module. It provides more flexibility than any of the online college funding calculators with which I have worked.

Once we determine the appropriate funding level, we then must consider the most effective funding strategy. Over the last few years. Congress has given us some new and wonderful education funding programs (see Figure 5.12).

Figure 5.12

EDUCATION INCENTIVES			
INCENTIVE	TAX BENEFIT	HIGHER EDUCATION EXPENSES COVERED	PHASEOUTS
Qualified Tuition Plans	Up to $110,000 or more can be contributed to a tax-deferred account per beneficiary. If not used for education, then earnings subject to 10% penalty. Can be rolled over to other beneficiaries.	Tuition, fees, books, supplies, equipment, room, and board.	Not Applicable.
HOPE Scholarship Credit	Credit of $1,500 per student for each of the first two years of postsecondary education. Credit is 100% of first $1,000 of expenses and 50% of second $1,000 of expenses. These amounts could be indexed for inflation beginning in 2003.	Tuition and related expenses of taxpayer, taxpayer's spouse, or taxpayer's dependent. Not room, board, books, student activity fees, athletic fees, insurance expenses, or transportation expenses.	Phased out for single taxpayers from $40,000 to $50,000 ($80,000 to $100,000 for joint filers).
Lifetime Learning Credit	Credit of 20% of up to $5,000 ($10,000 after 2003) of higher education expenses paid by the taxpayer. Cannot be used in year HOPE Credit is claimed.	Same as HOPE Credit.	Same as HOPE Credit.
Education Savings Account	Up to $2,000 per year can be contributed to a tax-free account. Limited to $2,000 per beneficiary (child). Not taxable when used for beneficiary's education expenses. If not, then subject to additional 10% penalty. Can be rolled over to other beneficiaries.	Tuition, fees, books, supplies, equipment, room, and board. Also, qualified elementary and secondary education expenses, such as tuition, fees, academic tutoring, and special needs services, and computers or Internet access fees during any school years of the beneficiary.	Phased out for single taxpayers from $95,000 to $110,000 of AGI and for joint filers from $190,000 to $220,000 of AGI.
Interest on Education Loans	Above the line deduction for interest on student loans. $2,500.	Tuition, fees, books, supplies, equipment, room, and board.	Phased out for single taxpayers from $50,000 to $65,000 of AGI and for joint filers from $100,000 to $130,000 of AGI.
Educational Savings Bonds	Interest earnings can be withdrawn tax-free if used for education.	Same as HOPE credit, but taxpayer must be at least age 24.	Phased out for single taxpayers from $57,600 to $72,600 of AGI and for joint filers from $86,40 to $116,400 of AGI.

Reprinted with permission from *101 Tax Saving Ideas* (Wealth Builders Press, 6th edition, 2002), by Randy Gardner, LL.M., CPA, CFP, and Julie Welch, CPA, CFP.

Coverdell Education Savings Account (ESA)

The first great option we have available is the Coverdell Education Savings Account (ESA), previously called an Education IRA. When ESAs were first introduced, it allowed people to save $500 per year per child in a tax deferred investment account. Recently the laws were greatly improved by increasing the allowable contribution rate to $2,000 per child per year.[10] Before, we found if difficult to invest $500 conveniently. Our investment options are greatly enhanced now that the maximum annual-per-child contribution has been increased to $2000.

The primary features and benefits of the Coverdell Education Savings account are very similar to those of Roth IRAs:

- You don't get a deduction at the time of contribution; however, the earnings grow tax-free, and if the funds are used to pay qualified education expenses, they are not taxed upon withdrawal.

- The child is the owner of the account.

- Maximum contribution is $2,000 per year per child.

- Contributions can be made until the child/owner reaches age 18.

- Contributions may be made until April 15 of the following year.

- Anyone with income less than $110,000 ($220,000 if married filing jointly) may contribute on behalf of the child.

  - Full contribution is allowed if income is less than $95,000 for single taxpayers and $190,000 if married filing jointly.

  - Phase-out occurs between $190,000 – $220,000 for those who are married filing jointly. For all other taxpayers, phase-out occurs between $95,000 - $110,000.

  - Parents ineligible to make an ESA contribution due to income level may gift funds to another family member, such as a grandparent, who meets the income requirement and can in turn make the annual contributions.

- Money contributed to an ESA can qualify for the gift tax annual exclusion.

- Balance of account generally must be distributed by the time the child is age 30.

  - Distributions are tax-free and penalty-free if used to pay for qualified education expenses. (Qualified education expenses include any qualified elementary, secondary and post-secondary school tuition, fees, books and supplies. Room and board for a full-time college student may also be considered qualified education expenses.)

  - The child may transfer the account tax-free and penalty-free to an ESA of a family member or their own child.

  - Distributions for any other purpose are subject to tax and penalty.

- You may claim the Hope Scholarship Credit or the Lifetime Learning Credit for part of the educational expenses and use tax-free ESA distributions for the expenses over and above the credit taken.

Section 529 Plans

Qualified tuition savings plans (Section 529 plans) have evolved into one of the most attractive college savings programs available to middle Americans. Contributions grow tax-free until distribution. Distributions are also tax-free if used to pay for qualified education expenses.

Contributions to a Section 529 plan can be significantly greater than those allowed in an Education Savings Account. Contributors may also be able to take a tax deduction on their state income tax return for the year in which the contribution is made if they are residents of the state sponsoring the plan. One can make contributions to any state's qualified tuition savings plan, however, no state income tax deduction is granted unless the contributor resides in that state.

The amount you put into a qualified tuition plan is considered a gift, unlike contributions to ESAs. The maximum contribution you can make to a plan is set by the state sponsoring the plan.

The web site www.SavingforCollege.com is an excellent resource on 529 plans. They provide proprietary "5-Cap Ratings" on all 529 plans offered. This site also allows one to conduct a side-by-side comparison of all 529 plans based on criteria that is important to you and your client. It is an extremely valuable comparison tool.

UTMA/UGMA

With the other education savings plans available today, we find no use for UTMA/UGMA (Uniform Transfer to Minors / Uniform Gift to Minors) accounts. With the 1986 tax law changes, the advantages of these accounts became extremely minimal – too minimal, in my opinion, for parents to give up control of assets. However, a lot of our clients still have them. Most were set up prior to 1986.

We must be aware that taxable income and capital gains distributions come from UTMA/UGMA accounts. They may have to be reported on the parent's tax return if the child is under age 14. These accounts are not tax-deferred or tax-free education savings plans and pale in comparison to the Section 529 and Coverdell Education Savings accounts now available.

Many clients have asked if they can take money out of over-funded UTMA/UGMA accounts to keep it away from a child nearing age of majority. The answer is no, they can't. These are already the children's assets. As guardians of minor children, parents must protect these assets. Parents have a legal obligation to provide for the care of their children. Unfortunately, I know of no court case that has defined just exactly for what reasons a custodian can remove assets from a child's ownership.

Financial Aid

Financial aid planning is an important subspecialty of college planning. Regardless of whether our clients have the assets to pay for their child's college expenses, it is generally advisable for them to apply for financial assistance with the federal and state governments, and institutional assistance, as well.

I do not consider myself to be a financial aid specialist. I outsource this part of my services to Collegiate Funding Solutions (www.cf-solutions.com). As a licensed provider of "a college-funding Solutions Plan" from Collegiate Funding, I can efficiently provide an extremely useful service. Most Middle Americans can greatly benefit from implementing the basic strategies revealed in a "Solutions Plan." These simple, but often-overlooked techniques will enhance the amount and possibility of receiving financial aid for the student.

Practitioners serving the Middle Market should know the deadlines and process involved in applying for financial aid. With appropriate lead-time, we may be able to lower the "Expected Family Contribution." Simple income and asset transfer techniques can result in hundreds of dollars saved for the client.

Education funding is one of the top three financial objectives of mainstream Americans. Financial aid is a significant factor for most clients being able to achieve their dream. Practitioners who elect to specialize in college funding must dedicate themselves to continual education in the area of financial aid, or outsource this part of their service. As mentioned above, I outsource to Collegiate Funding Solutions, Inc. I find their services to be cost-effective, thorough and very educational.

As we discussed earlier, parents must often compromise their retirement objectives in order to accomplish their desire to pay for their children's college education. Generally, when we are talking about this type of compromise, college is many years away. But, unfortunately, many parents don't have a lot of time to plan and save. They have three children ranging in age from 12 to 16. Their compromise may have to come from their children. They may have to pay for these costs out of cash flow, somehow, or they may have to borrow money personally.

When borrowing money to pay for college expenses, I first want to see the student take out Stafford (federal unsubsidized) loans. These student loans are *not* need-based. The student can receive this loan regardless of whether the family qualified for financial aid. Currently, the interest rate on these loans is at an all time low of 4.06%. Repayment of the principal of Stafford loans begins six months after the student graduates. The next best option for college financing is generally Federal PLUS (Parents' Loans for Undergraduate Students) loans. These are unsecured loans and the current interest rate is 4.86%. Interest on student loans is also tax deductible in many cases. If additional borrowing is necessary, we consider a home equity line of credit and then a 401(k) plan loan, while remaining conscious of the need for balance between the education and retirement funding objectives.

Financial Independence / Retirement

Performing a retirement capital needs analysis will answer the question, "how much is enough?" But we must first know what the client's retirement lifestyle might be like. Will the client stay in their current home or will they downsize at or during retirement? Do they plan to travel or take up an expensive hobby once they have more leisure time? Some costs may go down at retirement, but very few retirees actually spend less than they did before they retired – unless they have to.

For most clients, we project that they will need a least 100% of what they currently spend for basic living expenses. We allow debt service payments to continue on their current amortization schedule. The cost of other periodic expenses such as home repairs, vacations, and the replacement of vehicles are added to the projection. Do we need to add the cost of health insurance or long-term care insurance? Which expenses cease in the latter years of retirement? Elderly adults tend to spend much less on basic living expenses and entertainment than younger retirees. However, I am reluctant to project that living expenses will go down in the future. The cost of health care has increased significantly faster than most other expense items. The reductions experienced in some areas may be offset by increased health care costs.

It is estimated that elder seniors spend approximately ⅓ of their monthly income on health care expenses. I once ran a retirement scenario that illustrates this potential inevitability. My client spends $5,500 per month on basic living expenses including her health insurance, prescriptions and other related medical costs. I inflated living expenses at 3%. However, as a very knowledgeable consultant to the health care industry, she was uncomfortable with that assumption for medical expenses. As a result, my client asked me to separate the health care costs from her other expenses, and inflate just those costs (health care) by 10% per year instead of the 3% per year I had been using for all living expenses. It was shocking how much this impacted her total living expense needs later in life. Heath care costs made up half of her income need at mortality.

Retirement Capital Needs Computation

We utilize MoneyTree's EasyMoney module for most of our financial planning analysis and projections. We also own MoneyTree's Golden Years and Silver Planner retirement projections modules, which are integrated with EasyMoney. Each module serves a different planning purpose. For "quick" projections and to graphically illustrate the impact of a change to basic assumptions, such as savings rate or inflation, Silver Planner is used. For clients with detailed cash flow planning needs, or for those who are nearing or in retirement, Golden Years is a very powerful tool. However, for most retirement projections we use EasyMoney.

MoneyTree also has a Monte Carlo simulation program. I find this analysis very informative. It helps us to remain ever conscious of the errors of averages. Remember, when we use averages, actual annual returns will be higher or lower then the average.

When we use static averages in our long-term projections, we must be very conservative. Unfortunately, some clients don't want to "buy-in" to what they feel are too conservative assumptions. Our initial retirement capital needs computation may indicate that the client will meet their retirement income objectives if they receive an annual rate of return of 7%, year-in and year-out. Sounds simple enough, doesn't it?

Monte Carlo simulation reveals the impact of volatility on this assumed rate of return. One may be able to achieve a long-term average return of 7% with limited or substantial volatility. These ranges of returns over time provide us with the "average" rate of return. Monte Carlo takes into account the assumed volatility of returns and plots out potential outcomes. If a series of bad results happen in the early years of retirement, the client may run out of money decades too soon. If the best results happen in the early years of retirement, the client may die with millions of dollars. However, the average result shows that they might narrowly achieve their objective.

Advisors, as well as clients, must understand the limits of static averages in financial planning projections. Monte Carlo helps illustrate the probabilities of achieving financial independence based on certain assumptions. We lower the static average assumption until the probability of success is fairly certain.

There are numerous software programs and retirement calculators on the Web, which consumers can use. Many of these programs are excellent tools. However, most are very simplistic and cannot handle the huge number of potential variables and planning options a professional advisor is trained to recognize and project.

The basic assumptions a professional advisor uses will generally be significantly more reliable than what a novice consumer might think is appropriate. My default assumptions are as follows:

- Clients will need at least 100% of their current income in retirement, and possibly more in the early years of retirement.

- Cost of living increases at no less than 3% per year.

- Long-term rates of return on retirement assets are no more than 4% above the inflation rate.

- Social Security projections

  - I do not project that clients under 40 will receive any Social Security retirement benefits.

  - I discount the projected amount of Social Security benefits for clients between 40-50 by 50%.

  - For clients over 50, we illustrate their projected retirement benefit. However, if clients can handsomely meet their retirement objectives without including Social Security, I will run a scenario without it. There are so many variables that can change long-term projections. I do not want to give clients the illusion that they have all this surplus wealth now. I don't want them to change the wonderful habits that will make their goals possible.

  - I use an inflation assumption on Social Security income of 1% per year.

- I do not assume tax rates will go down in the future.

- I project life expectancy to at least age 100.

As I discussed earlier in this chapter, most clients have to achieve some compromise in their financial objectives. Virtually no one can have everything they might want, no matter how much money they have. We all must decide what is most important to us.

Earlier in this century, average life expectancy was *much* shorter then it is now. When the Social Security program was introduced, recipients were only expected to receive benefits for a couple of years. Now many Americans will live longer in retirement than they spent in the workforce.

However, most Americans still hope to retire by age 65. This objective may be unrealistic. The capital needed to fund retirement income for 35 years is staggering. Most middle Americans will not be able to maintain their standard of living for such a long period of time. They must work longer, have additional income after "traditional" retirement, reduce their living expenses or save a substantially larger asset base than they might be able to accumulate.

A professional advisor must help clients balance their objectives with reality.

I am seeing a trend with clients who want to "retire" from their current careers in their 50's and 60's, but continue to earn an income doing something they really love. Most of the time this means that they may have much less income. Balance and quality of life are most important to them. They are willing to work much longer than traditional retirement ages if they can do what they truly love.

I once had the pleasure of working with a couple in their mid-40's who could leave their fulltime professional careers and live the life they dreamed. They had become successful part-time artists. They plan to enjoy this work indefinitely. In our retirement planning projections we determined that they must cover their basic living expenses with income earned from their artwork until at least age 75. This part-time income, along with their inherent frugality made it possible for them to leave the hectic pace of their former careers and still have a high probability of achieving financial independence.

Qualified Retirement Plans

Virtually every middle American that I've worked with needs to save more to achieve their retirement objectives. They also have access to a qualified retirement plan through their employer, or they could establish a qualified retirement plan as self-employed individuals. Often, middle Americans are not fully utilizing these vehicles. I believe the underutilization of qualified retirement plans is a result of:

- Ignorance regarding how the plans work

- Underestimating the benefits of utilizing these plans

- Lack of understanding of just how much clients must save in order to achieve their retirement objectives

Throughout the planning process, we calculate the savings requirement and help educate clients on the mechanics and value of their qualified retirement plan. Retirement plans are the best tax shelter around. Many employer-sponsored retirement plans also provide a matching contribution (or a percentage-based contribution, based on the employee's contributions) to participants. This is like finding "free money" and clients who are not fully taking advantage of a retirement plan with an employer match need to be educated about the opportunity. These plans usually have hardship withdrawal provisions; they may also have loan provisions.

Generally, consumers are uncomfortable investing in something they do not understand, or something they feel they are locked into. As professional advisors, we can help eliminate the mystery of qualified retirement plans and illustrate the substantial benefits of tax-advantaged retirement savings vehicles for our clients.

I use "One-Sheets" to illustrate the value of investing through their 401(k) versus a non-tax deferred retirement vehicle (see Figure 5.13).

Figure 5.13

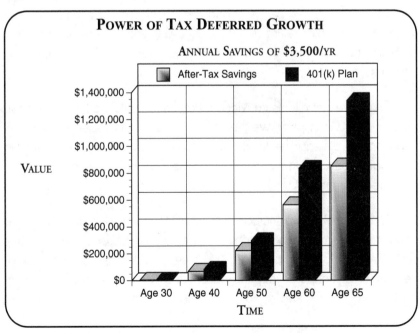

131

The most common type of qualified retirement plan available to employees is the 401(k) plan. The maximum percentage of salary that can be deferred into a 401(k) plan (according to the government) is now 100%, however, each employer plan may have a lower limit. The maximum amount of salary you can defer into a 401(k) plan for 2002 is $11,000 if you're under 50 years of age, and $12,000 if you're 50 and over. In 2003, the contribution limit increases to $12,000 for individuals under age 50 and $14,000 if you're 50 and over.

Many consumers are unaware that all of the money that they defer into a 401(k) plan is *theirs* if they leave the company. Many employers will also match a portion of the amount the employee contributes to the plan. Commonly, an employer will provide a matching contribution of 25% to 50% of the first 5% or 6% of salary contributed by the employee. Only employer contributions are subject to a vesting schedule.

It's hard for an employee to go wrong participating in a company's 401(k) plan when the employer provides a matching contribution. Even if the investment options are paltry, the matching contribution can provide a substantial return on investment. If the participant invests his or her contributions into a stable value sub-account and receives a minimal return of 4 to 5% per year and they receive a 25% matching contribution, their total return is nearly 30% per year. There are no other vehicles that can provide this type of investment return with such minimal risk.

Once we get clients convinced that they should participate in their employer's 401(k) plan, we then have to help them increase their contributions to at least the level the employer matches. I use the simple techniques outlined in Figure 5.14 ("Save That Raise") to coach clients in increasing their 401(k) contributions.

Once clients have increased their 401(k) plan contributions to the amount of the matching contribution, we then encourage them to make Roth IRA contributions, presuming (1) they need to save additionally for retirement (which is usually the case), and (2) they're eligible to contribute to a Roth. If they're not eligible to make a Roth contribution, we generally recommend that they increase their 401(k) contribution to the maximum allowed by law, or their retirement funding requirement, whichever comes first.

In some circumstances, clients have minimal investments outside of qualified retirement plans. In these cases, we recommend that clients first contribute to their 401(k) plan in the amount the company will match, then make Roth IRA contributions, and then invest any additional savings for retirement in their personal ownership. This is not the most tax-effective investment strategy, but it does provide considerably more flexibility and therefore may be more palatable to the client.

There are ways to minimize current taxation on personal investment assets. We'll discuss ways to manage the tax effects on these assets later in this chapter. The most important factor is that the clients save the required amount needed to achieve their retirement objectives.

On the rare occasion that a client has "maxed out" their 401(k) plan, has a reasonable amount of investment assets outside of qualified retirement plans, and is not eligible to make a Roth IRA contribution, but still needs to save additionally for retirement, we recommend nondeductible IRAs.

Figure 5.14

Save That Raise!

- Consider increasing your 401(k) contribution each time you receive an increase in your salary.

        Example: You receive a 2% cost-of-living increase.
                         Subsequently, you increase your 401(k) contribution by 3%.

                         After factoring in your tax savings, your net take home pay hardly changes. But you are saving an additional 3% of your salary to help meet your long-term goals.

- Another strategy is to make a deal with yourself to spend one-half of any salary increase and invest the other half in your 401(k) plan.

Figure 5.15

IRA CHOICES FOR 2001 AND LATER

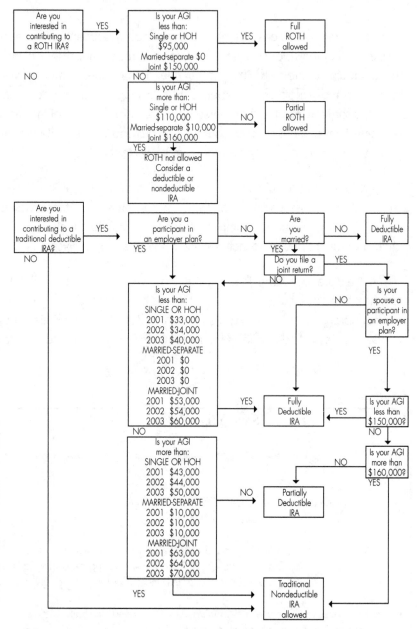

NOTE: You, and/or your spouse if you are married, must have earned income of at least the amount you contribute to your total IRAs. Reprinted with permission from *101 Tax Saving Ideas*, (Wealth Builders Press, 6th edition, 2002), by Randy Gardner, LL.M., CPA, CFP, and Julie Welch, CPA, CFP.

Figure 5.16

IRA vs. Taxable Account

You are in the 34% (27% Federal and 7% state) tax rate bracket. You earn 10% (6.6% after tax) (10% x (1 - 34%)) on your investments. You make $3,000 contributions at the beginning of the year for 20 years to the following accounts:

	Roth IRA	Traditional Deductible IRA	Traditional Nondeductible IRA	Taxable Account
Annual contribution	$ 3,000	$ 3,000	$ 3,000	$ 3,000
Tax savings ($3,000 x 34%)		1,020		
Cumulative contributions	60,000	60,000	60,000	60,000
Account value – Year 20	189,007	189,007	189,007	125,517
Tax on distribution ($189,007 x 34%)		(64,262)		
(($189,007 - 60,000) x 34%)			(43,862)	
Net cash from tax savings including interest earned		42,676		
Net cash	$189,007	$167,421	$ 145,145	$ 125,517

Thus, if your tax rate stays the same for all 20 years, and if you have a choice between the above accounts (based on your income level and your participation in a retirement plan), your first choice would be to make your contributions to a Roth IRA.

However, if your tax rate decreases after you retire, a traditional deductible IRA may be better. Assume your Federal tax rate drops to 15% (22% including the 7% state tax rate) in year 20 when you withdraw the money.

	Roth IRA	Traditional Deductible IRA	Traditional Nondeductible IRA	Taxable Account
Annual contribution	$ 3,000	$ 3,000	$ 3,000	$ 3,000
Tax savings ($3,000 x 34%)		1,020		
Cumulative contributions	60,000	60,000	60,000	60,000
Account value – Year 20	189,007	189,007	189,007	125,517
Tax on distribution ($189,007 x 22%)		(41,582)		
(($189,007- 60,000) x 22%)			(28,382)	
Net cash from tax savings including interest earned		42,676		
Net cash	$189,007	$190,101	$160,625	$ 125,517

In this case, your first choice would be to make your contributions to a traditional deductible IRA.

If you're self-employed, you can establish a retirement plan for yourself and make tax-deductible contributions. Self-employed people can set up a Keogh plan or a Simplified Employee Pension Plan (SEP) or a SIMPLE plan. The chart in Figure 5.17 compares the basic features of these plans.

Figure 5.17

RETIREMENT PLAN ALTERNATIVES FOR 2002

Plan Type	Contributions	Distributions	Phaseouts
Individual Retirement Accounts (IRA)	Limited to $3,000 ($3,500 if age 50+) per person or rollover amount. Deductible if not active participant in qualified plan or if under phase-out levels.	Taxable unless contributions were not deductible. May be subject to 10% penalty tax unless taxpayer is 59½, dead, disabled, first-time homebuyer, receiving over life expectancy, using for higher education expenses, or using for deductible medical expenses.	If active participant, $34,000 of AGI if single ($54,000 if married). Rising to $50,000 for single and $80,000 for married by 2007. If spouse only is active participant, $150,000 - 160,000 of AGI.
Roth IRA	Limited to $3,000 ($3,500 if age 50+) for IRAs and Roth IRAs, or rollover. Not deductible. May be made after age 70½. Conversion opportunity.	Not taxable. May be subject to 10% penalty if made early.	Phased out for single taxpayers from $95,000 to $110,000 of AGI and for joint filers from $150,000 to $160,000 of AGI.
Simplified Employee Pension Plan (SEP).	Deductible up to the lesser of $40,000 or about 20% of compensation. Discrimination rules apply.	Taxable. May be subject to 10% penalty if made early.	Not Applicable.
Keogh Plans	Deductible. Depending on the plans, about 20% of earnings. Discrimination rules apply.	Taxable. May be subject to 10% penalty if made early.	Not Applicable.
401(k) Plans	Exclusion from wages up to lesser of 100% of wages or $11,000 ($12,000 if age 50+).	Taxable. May be subject to 10% penalty if made early.	Not applicable, but special rules apply for highly compensated employees.
SIMPLE Plans	Deductible up to $7,000 ($7,500 if age 50+). Requires employer match for most employees.	Taxable. May be subject to 10% penalty if made early.	Not Applicable.

Reprinted with permission from *101 Tax Saving Ideas*, (Wealth Builders Press, 6th edition, 2002), by Randy Gardner, LL.M., CPA, CFP, and Julie Welch, CPA, CFP.

Only after all of the above retirement funding options have been maximized and the clients have developed a fairly substantial, tax-efficient personal portfolio will we consider annuities as a retirement funding vehicle.

PLANNING FOR LIFE'S TRANSITIONS

Many clients first contact me because they're going through some type of life transition. They may be starting their first job or changing careers. They may be newly married, starting a family, preparing for or recently divorced, or preparing for retirement.

Usually something in an individual's life (or current market events) prompts them to seek out the advice of a financial planner. Sometimes people assume that because I will allow a client to engage me for a very limited scope of services that I do not even discuss the rest of the client's financial situation with them.

Regardless of the event that motivated a prospective client to call, I always go through a thorough data gathering process centered on our Confidential Questionnaire (see Figure 5.1) at each initial meeting.

My objectives for the initial meeting are:

- Determine the scope of services that should be provided at this time

- Provide a fee quote

- Request additional data needed to complete the project

- Schedule the presentation meeting

Prospective clients may have contacted me for input on their 401(k) plan allocation. However, by the time we have discussed the information provided on the Confidential Questionnaire we generally determine that there several other areas that need to be addressed at this time as well.

Clients rarely balk at the services I recommend or my fee quote. This is probably due to the fact that I am very conscientious of their needs, priorities and resources. I try to put myself in their shoes. If I only had $4,000 in the bank and $200 dollars a month discretionary income, how much would I be willing to spend on a financial advisor's services at this time? What services are really essential? What can the client do to keep the cost down?

As I've mentioned before, I would much rather help a client with one or a few areas of their financial situation, than miss out on the opportunity to help them at all.

The client who is changing careers or just starting a new job may need advice on completing their W-2 form, taking full advantage of the employee benefits plan, and how to allocate 401(k) contributions.

If a client is leaving a current salaried position to start a business of their own, we must consider additional issues. We strongly recommend that a home-equity line of credit be established before leaving current employment, if one is not already in place. We must consider options available for medical and disability insurance. Can this individual be covered on their spouse or domestic partner's group plan? Can the employer-sponsored medical or disability insurance be converted to individual policies? If these options are not available, approximately how much will it cost to adequately replace this insurance protection? Eventually, we will need to consider establishing a qualified retirement plan to maximize the self-employed individual's retirement funding options.

For those clients who are newly married or just starting a family, our primary focus will be on current and near-term cash flow needs. How has the merger of two individual's financial lives set the stage for their financial planning together? Many of these issues need to get out in the open. My role is to help clients recognize how their financial lives have changed and what steps we need to be taking now to help them fulfill their long-term financial objectives.

Unfortunately, many clients first come to me immediately after divorce. I say this is unfortunate because often times they may have been much better served seeking out the advice of a financial planner *prior* to negotiating their divorce settlement. I do not hold myself out as a divorce-planning specialist. In the event that a prospective client needing specific divorce planning expertise contacts me, I will refer this individual to a colleague who specializes in this area. Once the divorce is final, I am more than happy to enter into a traditional financial planning relationship with this client.

For clients who've already divorced, we often need to focus their attentions on redefining themselves as an individual financially. What are their expenses? What income sources are there? What are the most immediate and pressing needs of this client? What are his or her financial and life goals? We must spend a considerable amount of time working out the current cash flow needs before we can start planning seriously for the future.

These types of engagements often involve several meetings spread over many months. Occasionally, people come to me looking for a miracle. I had an initial meeting with a prospective client who had retired from teaching 3 years earlier. She was receiving her full teacher's retirement benefit, but that only provided her with about ½ of the income she needed. So she went back to teaching fulltime, with another school district, and continued to draw her pension. She spent all of her income. She hoped that I could invest her IRA assets – $56,000 – so that she could afford to quit working in three years when she turns 65. I could tell that she would likely run out of money within 5 years, if she didn't work longer, save more, *and* spend less. That was not the news she wanted. She wanted an investment miracle.

I gave her a copy of *Your Money or Your Life* and encouraged her to start making reductions to her budget now and save more for retirement. She also needed to consider working longer if she couldn't greatly reduce her expenditures. There must be an adjustment in lifestyle. It will either come when she ultimately retires or the adjustments can begin now. It would be easier to tolerate if these adjustments were gradually implemented over time.

Unfortunately, too many Americans go into retirement with a warped perspective regarding how much money they will need to maintain their standard of living. Without the assistance of a qualified financial advisor, these retirees may have a very rude awakening. They fail to appreciate the devastating effects inflation can have on their standard of living over time. They expect the current interest rate environment to remain unchanged. Their retirement plans may work out okay – if they don't experience any market downturns. Many clients who retired three years ago are now questioning whether they made the right decision.

Recently, I've seen a lot of clients who had adequate cash flow when interest rates on fixed income investments were higher. However, these clients now may be receiving less than two-thirds of the income they received just a few years ago. If they had any money in the stock market, it has also lost ground. These retirees are facing the hard realities that too many Americans have faced in the past. Without the guidance of a personal financial advisor, many people retire before they are financially able to do so, and/or they invest their retirement nest egg inappropriately.

About three years ago I allowed myself to get into a debate with a prospective client who, with some limited knowledge, had convinced himself and his wife that they could retire in 10 years and maintain their current standard of living. They had about $500,000 in investment assets when we met. The gentleman concluded that in 10 years, when they were age 60, they should have about $1,400,000. This was based on his assumption that he could earn 10% per year, year-in and year-out, on these investments. He knew that the stock market has averaged about 10% per year over time, and that is what he was basing his calculation on.

Their objective was to have $100,000 per year in after-tax income. So he determined that they needed $1,400,000 at retirement to provide $140,000 (10%) gross earnings, which would yield about $100,000 after-tax.

I tried to explain why this strategy had little hope of success. Primarily, they can't count on 10% rates of return year-in and year-out, and they had not factored in the effects of inflation. The gentleman felt that if they received $100,000 per year in after-tax income, they should be able to handle whatever inflation comes their way. He felt that "a good financial advisor" could make certain that they received a "measly" 10% per year return (remember this was in 1999). Needless to say, I told them I couldn't deliver those results with any degree of certainty and anyone who said they could, shouldn't be trusted. We parted company and I haven't heard from them since.

Financial planning is all about setting goals and plotting out a course that will most efficiently help us achieve our goals with a high probability of success. However, there may be events in our lives that abruptly change our course. The death of a family member, the loss of a job and long-term illness can all have a major impact on our lives. However, they don't necessarily have to have a major impact on one's financial plan. We should do our best to prepare for these events by adequately insuring our families and having what we believe is an appropriate level of cash reserves.

INVESTMENT PORTFOLIO DESIGN

The first step in designing an investment portfolio is determining the objectives for the assets. For what purposes are the funds being accumulated? When will the funds be needed? Some objectives must be funded immediately (i.e., *needs*). Other objectives are *desires* that the client hopes to accomplish in the future; these can be funded over time.

There may be many objectives and time horizons that apply to a client's investment portfolio. Clients will probably have assets that need to be available in a few years to replace a car, pay for college expenses or pay for a wedding. Other assets may be earmarked for longer-term objectives (e.g., buying a retirement home), and still other assets must be available to fund retirement living expenses.

As mentioned previously, we all must prioritize our objectives and determine what we are willing to sacrifice in order to achieve our most important objectives. We can't have everything we may want. The greatest value a professional advisor can provide is assisting clients with prioritizing their goals and developing a strategy that most effectively achieves the goals that are most important to the client.

Determining Risk Tolerance

In my opinion, determining a client's tolerance for risk is a very subjective art. Human beings tend to be overly confident when their most recent investment experiences have been very positive. Conversely, investors often become overly pessimistic when their recent experiences have been very negative.

My firm utilizes a Risk Tolerance Questionnaire (see Figure 5.18). We had an industrial psychologist (one who specializes in developing questionnaires for the financial services industry) create our Risk Tolerance Questionnaire. The goal of the questionnaire was to make it short enough that a client would complete it, and thorough enough to provide meaningful information.

Figure 5.18

The Garrett Planning Network, Inc.

Risk Tolerance Questionnaire

Show how much you **Agree** or **Disagree** with each of the following investment statements by marking the appropriate box at the end of each sentence.

	Disagree				Agree
I can accept minor fluctuations in my account value in exchange for more income.	❏	❏	❏	❏	❏

	Disagree				Agree
I can accept a small risk of loss and somewhat larger fluctuations in my account value in exchange for conservative growth opportunity and the possibility of more income.	❏	❏	❏	❏	❏

	Disagree				Agree
I can accept a greater risk of loss and greater fluctuations in my account value in exchange for more aggressive growth opportunities.	❏	❏	❏	❏	❏

	Disagree				Agree
I can accept the risk of significant losses and large fluctuations in my account value in exchange for very aggressive, rapid growth opportunities.	❏	❏	❏	❏	❏

Figure 5.18 (Cont'd)

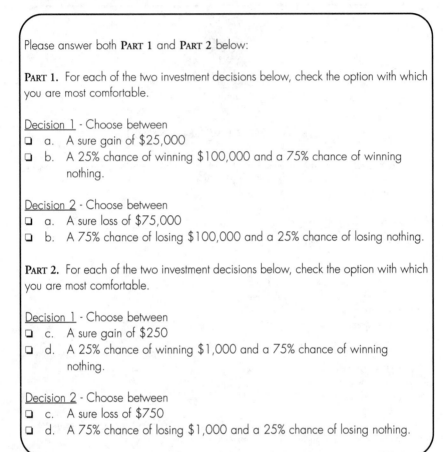

Please answer both **PART 1** and **PART 2** below:

PART 1. For each of the two investment decisions below, check the option with which you are most comfortable.

Decision 1 - Choose between
- ❑ a. A sure gain of $25,000
- ❑ b. A 25% chance of winning $100,000 and a 75% chance of winning nothing.

Decision 2 - Choose between
- ❑ a. A sure loss of $75,000
- ❑ b. A 75% chance of losing $100,000 and a 25% chance of losing nothing.

PART 2. For each of the two investment decisions below, check the option with which you are most comfortable.

Decision 1 - Choose between
- ❑ c. A sure gain of $250
- ❑ d. A 25% chance of winning $1,000 and a 75% chance of winning nothing.

Decision 2 - Choose between
- ❑ c. A sure loss of $750
- ❑ d. A 75% chance of losing $1,000 and a 25% chance of losing nothing.

Figure 5.18 (Cont'd)

PLEASE ANSWER THE FOLLOWING QUESTIONS:

For your current investments, what has been your annual rate of return? _____

Have you been satisfied with that return? _____

If no, why not? _____

What percentage of your portfolio can you afford to lose or how much money can you afford to lose in any one year? _____

What action would you take if the market dropped 50% from its present value?_____
_____

Regarding your finances, what, if anything, do you spend the most time thinking about?
_____
_____

Are there things in your financial life that you wish you had done differently?
_____
_____

Are you pleased with your ability to manage and shelter your income from taxes?
_____

Are you pleased with the diversification and performance of your portfolio?
_____

What is the best and worst investment decision you have ever made?

Best: _____

Worst: _____

Are there any investments that you will NOT sell for past performance, personal or social reasons?
_____

Are there any investments that you will NOT buy for social reasons?
_____

We then provided this questionnaire to hundreds of clients, anticipating that we'd be able to draw some conclusions about the responses provided on the questionnaires and the clients' tolerance for risk. Early on, I'd hoped we would be able to generate a workable scoring system. Unfortunately, the only scoring that can be automated is on pages one and two of the questionnaire. Page three consists of essay questions, and this is where I generally get the most valuable information.

The survey revealed that investors' attitudes toward risk are much more subjective then we wish they were. We might like to have clients complete a questionnaire that would allow them to respond to each question simply by checking a box. Scoring becomes much less subjective when clients have to choose "True" or "False," or (A), (B), (C) or (D). However, the validity of the result becomes suspect if clients must choose their response from a limited number of options. The accurate response might be "sometimes," "it depends," or "possibly" rather than an absolute "always" or "never."

I find that I have to blend a lot of subjective and objective information together to form a conclusion about someone's risk tolerance. I rely not only on the Risk Tolerance Questionnaire, but also on comments the client(s) may have made during our initial meeting, the structure of their current portfolio, and their motivation for contacting me.

Behavioral finance teaches that human beings are most highly motivated by recent events. Consequently, I want to hear from the client(s) and see in their own handwriting how they feel about certain events and issues. I extrapolate from all possible sources: current portfolio allocation; recent trading activity; dialogues about priorities, and the need for security; and the formal Risk Tolerance Questionnaire.

Asset Allocation

I then classify the client(s) according to one of five model allocations, ranging from conservative to aggressive. I find that most of this determination is subjective. However, I rely heavily on the responses to their Risk Tolerance Questionnaire (primarily page 3) and their comfort level with their current portfolio allocation.

Our model portfolios (see Figure 5.19) begin with broad allocations between fixed-income and equities, and between foreign and domestic securities. We then further allocate between large and small cap, and growth versus value. For our model portfolios, the allocations are fairly generic. We don't make global allocation decisions on how much we might direct funds toward international fixed income, emerging markets, real estate, etc. For the models, we limit the allocations to very traditional, broad-based asset classes.

Figure 5.19

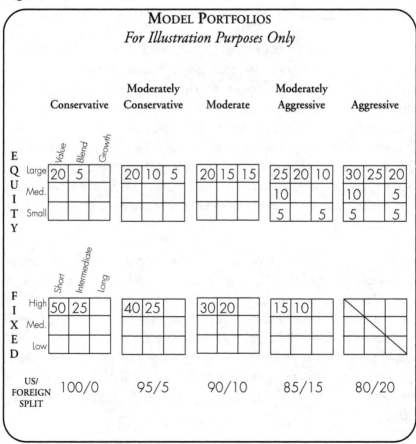

147

With the type of relationship I have with clients (i.e., providing advice on an as-needed basis), I want to do my best to provide them with an asset allocation that will *serve them well over time*. I never know how often or when I'll see them again for a review. I *want* my broad allocation decisions to stand the test of time (the key word here is *want*). They are based on my judgment about the future and my interpretations of the client's risk tolerance level. Needless to say, it is very subjective.

I am not a money manager – I am a financial planner. My objective is to achieve consistent, predictable returns over time on the entire portfolio to help the client achieve his or her financial objectives. Consequently, I want to use assumptions in my long-term projections that have a very high probability of achieving the desired outcome.

I'm a true believer in asset allocation, but I'm not comfortable with the way many advisors use optimizer software programs. I've subscribed to the top optimizer programs over the years. I appreciated having that kind of resource available – not to design recommended portfolios, but to test how different portfolio allocations would have performed over various periods of time. To make the optimizer a predictive tool, however, I'd have to know what historical time period most resembles the period we're moving into now. I can't predict the future – and neither can you. (I still haven't learned how to use the crystal ball on my conference table!)

I find Roger Gibson's book, *Asset Allocation: Balancing Financial Risk* (McGraw-Hill Trade, 2000), to be an excellent resource for advisors. Many of the graphics he provides in this book can be useful in helping clients understand and appreciate the value of a *truly* diversified portfolio. Refer to Figure 5.20 for examples of illustrations of individual asset classes versus more diversified portfolios over time (These graphics were reprinted with permission from the *Tools & Techniques of Financial Planning*, The National Underwriter Company, 6th edition, 2002, pp. 48, 55.)

Figure 5.20

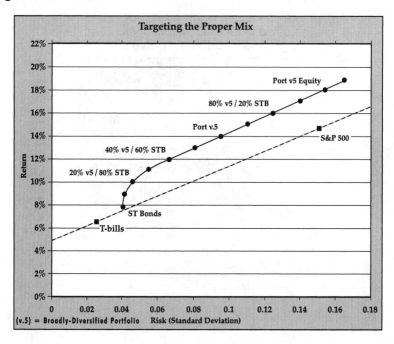

"The reference portfolio (v.5) has been diversified into eight equity segments. Seven of those segments have outperformed the S&P 500 Index on a historical basis, and one is the S&P 500 itself." (See *Tools & Techniques of Financial Planning*, p. 46.)

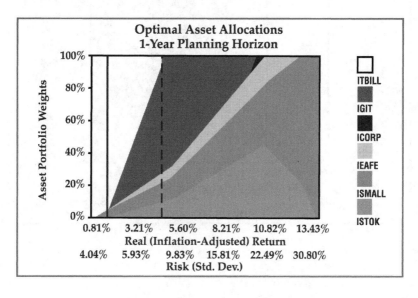

Figure 5.20 (Cont'd)

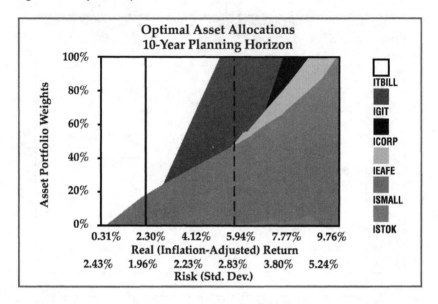

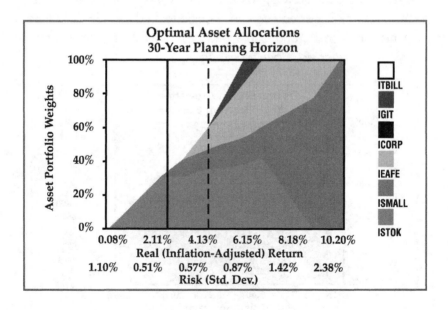

Figure 5.20 (Cont'd)

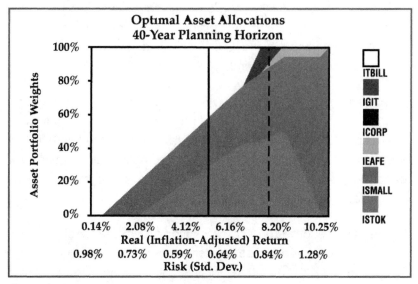

Legend

ISTOK	Inflation-Adjusted S&P 500 Stocks
ISMALL	Inflation-Adjusted Small-Cap Stocks
IEAFE	Inflation-Adjusted Foreign Stocks
ICORP	Inflation-Adjusted Corporate Bonds
IGIT	Inflation-Adjusted Intermediate Term Government Bonds
ITBILL	Inflation-Adjusted T-Bills

As stated earlier, I want to provide clients with a portfolio allocation that will serve them well over time, but I never know how often, or when, I'll see them again. Given that fact, I don't feel that an "active" investment strategy is appropriate for most Middle Market clients. Because active investment strategies should be continually monitored, I feel these strategies are appropriate only for clients who engage their advisors for continual and ongoing investment supervision.

Accordingly, I typically use passive investment strategies in the implementation of clients' portfolio allocations. For equity exposure, I utilize mutual funds exclusively. For the fixed-income component of the portfolio I usually recommend individual securities (if the portfolio is large enough to warrant individual securities). For smaller allocations to fixed-income, or to provide specific exposure to convertible bonds or high-yield securities, I use mutual funds.

Index funds (e.g., the Vanguard 500 Index and the Vanguard Total Stock Market Index) are my vehicle of choice for core U.S. large-cap or broad market exposure. In my opinion, it is very difficult for an actively managed large-cap blend U.S. stock fund to compete over time against a low-priced index fund.

However, to tailor the portfolio in the manner I feel is appropriate, I'll complement the core exposure with actively managed mutual funds. For example, over the last several years my firm has maintained a bias toward value funds. I use vehicles such as Thornburg Value, Ameristock, Dodge & Cox Stock, Clipper, T. Rowe Price Equity Income and Weitz Value Funds for this type of exposure.

I feel that the large-cap U.S. stock market is extremely efficient, yet one may be able to capitalize on inefficiencies in the small-cap market and foreign markets. Therefore, for international and small-cap exposure, I prefer actively managed mutual funds over index funds.

There is ample academic research illustrating the benefits and simplicity of passive investment strategies. I'm a firm believer that once the appropriate asset allocation has been determined, the best method of implementation for the portfolio is to use a long-term, buy and hold approach. This is especially true for clients whom we serve on a periodic or as-needed basis. We need to help clients determine their risk tolerance level, the appropriate asset allocation, and the specific vehicles with which to implement the recommended allocation.

Tracking Performance

At the beginning of each year, we undergo a very intensive, methodical mutual fund screening process utilizing Morningstar's® Principia Pro™. We screen for the top performing mutual funds on a risk-adjusted basis in each category of Morningstar's® 9-Box Style Grid™. Once we've narrowed the available options from hundreds of funds to a few dozen, we do further research, including cross-referencing with Litman/Gregory's investment consulting service, Advisor Intelligence (www.AdvisorIntelligence.com), to select the funds that will go on our recommended list.

I maintain at least four different recommended mutual fund grids: (1) domestic equity; (2) foreign equity; (3) taxable bonds; and (4) tax-exempt bond.

My recommended fund lists are much longer than those of most traditional advisors. I find it most efficient to pre-screen select funds from the major fund companies providing 401(k) plans because so many of my clients participate in 401(k) plans. Consider adding your select funds from each of the 401(k) plans you review on a grid of its own, labeled "Top 401(k) Plan Picks." The next time you work with a client who has those same investment options, you will already be aware of the funds you like. Most of your time will be spent on the allocation decision, rather then the specific investment decisions regarding the 401(k) plan assets.

You can keep track of your recommended/watch list funds' performance relative to their peers with any of the online portfolio tracking tools. I use the Mutual Fund Education Alliance's web site (www.MFEA.com) to track funds. I'll label the portfolio "Large Value" and enter one share of each mutual fund on my recommended/watch lists for that Morningstar® category into the portfolio. I also add "Most Popular" funds and benchmarks to each portfolio. With this information I can quickly determine how my fund selections are competing against a peer group and benchmark on any given day, during the last month, and year-to-date. I have a quarterly subscription to Morningstar's® Principia Pro.™ I find it very valuable to have instant access to peer group comparisons through my online portfolio tracking tools.

I've also assisted clients in setting up online tracking portfolios for themselves. We've used the Mutual Fund Education Alliance (wwwMFEA.com), Quicken (www.Quicken.com), and Morningstar® (www.Morningstar.com). We've also coached clients on using their discount broker's website and portfolio tracking tools. This coaching can be provided in my office or I can go to their computer "virtually" through our subscription with WebEx, a virtual conferencing service (www.webex.com).

How to Work Effectively With a Discount Broker

I've found that clients who are interested in saving money are more than willing to set up an investment account directly with a mutual fund company (either online or over the phone). Clients can easily consolidate and implement a diverse portfolio of securities through a discount broker. We work primarily with Schwab, Vanguard, Waterhouse and Fidelity. I have my personal preferences, but the main objective is to find a discount broker who can most effectively and affordably fulfill the client's needs.

For example, if we'll be using a lot of Vanguard funds, we recommend that the clients establish an account with Vanguard Brokerage Services. Not only can the clients purchase Vanguard funds at no fee, but within the same account they can also hold positions in virtually any other no-load fund. It's a simple, yet diversified approach – that's why I love mutual fund marketplaces.

Unfortunately, Vanguard doesn't have any local reps in our area, so a client must be comfortable completing all the paperwork (i.e., to establish new accounts and transfer assets) themselves.

My firm's discount broker of choice is Schwab. We have developed a wonderful working relationship with our local retail branch offices. Our primary contact, Dominick Lopez (at the Kansas City Country Club Plaza branch), works directly with many of our clients. Clients provide Dominick with detailed, written instructions from our firm, and he prepares all of the paperwork, processes the transfers, and places the trades. If he has any questions, he calls me. Now my clients and I have someone who will gladly take on the responsibility of the logistics of portfolio implementation, and nobody pays extra for this service. Clients have commented favorably on this personalized, attentive service. In order for clients to hire me to provide those same services, they would have had to pay an additional fee of several hundred dollars. This is yet another way I can provide just what the client needs from me at an affordable price. Again, the frugal planner mindset comes into play.

Creating an alliance with a discount brokerage house — especially when you can establish an alliance with a professional, branch office representatives who offer affordable, personalized service — is a winning situation for all parties involved. I no longer have to fill out forms, follow-up on transfers, and place trades — nor do I miss those activities. Far too often I underestimated the amount of time it actually took to finish implementing various projects. As a result, when I provided fee quotes, I also underestimated the fees. The only thing I dislike more than filling out forms and resolving transfer problems is not getting paid for it.

The client also avoids the majority of the headaches involved with implementation when working with a representative from a retail discount broker's branch office.

And finally, the branch office representative and the brokerage company also benefit by bringing additional assets to their firm. If a client already has an account with a discount broker and it's working well for them, I attempt to use that brokerage firm to implement my recommendations. It doesn't matter to me with whom a client consolidates his assets. The only thing that matters is whether the client will be able to implement the recommended portfolio easily and cost effectively.

When I worked at various wealth management firms, I dealt primarily with the institutional side of discount brokerage firms. However, once I started working with clients exclusively on an hourly, as-needed basis I found working with retail branches to be much more effective for my clientele and business model.

When designing specific implementation recommendations for a client's investment portfolio I begin with the investment plans/accounts with the most limited or restrictive options. The "best" choices available within variable contracts and qualified plans are identified first. Next, we select cash reserve vehicles and tax-efficient investments for the client's personal portfolio. Finally, we utilize IRA assets to fill out the balance of the allocation (as shown below).

- Variable annuities and life insurance
- Employer-sponsored retirement plans
  - 401(k)
  - 403(b)
  - Deferred compensation plans
- Taxable portfolios
- IRAs

TAX PLANNING

I find that I have access to all the tax information and expertise I need by using (1) a quick reference chart provided to me annually by Julie Welch[11] (one of the CPAs on my list), (2) the current editions of Tax Facts 1 and Tax Facts 2 (published annually by the National Underwriter Company[12]), and (3) my network of tax advisors. (Federal income tax rates can be found in Appendix E.)

I don't hold myself out as a tax specialist. Fortunately, most of my clients have pretty basic tax situations. When I run into an individual needing higher-level tax expertise, I gladly refer them on to a specialist.

When I start working with a client, it's beneficial to have a copy of their most current tax returns – for various reasons. As discussed in the Cash Flow section (above), I most commonly derive basic living expenses by going through the following steps:

Start with: • Net paycheck (paycheck stub, year-to-date numbers)

Subtract: • Itemized deductions (Form 1040, Schedule A)
- Insurance premiums (insurance declaration pages)
- Investment commitments (paycheck stub, investment and retirement account statements)
- Liability payments (mortgage, loan and credit card statements)

When it comes to tax planning, we don't have too many options for reducing income taxes for most middle Americans. These individuals are generally employed homeowners. They may be able to take better advantage of their employer's retirement or flexible spending plan.

We may even be able to improve on the tax efficiency of their investment portfolio. Aside from these issues, however, missed tax deductions and tax credits are the most common tax planning opportunities that I encounter (see Figure 5.21).

Figure 5.21

ITEMIZED DEDUCTIONS AND COMMONLY MISSED OPPORTUNITIES

- Medical Expenses

  - Medical and dental expenses over 7.5% of AGI are deductible from adjusted gross income, unless the expenses are reimbursed.

  - In 2002, self-employed individuals may deduct up to 70% of their health-insurance costs on their federal income tax return, and some states allow a deduction for the other 30% on the state income tax return. In 2003, self-employed individuals may deduct up to 100% of their health-insurance costs on the federal return.

- State and Local Income Tax Payments

  - Pay state 4th quarter estimated taxes by December 31st.

- Real Estate and Personal Property Taxes

  - Not only can you deduct the real estate tax on your home on your federal income tax return, you can also deduct taxes paid on vacation homes, time-shares and raw land.

  - Personal property taxes paid on vehicles, motorcycles, boats and motor homes are deductible as well.

- First and Second Home Mortgage Interest

  - Motor homes, vacation homes and some boats may qualify as a second home.

  - Home equity loans may also be deductible up to $100,000.

- Points Paid in the Year Home was Purchased

  - If points are paid when refinancing, these points may be deducted over the life of the loan, and any remaining balance may be deductible if the home is sold or the mortgage is refinanced again.

Figure 5.21 (Cont'd)

- Investment Interest Paid

    - Investment interest is deductible up to the amount of net investment interest earned; the balance can be carried forward.

    - One can elect to treat capital gains as ordinary income to increase net investment interest earned.

- Charitable Contributions

    - Cash contributions are deductible – taxpayer must keep records.
    - Contributions of $250 or more require a receipt from the charity.
    - Donations of professional services or labor are not deductible.
    - Non-cash contributions are also deductible – must keep records.
        - If non-cash contributions are $500 or less, that amount must be recorded on Schedule A. Form 8283 must be completed for larger contributions of property.
        - Obtain a copy of IRS Pub 561 for information on determining the value of donated property.
    - Donate Appreciated Property.
        - Sell *depreciated property* and donate the proceeds.
- Casualty Losses
    - May be deductible. Subject to limitations.
- Miscellaneous Deductions
    - Employee Expenses
        - Unreimbursed employee expenses
        - Professional dues and subscriptions
        - Union dues
        - Tools and uniforms
        - Job hunting costs
    - Investment Expenses
        - Tax return preparation fees
        - Investment management / financial planning fees
        - Custodial fees
        - Investment books, subscriptions and software
        - Online fees for tracking investments
        - Safe deposit box rental fees
    - Maximize by bunching deductions into one year.
- Moving Expenses

Tax Issues, Opportunities and Pitfalls for
Non-Traditional Couples

From an income tax standpoint, unmarried partners who earn similar incomes are actually better off than married couples due to the "marriage penalty."

Unmarried partners may be able to arrange their tax-deductible expenses so that the higher wage earner pays for the *tax-deductible items* and makes the charitable contributions for the couple, while the other partner claims the standard deduction. On the other hand, legally married counterparts can't take an itemized deduction *and* a standard deduction.

When opening a joint investment account, consider *whose Social Security number is listed* as primary on the account. If all else is equal, use the Social Security number of the partner in the lowest income tax bracket. That person will receive the Form 1099 and be required to report the income on their tax return.

Older, unmarried couples can earn larger amounts of income than married couples before their Social Security retirement benefits become subject to taxation.

When two people marry, or have a similar committed, long-term relationship, it is often their desire to *"merge"* their finances and own property jointly. But, be aware of the potential for inadvertent gifting. *Transferring assets to another individual is a gift.* Married individuals are allowed to claim *unlimited marital transfers* (which are not subject to gift tax); however, unmarried people are not afforded that luxury.

If one party owns a home individually, and then re-titles the asset to joint ownership, that person has *effectively made a gift* of one-half of the home to the other person. There is no problem if the other person is their legally wedded spouse. However, if the other party is not the spouse, a gift tax return must be filed if the value transferred is over $11,000 (as indexed) in any one year.

One strategy that's sometimes used when a couple wishes to transfer an asset from individual to joint ownership is to work with an attorney to draft a document that spells out the terms of the ownership transfer. For instance, if an asset valued at $50,000 was to be transferred to another person, the transfer could be set up to legally occur over a period of five years, with $10,000 being transferred to the co-owner each year. The agreement should specify the terms of the transfer in detail and what is to occur in the event of premature death, or separation of either party.

More commonly, employers are offering their unmarried workers health and other benefits for their "domestic partners." Nearly one out of every four large companies (5,000+ employees) provides health benefits to non-traditional partners, and dozens of cities and counties and a few states provide domestic partner benefits to their employees.[13] However, these benefits are taxable to the employee.

With domestic partner benefits, employees pay for their cost of the coverage with *post-tax dollars*, and then must pay taxes on the employer's share of payment for the benefits as *added income*. Married employees, on the other hand, pay no taxes on the traditional benefits they receive.

I've mentioned the primary factors regarding income taxes that one must consider when planning for "non-traditional" clients. For excellent information on all aspects of planning for couples who are not legally married, I recommend Harold Lustig's book, *4 Steps to Financial Security for Lesbian and Gay Couples.*[14]

Common Income Tax Problems

The most common income tax problems I see with employed individuals are inappropriate withholding and tax-inefficient investment portfolios. The most common tax problems I encounter with self-employed individuals are failure to deposit adequate funds in an escrow account to cover estimated tax payments and failure to file payroll taxes in a timely manner.

I recommend that Schedule C wage earners set aside 33% to 40% of their gross income each time they are paid into a money market account earmarked exclusively for tax payments. I also suggest they add a consistent percentage of their gross wages to their retirement plan each time they get paid. What is left, is their "net pay" and can be used to cover the "here and now" living expenses.

Unfortunately, if a client doesn't have the funds, they don't pay their taxes in a timely fashion. Clients occasionally owe back taxes, penalties and interest totaling thousands of dollars. Sometimes I need to refer these individuals directly to a tax attorney or CPA to resolve these problems with the IRS. Other times we simply need to help the client develop a workable plan to pay their back taxes, while progressing toward their other financial goals.

ELDER CARE ISSUES

In recent years, I've worked with a lot of older clients who are having difficulty maintaining sufficient cash flow. They may have chosen (or been forced) to retire before they were financially able to do so comfortably. Sometimes their cash flow shortfall is a result of the drop in interest rates on fixed income investments. For other individuals, the difficulty lies in the fact that the value of their investment portfolios, from which they are taking periodic withdrawals, has dropped significantly as the stock market has declined. Others may have incurred substantially more health related expenses than they anticipated. Whatever the cause, many older Americans do not have the income they need to maintain their standard of living.

It is not uncommon for the majority of an older American's wealth to be tied up in his or her home, bank account, or short-term certificates of deposit. When looking for opportunities to maximize cash flow, planners must first examine their investment portfolios. Too often seniors have substantial assets placed in very low-yielding accounts. We can enhance their cash flow simply by reallocating their current assets to fixed-income securities with higher yields. This can be accomplished while exposing the client to extremely minimal, or no, additional risk to their principal.

I frequently recommend higher-yielding money market mutual funds over checking, savings and bank money market accounts. I also recommend "ladders" of high quality individual bonds and certificates of deposit for enhanced cash flow.

Individuals who have had little or no exposure to the stock market may feel pretty smart and safe right now due to the current bear market. However, they may be exposed to more risk than they are aware. By taking an extremely conservative approach to investing their money, they may not have provided any opportunity for growth in their portfolio. Over time, the effects of inflation can deteriorate one's purchasing power. In less than 25 years, our current cost of living may double. If you're working with a 65 year old retiree who has just enough income now to support his *current* standard of living, how is he going to survive when he needs twice as much income *later* in life?

I believe that almost everyone should have some money invested for growth. Of course, if assets are allocated to growth investments, fewer assets will be available to generate current cash flow. Thus, we must help clients achieve a balance between their need for current cash flow and their need for long-term growth.

To achieve this goal, you might consider recommending preferred stocks, income-producing real estate, or natural gas royalty interests. These are vehicles that provide good current income and growth opportunities. Another option worth considering is a reverse mortgage. This strategy provides current cash flow by accessing the equity in one's home.

Social Security usually provides one-third to one-half of the income my clients need to maintain their standards of living. The rest must be generated from the client's assets.

Clients often ask me when they should plan to start drawing their Social Security retirement benefits. This answer will vary depending on whether the client still has earned income, their age, how long they expect to live, and our faith that the Social Security system will remain unchanged.

For long-term projections, we assume that clients begin receiving Social Security benefits at age 62 or upon their retirement, whichever is later. We also project that they live at least until age 100. If they live beyond average life expectancy, clients would be far better off by deferring receipt of their retirement benefits (based on our current Social Security system). The present value of the higher benefit is by far greater if our life expectancy assumption is accurate. Therefore, it is prudent to illustrate receipt of a lower benefit if projecting life expectancy beyond average mortality assumptions.

For more information regarding the assumptions we use in projecting Social Security retirement benefits please refer back to the Retirement Capital Needs Computation section of this chapter.

Medicare

Americans who have attained the age of 65 have access to Medicare. Medicare Part A provides hospitalization coverage and is premium-free to qualified recipients (i.e., those who have 40 quarters of credit with the Social Security system). Part B covers other medical expenses and recipients pay a premium for this coverage.

Individuals should apply for Medicare benefits during the period beginning three months prior to turning age 65 and ending three months after turning age 65. If an individual has applied for Social Security retirement benefits prior to age 65, they will automatically receive a card acknowledging Medicare coverage in the mail prior to their 65th birthday. Recipients of Social Security retirement benefits will automatically be enrolled in Medicare Parts A and B. However, one can simply indicate on the card if one prefers to postpone receipt of Part B benefits.

If an employee is covered by their employer's health-insurance plan and they are over age 65, it is advisable for them to enroll in premium-free Medicare Part A. The employer group plan will be the primary insurer, and Medicare Part A will become the secondary insurer for hospitalization benefits. The client can wait until after retirement to obtain Medicare Part B coverage.

If a person is *not* covered by an employer's health insurance plan, and they do *not* enroll in Medicare during the initial enrollment period, they may be subject to a 10% penalty.

Most people should also obtain Medicare Supplemental Health Insurance ("Medigap") to adequately insure themselves during retirement. In 1992, federal regulations set uniform standards for all Medigap policies. Except in Massachusetts, Minnesota, and Wisconsin, there are 10 standard plans – Plan A through Plan J. At any time within the first six months after first enrolling in Medicare Part B, a client may purchase any Medicare supplemental policy without medical screening or underwriting based on health or pre-existing conditions.

As I mentioned earlier, most employed clients and their spouses have health insurance through their employer's plan. If the client retires at age 65 and goes on Medicare, will the spouse be able to continue group coverage if she is under age 65? What happens if the employee dies – will the spouse lose coverage?

Medicare provides very minimal assistance with long-term care costs. Medicare may cover the costs of the first 20 days of skilled nursing care, and a portion of the costs from day 21 through day 100. However, the patient must have first had a *qualifying* hospital stay.

For more information and excellent resources (e.g., booklets) to share with clients, visit www.Medicare.gov.

Medicaid

Medicaid provides health and long-term care insurance to individuals with very limited income and assets. The majority of residents in nursing facilities are either on Medicaid or their expenses are privately paid. Long-term care insurance is relatively new and that is one reason most nursing home residents do not have private insurance coverage for long-term care costs.

Transferring Assets

The primary purpose of estate planning is to effectively and efficiently transfer assets at death. However, traditional estate planning documents generally do not address the "softer" points of the asset transfer process.

I like clients to have the opportunity to write down how they feel about their loved ones, how they want their possessions to be distributed, and how they want their heirs to behave during this process. One of my estate planning referral sources calls this a "Family Love Letter."

The "love letter" is to be opened and read immediately following the individual's death. While these letters are not likely to be legally binding documents, they do provide instructions to family members regarding the deceased person's thoughts and preferences at the time immediately following death.

It is recommended that these "love letters" be shared with family members and heirs *prior to* death. Open and honest communication helps avoid potentially adverse situations. If every family member knows what the client wants, and the client and the other heirs know what each of the heirs want, many uncomfortable situations can be minimized or eliminated.

To encourage families to start talking about the "softer" points of the asset transfer process, I encourage clients to read *Who Gets Grandma's Yellow Pie Plate?* by Marlene S. Stum.15

Although I strongly encourage older adults to discuss the distribution of their assets *upon* their death with their family members, it may also be appropriate for clients to consider transferring some assets to their heirs *before* death. The heirs may benefit more by receiving the gift now, and the client may also enjoy *seeing* heirs benefit from the gifts.

However, I am reluctant to suggest that clients begin transferring assets to their heirs unless it is obvious that the clients will never need these assets themselves; too many unforeseen events could occur. It is our job as planners to minimize these unforeseen events, advise clients on the benefits and disadvantages of gifting assets while they are living, and help them determine if, when, and how much of their estates could comfortably be transferred to heirs now.

Older Clients and Financial Security Issues

Deterioration of health and loss of control or the ability to manage one's personal affairs are significant concerns for many older Americans. Clients may also experience emotional issues regarding their finances as they grow older.

Older clients often have an unrealistic fear that they will run out of money. Working with a professional financial advisor can help minimize the sense of financial insecurity for many older clients. With our professional guidance, they will know how much they can afford to spend, and how their assets should be allocated to ensure or enhance long-term financial security.

I recently worked with clients who began feeling very insecure about their financial future, and in mid-July 2002, they sold all of their equity investments. Three weeks later they called me to ask what to do.

A few years before, I had provided a retirement projection and a second opinion regarding their stockbroker's management of their investment assets. At that time, we found that the clients needed to achieve an average long-term rate of return on their investments of 7% to maintain their standard of living. They had also expressed that they could reduce their standard of living if need be. The stockbroker designed an appropriate and quality investment portfolio for the clients. I gave only minor suggestions for improvement. The clients implemented my recommendations through their broker, and continued to visit with him regularly.

Unfortunately, in recent months the clients had grown increasingly uncomfortable with the behavior of the stock market and their declining account values. They called their stockbroker on numerous occasions, and he encouraged them to "sit tight."

In July 2002, they called the broker to discuss their options, but he was on vacation. They viewed their broker as their continual and ongoing investment advisor and felt that it was his responsibility to tell them when to get out of the market. The clients were determined that they could no longer sit by and watch the value of their accounts decline, so they sold all of their equity positions and parked the proceeds in a money market account yielding about one-half of 1%. Unfortunately, they didn't call me before taking this drastic step.

I met with them a few weeks after they sold their entire equity position. They talked about the financial insecurity they felt. They also wanted a game plan to "know when to get out of the market." I stressed to them the risks that they faced if they did not achieve a 7% average rate of return in retirement. I pointed out that they must have some growth exposure to achieve that objective. The one-half of 1% they're currently receiving on a portion of their assets is not helping their long-term situation.

I tried to put into perspective the risks associated with *not* having one-third of their assets invested in equities by telling them:

"YES, THE STOCKS CAN, AND DID, GO DOWN SIGNIFICANTLY IN VALUE. HOWEVER, THESE ASSETS WILL NOT BE NEEDED FOR MANY, MANY YEARS AND, THEREFORE, MUST BE INVESTED FOR THE LONG HAUL. NO ONE CAN TIME THE MARKET. NOT BEING IN THE MARKET WHEN IT GOES UP IS MORE DANGEROUS FOR YOU THAN BEING IN IT WHEN IT GOES DOWN. KEEP IN MIND THAT JUST MISSING OUT ON A FEW 'GOOD' TRADING DAYS OVER THE COURSE OF SEVERAL YEARS CAN CAUSE ONE TO MISS THE LARGEST PERCENTAGE OF THE GAIN."

In order to achieve long-term financial security, this couple must have some equity exposure. They also need assurance as to the where their cash flow is to come from for the foreseeable future. Many advisors suggest holding three to ten years worth of cash flow in fixed-income investments that are scheduled to mature just when the money is needed. Over time, as this fixed income ladder depletes, one must replenish it by selling equities.

I find that a minimum of three years needed cash flow should be earmarked in cash reserves and fixed income investments. With at least three years worth of cash flow set aside, we can survive the downturns of most equity markets. Simply making it clear to the client where their income will come from when the equity markets are down can eliminate a great deal of financial insecurity. This strategy helped encourage the clients in the example above to get back into the market.

Planners must find a workable balance between short-term and long-term financial security. The greater danger faced by the couple in the above example is to their long-term security. Because they are only in their late 60's, I reminded them that in 25 years their living expenses could double. If they leave all of the money in secure, fixed-income investments, they will not have enough income to support their standard of living. This is long-term financial *insecurity*.

SOMETIMES WE MUST GIVE UP ON A LITTLE SHORT-TERM SECURITY TO ENHANCE THE CHANCE OF LONG-TERM SUCCESS.

ESTATE PLANNING ISSUES

Who needs to worry about estate taxes? Well, not many of my clients. But estate planning is so much more than minimizing estate taxes and expenses.

Estate planning also involves the efficient transfer of assets to heirs. It is important for families to discuss their desires regarding the disposition of their assets.

Thus, even though most of my clients do not have an estate tax situation, they generally need to update their estate planning documents. At a minimum, clients should have a will, a living will, health care directives, and a power of attorney for financial decision-making. Many clients could also benefit from a living trust, while others could also take advantage of more advanced estate planning techniques. I know enough about estate planning to recognize these planning opportunities and to refer these clients directly to an attorney who specializes in estate planning.

I provide my clients who have engaged me for estate planning guidance with a copy of the *Five Wishes* brochure published by the nonprofit organization Aging with Dignity (www.agingwithdignity.org). *Five Wishes* helps clients express how they want to be treated if they are seriously ill and unable to speak for themselves. It is unique among all other living will and health agent forms because it covers all of a person's needs (i.e., medical, personal, emotional and spiritual). Five Wishes also encourages discussing the client's wishes with their family and physician. *Five Wishes* lets the client's family and doctors know:

1. Which person the client wants to make health care decisions for them when they can't make them.

2. The kind of medical treatment the client wants or doesn't want.

3. How comfortable the client wants to be.

4. How the client wants people to treat him or her.

5. What the client wants their loved ones to know.

I encourage clients to review this brochure, complete it, and share it with their estate planning attorney when they are having their other estate planning documents drafted. This exercise can help clients evaluate their options and feelings about end-of-life issues in the privacy of their own homes.

Americans often procrastinate about getting their estate planning documents drafted and executed. They procrastinate because they don't realize the importance of these documents, or may not want to face the reality that all of us will die someday. I try to make the subject of estate planning simple, while stressing its importance. I describe in lay terms what I feel the estate planning attorney may recommend, and

I encourage them to schedule an appointment. I've gone so far as to schedule the appointment for the client during our presentation meeting. If a client requested, and paid me to, I would attend their meeting with the estate planning attorney.

The estate planning attorneys to whom I refer clients provide them with detailed instructions on how to re-title assets and change beneficiary designations on their current life insurance policies, IRAs and qualified retirement plans. Clients may also be advised to add transfer-on-death beneficiary designations to their personal brokerage accounts, their bank accounts and personal property.

WORKING WITH "SPECIALIZED PARTICIPANTS"

As you can see, I work with and rely on a host of "specialized participants" in the financial services industry. I am a financial planning "generalist." Middle Americans needs financial planning "generalists" to help them make better money management and financial planning decisions.

To effectively and profitably serve this market, a practitioner must develop strong strategic alliances with quality product and service providers. You should surround yourself with a network of qualified, trusted allied professionals. A financial planning "generalist" should know which products and services offered by various "specialists" are appropriate for her clients, and help the clients fill their needs by directing them to qualified "specialists."

To be profitable and effective working in the Middle Market, I have to focus on what I do best, which is:

• Advising,

• Consulting,

• Educating, and

• Coaching clients on the basic aspects of personal finances.

I outsource any project or analysis for which I am not currently competent to qualified advisors. I find that if I "stick to my knitting," I can profitably provide a much needed, and very valuable, service to my Middle Market clientele.

To effectively serve the Middle Market we must be very efficient financial planners and business operators. We've got to systematize and streamline everywhere we can. You should develop a systematic way to do *all* things involved in running your practice. As my business strategy coach, Kevin Poland, always reminds me, "a system is not a system, until it's documented." If you're building a business – even if it's only a business of one – you must *systematize and document* all processes so that they can be refined, improved, and repeated. These processes can be performed by you, an appropriate staff person (if someday you choose to expand), or they can be outsourced.

Remember that you must work *on* your business as much as you work *in* it. If you're not skilled or interested in certain tasks, then outsource them. For example, I outsource the following functions:

- Compliance

- Accounting and payroll

- Website development and maintenance

- Computer software and systems

- Ghostwriting / editing

- Marketing communications

- Clerical

- Janitorial services

- Lawn and garden care

We always have the option of not doing these things. Yes, it costs money to hire people to provide all of these services, but you've got to decide where your time is best spent. My lawn and janitorial service providers charge $12.50 an hour. However, when there's this untapped market out there full of folks who are willing to pay me $180.00 per hour, I've got to ask myself, "what is my job?"

I am a financial planner. I charge by the hour. The more hours I charge, the more money I make, and the more people I can serve. I am not a computer wizard, nor am I a great writer. I don't care for the bookkeeping part of the job. I won't even do my own tax returns. (I hate filling out the forms, and you can always learn something when working with a specialist.) I also hate compliance and doing payroll. Consequently, I outsource all of these services.

When we first establish our practices, we have to do all or most of these tasks. However, too many seasoned financial planners are swamped because they are still performing too many non-financial planning responsibilities. This is unfortunate because:

TO EFFECTIVELY SERVE THE MIDDLE MARKET, WE MUST BE VERY EFFICIENT FINANCIAL PLANNERS — AND BUSINESS OPERATORS.

Building a business is much more than building a clientele. It involves building a system of processes that will make it possible to provide great service to one's clients and to enjoy one's life.

We've discussed the evolution of financial planning. We've explored who the Middle Market really is, what they need and want, and how you can effectively position yourself to successfully serve this huge, and still virtually untapped market. We've looked at various practice models for serving this special niche and drawn some conclusions about which ones are best suited to delivering affordable, professional services. We've talked about this vast opportunity and why you should consider catering to the Middle Market. We've also addressed the financial planning issues that matter most, or are most common, to the majority of Americans today.

Now that you know why you'd want to establish an "All-American Practice," and how you might structure your business and serve your clientele, let's move on to discuss marketing your services as an "All-American Planner." In Chapter 6, I'll share the most effective marketing tactics and communications strategies for reaching – and appealing to – the validator and the Middle Market.

ENDNOTES

1. Joe Dominguez and Vicki Robin, *Your Money or Your Life: Transforming Your Relationship With Money and Achieving Financial Independence* (Penguin, September 1999).

2. John De Graaf, David Wann, Thomas Naylor, *Affluenza: The All-Consuming Epidemic* (Berrett-Koehler, June 9, 2001).

3. Jacqueline Blix and David Heitmiller, *Getting a Life: Strategies for Simple Living* (Penguin, January 1999).

4. Juliet Schor, *The Overspent American: Why We Want What We Don't Need* (Harper Collins, May 1999).

5. George Clason, *The Richest Man in Babylon* (Signet, January 2002).

6. SRI Consulting Business Intelligence, "More Households Have Inadequate Life Insurance," (March 12, 1999).

7. U.S. Census Bureau, Current Population Survey, March 2000 and 2001. See also Charles T. Nelson and Robert J. Mills, "The March CPS Health Insurance Verification Question and Its Effect on Estimates of the Uninsured," (U.S. Census Bureau, August 2001); www.census.giv/hhes/hlthins/verify/html.

8. This document can be viewed at www.insurance.wa.gov/readonline.htm.

9. U.S. Census Bureau, Current Population Survey, March 2000 and 2001.

10. IRC Sec. 530(b)(1)(A)(iii), as amended by The Economic Growth and Tax Relief Reconciliation Act of 2001.

11. Julie Welch, CPA, CFP™ and Randy Gardner, LLM, CPA, CFP™ write a guide for consumers and their advisors entitled, *101 Tax Saving Ideas* (Wealth Builders Press, 2002).

12. *2002 Tax Facts 1 & 2002 Tax Facts 2*, (The National Underwriter Company; www.nuco.com.).

13. Lambda Legal, "Details About Domestic Partner Benefits" (September 28, 1997).

14. Harold Lustig, *4 Steps to Financial Freedom for Lesbian and Gay Couples* (Fawcett Books, June 1999).

15. Marlene Stum, *Who Gets Grandma's Yellow Pie Plate?* (Minnesota Extension Service, February 1, 1999).

Chapter 6

MARKETING YOUR FINANCIAL PLANNING SERVICES TO THE MIDDLE MARKET CONSUMER

PROFIT IN BUSINESS COMES FROM REPEAT CUSTOMERS, CUSTOMERS WHO BOAST ABOUT YOUR PROJECT OR SERVICE, AND THAT BRING FRIENDS WITH THEM.

– W. Edwards Deming

There's no shortage of marketing information in the business world today, especially in the financial services industry. Peruse any industry discussion board and you'll see a plethora of comments debating the pros and cons of various marketing methods – cold calling, neighborhood canvassing, mall crawling, direct mail, display advertisements, networking, seminars, sales presentations and more. Attend any industry conference and you'll be privy to a session or two on sales and marketing strategies. Read our industry magazines (or just open your e-mail) and you'll be exposed to a host of tips and assertions about the best way to market your services (and the best services *to help you* market your services).

Each speaker, colleague and writer has his or her own assertions of "what works" based on personal experiences, biases and preferences, training, background and business model. Wherever you go you'll hear dozens, if not hundreds, of ideas and approaches. Some strategies will make a lot of sense to you, while others may turn your stomach. Are they all worth trying? Are you a wimp if you hate the thought of cold-calling or neighborhood canvassing?

The purpose of this chapter is to share my observations and experiences regarding what works – and what doesn't work – in marketing financial planning services to middle Americans.

Over the years, I've tried a variety of marketing methods and exchanged ideas with numerous successful colleagues (and not-so-successful colleagues) to find out what they do to market their services to glean best practice ideas for specific service models. I'm pleased to have the opportunity to share what I've found to be the best ways to build and sustain a financial planning practice centered around meeting the needs of middle America.

As in any business, there are some basic marketing principles that hold true no matter what your product, service or business model is. There are, however, some distinctions that make marketing-to-the-middle unique. In this chapter, I hope to help you sort through the various options and opportunities you are likely to encounter as you formulate your marketing plan.

CREATING YOUR MARKETING PLAN

Once you've decided to target and serve the Middle Market, it will be important to lay a solid marketing foundation and focus squarely on what works. No entrepreneur wants to waste time and resources on high-dollar/low-return endeavors. But, sadly, many entrepreneurs do just that. Why does this happen? How do they get so far off track? In my opinion, they simply lose sight of what matters most. Most likely, they either failed to plan or failed to follow their plan. It's easy to fall for the "strategy du jour" (or the "stock du jour," for that matter) if you lack a long-term, strategic plan.

If you're serious about building a long-term successful practice, you need to have a strategic *written* marketing plan. Putting our goals – and the strategies designed to help us reach those goals – in writing makes them real for us. The subconscious mind goes to work and seeks the target you've written down. We make a stronger commitment to our goals when they are written down because we can measure and track our written plan and determine when we are off track. Of course, the real power lies in not only writing down your goals and how you'll achieve them, but in following through in a disciplined way to *accelerate* the realization of your goals.

Also, much like the process of financial planning, *the process* of market planning may be as important as the finished plan and its results. It's the process that forces us to think in terms of "the big picture," not just the individual marketing components. A thoroughly developed marketing plan provides a blueprint to guide us, day-in and day-out, as we create and disseminate the various components. It should also outline how all the components will work together, in a cohesive way, to realize our goals.

Starting to sound a bit like the benefits of creating a personal financial plan, isn't it?

Creating the marketing plan will force you to reflect on who you are, who you will best serve, what you will provide, and how you want to do business. It will help you analyze your strengths and weaknesses and should clarify your goals. As you become clear about your mission and personal passion, you will become a better communicator when articulating the value of your services and advice. Finally, if you revisit and refine your plan on a periodic basis, you will refocus and remind yourself of your goals and how you need to make them real. This type of focus will move you closer to your goals and help you reach your desired milestones more rapidly.

Your marketing plan can be simple or elaborate, but it should concretely outline who you will serve (your market), your mission, the services you will offer, why you are different (your message), and how you will reach your clients (your marketing methods). Just remember "the 3 M's" – (1) your *market*, (2) your *message*, and (3) your *methods*. That's the order in which you should think through your plan. Too many advisors jump right to their "methods," without giving adequate thought to their "market" and their "message."

Figure 6.1

"THE THREE M'S"

YOUR MARKET – Define your market. Who do you want to serve and why? Really delve into it. Try creating a detailed composite of your ideal clientele. What do they like to do? Where do they congregate? How old are they? Where do they live? What's important to them? What do they have in common? What do you have in common with them? Write it down!

YOUR MESSAGE – Generate your vision for your practice. Reflect on who you are. What are your strengths? What do you stand for? What are you committed to? Who will you partner with to achieve results? How do you serve your clients? Who have you helped before? What successes have you had? What do you bring to the table that other advisors don't? What is your purpose? How can you communicate that unique purpose? *Why* do you do *what* you do? Get passionate! Start crafting your own story. Become the master of telling that story. Write it down!

YOUR METHODS – Consider all the marketing methods and tactics you hear and read about. Which ones seem to make the most sense for you, your defined market(s) and your community? Are you "a natural" at seminars? Are you comfortable using the telephone to spread the word and tell your story? How can you become more active in the circles in which your targeted market(s) travel? Who can you partner with to become known in those circles? How can you create apostles who'll spread the word and tell your story? What do you need to do to create raving fans of your current clients? How can you create media relationships and leverage your press coverage? What's your timeline for success? Where can you best utilize your unique skills and abilities? Write it down!

MARKETING METHODS PORTFOLIO

Now that you've done the "hard work" – reflecting on yourself and defining your market(s) – it's time to start thinking about your diversified portfolio of marketing methods.

As financial planning professionals, we would never suggest that our clients put all their eggs into one basket; instead, we would suggest a diversified portfolio of investments that should work together over time to realize their long-range goals. Your marketing plan should also utilize a variety of methods that will compliment and build on one another. Sometimes one portion of the portfolio will yield the best results, then the pendulum will swing and another portion of the portfolio will start yielding the best results. Different components of your marketing method portfolio will (and should) mature at different times.

On the other hand, overdiversification (both in investing and in marketing methods) can be detrimental. Strategic focus can be good. Ask yourself which approaches make the most sense *for you* (consider your budget, your temperament and your natural strengths), *your community* (rural or urban, niche markets within the larger market called Middle Market), and *your commitments* (what's your timeline for success, how much fire do you have in your belly?). Then jump in and formulate a portfolio of marketing methods that, *together and over time*, will help you work toward those goals.

A portfolio of marketing approaches might look like the pie chart shown in Figure 6.2:

Figure 6.2

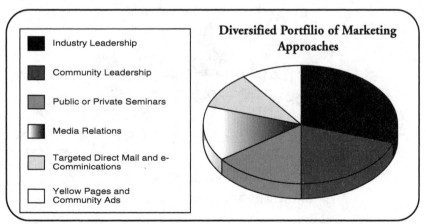

Diversified Portfilio of Marketing Approaches

Industry Leadership

Community Leadership

Public or Private Seminars

Media Relations

Targeted Direct Mail and e-Comminications

Yellow Pages and Community Ads

After you design your marketing methods portfolio and decide how you'll allocate your time and money, then detail the specific activities, expenditures, steps and commitments connected with each section allocation. (We'll be discussing some of those options and activities later in this chapter.) While some activities will be common to all financial planners, many will be as unique as you and your community are.

OWN YOUR PLAN

When all is said and done, you should *own* your market plan. It should inspire and motivate you! If you own your plan, it will be easier to implement the plan, stick to it and measure its results. But first you've got to own it. One of the traps I see planners falling into is paying a professional, or having an assistant, produce a marketing plan for them. While some professional market planning and/or staff assistance may be beneficial, there is much benefit to be found in rolling up your sleeves and grappling with some of the tough questions yourself. It puts you in the self-discovery and "ownership" process. Then, if needed, you can partner with a professional or a trusted colleague, or use a staff person, to help you polish, refine and implement the plan.

© 1999 Ted Goff

"Our study concludes that this is
the percentage of our customers
who will buy from us without any
effort whatsoever on our part."

WORK YOUR PLAN

Another pitfall planners may fall into is getting so busy working *in* the business that they fail to work *on* their business. My Certified E-Myth™ coaching consultant, Kevin Poland (from Tampa, Florida) helped me to remain ever conscious of this pitfall. One tip I learned early on is to make an appointment with myself each and every week to spend time working on and/or refining my marketing plan. Initially, we may be good at "working our plan" and getting results. The danger is that we may get busy with our workload or mistakenly assume we have a full and steady pipeline of interested clients and great referral sources.

Marketing is a communications issue, an art form. Building relationships is important, too. We have to work at keeping our relationships intact; that takes time and continued attention. Likewise, we have to work at keeping our marketing program and its corresponding relationships intact. My marketing coach, Marie Swift, principal of Kansas City-based Impact Communications, consistently reminds me that, "it's not just *marketing*...it's marketing *communications*."

So, be persistent and committed to building relationships.

When we ignore the ongoing marketing aspects of our business – and the underlying relationships – it may take some time, but eventually we'll feel the pain. We have to keep making deposits to our "community goodwill bank." Just like dollar-cost-averaging, we must religiously invest our time, energy and money back into our marketing program, through thick and thin, to realize the best results.

Once the marketing plan has been created, it's important to *work* your plan, and to revisit it periodically to fine-tune and improve the plan. Just like a good financial plan, the marketing plan should become a living, breathing document. Don't just write the plan and stick it on a shelf. Take it out, dust it off, and rework it every six to twelve months.

HOW MUCH TIME AND MONEY SHOULD I SPEND?

At a minimum, even when your pipeline is full, plan on devoting 25% of your time to marketing activities.

I'm often asked what percentage of revenues a financial planning start-up should expect to invest into marketing activities in the first one to three years of business, but there are so many variables involved that I can't provide a firm answer in this book. Marketing gurus will tell you to plough roughly 30% of your annual revenues back into your marketing endeavors, but that would be more than I (and many of my colleagues) invested into our initial marketing campaigns. In some cases, however, I've heard of start-up budgets that meet or exceed that guideline due to unique factors related to the advisor and/or the community.

Later in this chapter, we'll discuss the most cost-effective ways to market to middle Americans and do-it-yourselfers.

MARKETING PLAN TEMPLATES

While there are many good marketing plan templates available on the web and for purchase, I've included a blank one-page marketing plan document on the CD-ROM to get you started. Of course, I'd recommend that you do much more than create a simple one-page marketing plan, but this is a good first step. You can see the basic, one-page marketing plan outline in Figure 6.3. My tips for filling it out are explained in the next section, "Steps to Creating Your Marketing Plan."

STEPS TO CREATING YOUR MARKETING PLAN

Step 1: Target Market Definition / Parameters

Define your market. Who do you want to work with and why? Describe your ideal clientele. Provide demographics and psychographics. Go to http://www.census.gov to research demographic

Figure 6.3

BASIC OUTLINE FOR MARKETING PLAN

STEP 1: TARGET MARKET DEFINITION / PARAMETERS

STEP 2: OBJECTIVE / MISSION

STEP 3: MARKETING METHODS / TOOLS

STEP 4: TIME AND MONEY BUDGET

STEP 5: TIMETABLE / STEPS

---

information. Use your keen powers of observation and personal vision for your business to create your psychographics (i.e., your ideal client composite). In addition to describing your ideal clientele, reflect on and explain whom you will not serve and why. Under what circumstances would you turn down a client engagement?

Step 2: Objective / Mission

Generate your vision for your practice. Reflect on who you are. What drives you? What are you committed to? How can you communicate your unique value and purpose? Use passionate, lively words that "light you up." Your mission statement should consistently inspire you. Your *mission* will become a key part of your *message*. Remember to think in this order: (1) your market; (2) your message; and (3) your methods. Think of your mission statement as your personal "lighthouse." Will it send a strong beacon and guide you safely to shore in tough times? Can you enthusiastically share your mission statement with clients as well as allies and/or staff members? Do other people "light up" when you share your mission statement with them?

Step 3: Marketing Methods / Tools

Now that you've defined *your market* and started crafting *your message*, next start outlining your goals and objectives. (Remember, objectives are more accessible than goals.) This will lead you into outlining *your methods*. How you will reach your market – letters, telephone calls, postcards, business expos, networking, or advertising? Remember, more isn't necessarily better. And you don't have to use every tool. Pick three or four methods that appeal to you (i.e., activities that are a natural fit for your skills and abilities), and start doing them really well. Then branch out so that you have a diversified portfolio of marketing methods. Think of your methods as "your marketing tool belt." The tool belt should contain enough tools to get the job done, but not so many as to weigh you down. You may need a staple gun, a screwdriver, a hammer and some nails to start with. Later, you can add more sophisticated and costly tools to your belt as you become proficient using the fundamental tools (or as your vision guides you).

Step 4: Time and Money Budget

Effective marketing doesn't have to cost a lot of money. Your marketing plan is *yours*. You can choose tools that require you to spend time instead of money. My personal choice is to invest the least amount of money possible in my marketing endeavors. Does this mean I don't spend any money on marketing? Does that mean my materials look shabby? No, but I choose to spend far more *time* doing marketing-related activities than I do money. This is a relationship business and relationships generally take more time than money to keep them flourishing. Outline your money budget, your time investment, and parcel that into your schedule. Then stick to that time and money budget religiously.

TIME:

Networking Activities	3 hours per week for 6 months
Direct Mail / Calling Campaign	4 hours per week for 18 months
Seminar Program	2 hours per week for 12 months
Plan Administration	1 hour per week for 24 months
TBD Marketing Tasks	2 hours per week, indefinitely

MONEY:

Networking Activities/Dues	$100 per month for 6 months
Direct Mail / Advertising Campaign	$300 per month for 18 months
Seminar Programs/Materials	$75 per month for 12 months
Plan Administration	$0 per month for 24 months

Step 5: Timetable and Steps

For each objective, list the steps needed to attain the objective. Break down all steps to the smallest tasks possible. Determine the order in which you'll do them. For instance:

Week 1 – Gather names
Week 2 – Write introductory letter
Week 3 – Generate and send 50 letters
Week 4 – Make 10 follow-up telephone calls each day
Week 5 – Review and evaluate letter mailing and calling plan

Create deadlines for yourself and stick to them. Pretend your life depends on getting those marketing pieces sent out, telephone calls made, and lunches scheduled (actually, it's not far from the truth!). Find simple ways to reward yourself when you stay on track and, perhaps, more elaborate ways to celebrate your larger successes. Find a committed listener or accountability partner to hold you to your stated goals.

Finally, develop a simple way to track your progress and measure your results. I like working with a specialized way of producing specific, measurable goals called "Bull's Eyes." Over the years, I've had the privilege of working with Bull's Eye's originator and trainer, Tom Werder. (For more information on Tom's book, *The Bull's Eye Principle: How to Lead and Manage People to Extraordinary Results*, go to: http://www.tom werder.com/1.htm.) Tom's simple yet effective methods have helped me to create and hit many personal and business Bull's Eyes. The beauty of tracking specific, small tasks to measure your Bull's Eye success rate is that you can see in pretty short order just where you need to improve and what you need to refine to achieve your goals. Immediate and constant feedback can serve as a powerful rudder for your enterprise. (Never forget that even if you are a company of one, you are your own enterprise.)

In summary, we have established that it is vital for you to create and maintain a written marketing plan. Whether your marketing plan is five pages or 50 pages, it is important for you to reflect on who you are, who you best serve, what your mission and key marketing messages are, and how you will implement the plan and measure its success. As planners, we undoubtedly counsel clients that having a written financial plan is the best way to realize success. The same holds true for us, too. Creating a written plan gives substance to our thoughts. A good marketing plan points us in the right direction and gives us a road map to follow, complete with instructions for reaching our destinations.

WHAT IS MARKETING?

Let's back up just a bit and address the question, "what is marketing and how does it differ from sales?"

The American Marketing Association defines "marketing" as follows:

> "MARKETING IS THE PROCESS OF PLANNING AND EXECUTING THE
> CONCEPTION, PRICING, PROMOTION, AND DISTRIBUTION OF IDEAS,
> GOODS, AND SERVICES TO CREATE EXCHANGES THAT SATISFY
> INDIVIDUAL AND ORGANIZATIONAL OBJECTIVES."[1]

The Oxford Dictionary and Thesaurus defines "marketing" as:

> "ACTIVITY OR PROCESS INVOLVING RESEARCH, PROMOTION, SALES
> AND DISTRIBUTION OF A PRODUCT OR SERVICE; SELLING OR BUYING
> IN A MARKET."[2]

The marketing communications consultant I've had the benefit of working with since 1998, Marie Swift of Impact Communications, takes the definition of "marketing" one step further:

> "MARKETING IS ANYTHING THAT IMPACTS A CLIENT'S OR [A] POTENTIAL
> CLIENT'S VIEW OF YOU AND YOUR COMPANY. IT'S EVERYTHING FROM
> HOW YOU ANSWER THE TELEPHONE, TO YOUR SIGNAGE AND HOW
> YOU [DECORATE YOUR] OFFICE, TO HOW YOU WALK, TALK AND DRESS.
> IT INCLUDES YOUR COMPANY'S BRANDING AND PRINTED MATERIALS,
> [AS WELL AS] YOUR WEB SITE AND E-COMMUNICATIONS. IT'S SHAPED
> BY THE DECISIONS YOU MAKE ABOUT WHAT SERVICES AND PRODUCTS
> YOU'LL PROVIDE, AND ANCHORED ON THE ESSENCE OF WHO YOU ARE
> AS A PROFESSIONAL. IT INCLUDES YOUR IMAGE, YOUR PUBLIC PERSONA.
> IT'S EVERYTHING YOU DO TO ATTRACT AND RETAIN BUSINESS."[3]

When asked how "marketing" differs from "sales," Marie will tell you:

> "MARKETING WORKS ON THE LAW OF ATTRACTION. IT'S MORE ART
> THAN SCIENCE. TO ATTRACT MIDDLE MARKET CLIENTS, YOU'LL WANT
> TO CAST A LARGE NET IN STRATEGIC SPOTS WHERE THE 'SCHOOLS OF
> FISH' LIKE TO CONGREGATE. SALES IS MORE LIKE SPEAR FISHING — IT'S
> USUALLY A ONE-ON-ONE OR SMALL GROUP ENDEAVOR. IT HINGES ON

YOUR PERSONAL COMMUNICATION SKILLS AND WORKS ON THE POWER OF PERSUASION. IT IS MORE SCIENCE THAN ART, BUT CAN BE ELEVATED TO AN ART FORM WHEN DONE RIGHT. BUT BOTH ARE IMPORTANT TO YOUR SUCCESS."[4]

What style and image reflects your business? How can you best attract and retain Middle Market clients? Let's look at what makes "marketing-to-the-middle" unique.

SERVING THE MIDDLE MARKET

In serving the Middle Market, it is critically important to efficiently reach out to your ideal clients and effectively communicate your key marketing messages in a consistent, confident and easy manner.

People today are simply bombarded with too much information. Time is short. Priorities get muddled. Competing agendas and multiple commitments chip away at our focus. At times life can seem overwhelming.

Average Americans know they need professional financial advice, at least on an occasional or periodic basis. But they frequently don't know where to find help. They may think that no professional independent advisor will work with them either because they don't have sufficient investable assets to meet the advisor's minimums, or simply because they don't want to turn over their assets to be managed.

As a result, many middle Americans and do-it-yourselfers resign themselves to "going it alone" – just doing the best that they can. They don't realize there are professionals like you and me who are not only willing, but eager to serve them. Their lack of awareness leads them into the sea of noise and competing interests (e.g., web sites, periodicals, friends and family).

As stated in Chapter 2, this vast, untapped market has been overlooked and underserved for so long that even savvy "Gen-X" professionals may cry out "we have no where to turn for help and advice." See Figure 6.4.[5] (The news release also contains some interesting survey findings about "Gen-Xers" and do-it-yourselfers in general.) This demographic sees the value in having at least an occasional financial check up, and obtaining specific advice on an as-needed basis. Just as they see their dentist on a periodic or as-needed basis and call him or her "their dentist," they'd like to establish a relationship with a trusted financial advisor to round out their advisory and professional services team (i.e., CPA, attorney, doctor, dentist, etc.). Even if they only see you once a year, they will think of you as "their financial advisor."

So, the first thing to do — and what may matter most in all of your marketing endeavors — is to really *want* to serve this market. When you have decided that this is your calling and desire, you will begin to communicate with clarity and passion the many compelling reasons that you are the right advisor for this niche.

The next most important thing is to become active in your community. Look for ways to "see and be seen" by the people you want to serve (and the other professionals who will introduce you to potential clients). Move in the circles where the greatest number of potential clients will see, and get to know you, as a resource for the "average person."

Start saying, "I help average Americans, like you and me, make smarter financial decisions," and then elaborate on just how you do that. Become a good storyteller. People (including the media) love stories! Having a simple, consistent message — a story you can tell and re-tell time and time again — will help you differentiate yourself from other would-be suitors.

To stand out in the sea of daily noise and competition, deliver a consistent, simple, passionate message. Emphasize that you *enthusiastically* specialize in working with average Americans and the Middle Market. While you might fear you are beginning to sound like a broken record, repetition of your key marketing messages is essential, both in print and verbal communications.

Figure 6.4

The Garrett Planning Network, Inc.

6750 West 75th Street, Overland Park, KS 66204, Suite 3B. Toll Free: (866) 260-8400
Web: www.GarrettPlanningNetwork.com / E-mail: media@GarrettPlanningNetwork.com

NEWS

FOR IMMEDIATE RELEASE
July 20, 2001

Contacts: Marie Swift, Principal / Impact Communications
Phone: (913) 649-5009 / E-mail: marieswift@impactcommunications.org

Sheryl Garrett, Principal / The Garrett Planning Network, Inc. (GPN)
Phone: (866) 260-8400 / E-mail: media@garrettplanningnetwork.com

SURVEY, ARTICLE SAY GEN-XERS DISTRESSED
BY LACK OF FINANCIAL ADVICE

*Network of By-the-Hour Financial Planners Seeks to Remedy Situation,
Offer As-Needed Financial Planning Services and Advice to All
Interested Consumers*

(OVERLAND PARK, Kansas) – On CBS.MarketWatch.com, in his July 17, 2001 article "Rich Gen-Xers in Distress," writer Thomas Kostigen says: "Wealthy young adults are crying out for help but are being largely ignored by financial counselors. Two-thirds of Generation Xers, people age 22 to 34, who don't use a financial adviser, want one. Yet, not many investment professionals have focused on Generation X, says a report that surveyed people in this age group with $100,000 or more to invest. Sixty-three percent of those surveyed by New York Life Investment Management said they get their financial information from the Internet. But that's not advice. And a lot want to get their advice from a financial geek rather than a gadget."

Figure 6.4 (Cont'd)

The survey results strongly indicated that Gen-Xers using an advisor felt the relationship provided a satisfying level of financial security and stability, the article said. "Wall Street, however, has been busying itself designing financial services programs and products for the Baby Boomers, the largest and wealthiest segment of the population. But Generation X is no slouch. Roughly one-third of millionaire households are headed by someone between 18 and 39, according to the New York Life report," says Kostigen in his article.

"Most financial advisors have demonstrated little understanding or interest in reaching these investors," says Sheryl Garrett, a CERTIFIED FINANCIAL PLANNER™ practitioner in Overland Park, KS. "Gen-Xers typically want validation of the decisions they make independently. They want help with retirement planning and investment choices," she said. "When I saw this need a few years ago, I began retooling my financial planning practice to reach not only Gen-Xers seeking validation and professional advice, but also any consumer – from the young to the middle aged to the already retired – who wants validation and professional advice without ongoing asset management fees, retainers, long-term contracts or commissions."

"The Marketwatch article says Gen-Xers are in need of advice when it comes to financial planning and that 58 percent of those surveyed lacked a comprehensive plan," continues Garrett. "The sad thing is, too many consumers – from ALL walks of life and income brackets – have been turned away from traditional financial planning and asset management firms with high minimums. Even if the consumer can meet the minimums imposed by these firms, a growing number of more sophisticated investors just don't see the value in paying for an ongoing, contractual financial advisory relationship. Nor can they justify additional brokerage fees and transaction costs. As a result, they have resigned themselves to going it alone. It is my strong opinion, however, that most people need at least occasional professional financial advice to build the brightest financial futures."

According to the Marketwatch article, the New York Life survey shows one-third of those polled will continue to plan and operate on their own, without the help of a professional adviser. The article also points to another problem: being "sold to" rather than being "consulted with" turns off many Gen-Xers and Baby Boomers. Nancy Moore, spokesperson for New York Life, is quoted as saying "Gen-Xers are more focused on trust and an advisor's willingness to communicate and give them advice."

Sheryl Garrett concurs: "Consumers do want an advisor they can trust, but many have had a hard time finding an advisor with whom they feel comfortable. This unfilled need – consumers who want professional financial advice but are discouraged because they don't know where to find the type of advice/advisor they need – moved me to start The Garrett Planning Network. Any consumer, young or old, affluent or struggling, can find an hourly, as-needed planner by visiting the "Consumer Leg" of The Garrett Planning Network site (http://www.GarrettPlanningNetwork.com). As founder of the network, it is my mission to raise consumer awareness and let the public know that there is a nationwide network of Fee-Only planners focused on providing professional financial planning and advice on an hourly, as-needed basis. Now 'average Americans' with more modest portfolios and incomes – and self-managing investors who may have larger portfolios and incomes – have somewhere to turn for professional, timely advice and as-needed, hourly financial planning services."

Help your current and prospective clients understand who you are and how you can help them by speaking simply and directly to their needs and concerns. Then get out in the community and start speaking with missionary zeal about *what* you do, and *why* you do it.

WHY I TARGET AND SERVE AVERAGE AMERICANS

I said earlier that it is important for you to *really want* to serve the Middle Market, the validator and do-it-yourself communities. My personal epiphany occurred about seven years into my career. I'd been a registered representative for a major financial services organization, and I'd earned the right to use the CFP® marks of distinction. I'd gotten my "sea legs" serving clients as an assistant to a successful fee-only financial planner, and later as a key staff planner for a large, independent wealth management firm. I knew I eventually wanted to be an entrepreneur. Over time, I evolved and became a partner in another successful wealth management firm.

While I enjoyed being a trusted advisor to a select group of affluent clients, it always bothered me to turn away the people who did not meet our firm's minimums. After all, I grew up in a fairly small town, in a disciplined and frugal middle income family with working class values. My roots simply tugged at my heartstrings until I determined that it was time for me to "return home."

Having made this decision, I was determined to set up my practice so that I could efficiently serve the underserved, help the validators, make my services affordable to people from all walks of life, and liberate myself from concierge-level responsibilities.

As a result of the changes that I made, I'm personally much more satisfied. I make a professional living, and I have plenty of time to enjoy my family, friends and my leisure time. I'm enormously pleased with the continual sense of satisfaction I receive knowing that I'm helping people – just like me – who might not otherwise have access to professional fee-only financial planning and advice. I'm not just adding another fraction of a percentage point to a wealthy individual's portfolio. Instead, I'm helping "real people" send their kids to college, build for the future, retire worry-free and enjoy a better night's sleep.

Come to think about it, I sleep better at night now, too.

SIMPLE IS OFTEN BETTER

Over the years, I've tested simple and fancy marketing materials. What I've found is that Middle Market consumers appreciate professional, but modest, marketing materials and lower-key tactics over slick, high-end materials and high-profile tactics. (Actually, high-end marketing pieces can be a turn off to average folks who may wonder where the money to produce them comes from!). While you want your marketing pieces to look and feel professional, it's important not to appear "over-produced." Average Americans respond better to simple, honest marketing messages and mid-level quality marketing materials. This is good news for the small planning firm or sole practitioner.

While you do need to invest some time and money in developing decent promotional materials, it may not be as expensive as you think to establish a solid presence in your community.

ESSENTIAL BRANDING DECISIONS

The modern notion of "branding" comes from the custom of branding livestock in the American West. Branding cattle conveys to the cowboy a clear and distinct mark of ownership. Branding your company and services should accomplish the same goal – to provide you with a clear and distinct mark of ownership. When potential clients see your advertising and marketing materials, you want them to think, "that's Henry James' company, no doubt about it."

But, while some may think of "branding" solely as the graphic identifier (i.e., your logo) or the tag line, those are only two elements in the branding process. "Branding" is the use of any and all techniques by which a company, organization or product distinguishes itself from others. It's how you express your value and your functions to your target markets.

Just as the cowboy sears his brand onto each of his cattle, your goal should be to burn your message into the minds of your target market. You need to decide in advance what you want your potential client to think or feel when she reads your marketing message, sees your logo, or hears your positioning statement. Over time, your brand should be instantly recognized and trigger an immediate association with your company and its competitive advantages.

So, what do you want to convey to your market? Are you:

- Just another financial advisor?

- The low-cost leader?

- A full-service solution provider?

- A flexible, needs-based resource?

- A comprehensive problem solver?

- An advisor to the affluent or elite?

- A Middle Market specialist serving regular folk?

What type of advisor are you? What type of service and/or focus are you going to use? What type of clientele are you willing to serve?

Branding is the *process* of identifying and differentiating your services to establish your uniqueness. If you've worked through some of the questions and processes described earlier in this chapter (especially in the area of creating your marketing plan), then you've already embarked on the branding and positioning decision-making process. Essentially, you've started developing your "company identity" – a large part of which is *you!*

Branding and positioning affect the messages and the materials we aim at current and prospective clients, the media, and our centers of influence. The essential elements of branding are:

- Identity

- Differentiation

- Uniqueness

Good branding helps your services be more easily remembered in the community. It provides strong links, and ties together all your promotional and marketing efforts. It unifies your public relations materials, yellow pages advertisements, community advertisements, radio spots, seminar productions, sponsorships, office décor and signage, newsletters and direct mail campaigns, e-communications, brochures and other collateral materials.

Think of branding as clearly and firmly establishing the identity of your company, product or services. A "brand" has promotional value and benefits associated with it. Questions to ask yourself during the branding process include:

1. What is your distinct personality?

2. What makes you different from all the others?

3. What statements can *only you* make in your promotions and marketing communications?

4. What statements do competitors dare not say (or don't bother to say) in their promotional and marketing communications?

5. What ideas, images and motivations can you use that will distinguish you from all others?

6. What are your personal preferences for style, color, verbiage and image?

Good branding is:

- **CONSUMER-ORIENTED.** A good brand is credible and sincere, and involves the client. It appeals to the client's self-interest.

- **FOCUSED ON ESTABLISHING ONE OR MORE COMPELLING REASONS FOR TRYING YOUR SERVICES.** A good brand presents a unique benefit and contains a promise of competitive advantage.

- **MEMORABLE.** A good brand is bold, and leaves a distinct impression. It links your company or name with the key selling ideas.

- **CLEAR AND COMPLETE.** A good brand says what it needs to say simply and clearly. It is uncomplicated and easy to understand. There are no alternative meanings or possibilities for confusion.

- **PERSUASIVE.** A good brand moves the client toward action or engagement of your services.

The good news is that just by targeting and serving the Middle Market, you've already established a key way to start differentiating yourself!

When I decided to target and serve the Middle Market and the do-it-yourself community exclusively, I created a tag line, logo, mission statement and key marketing messages during the development of my initial marketing plan. I thought long and hard about what made me different, and how my services and target market were different.

After reflecting on the questions and elements above, my staff and I found it fairly easy to brainstorm key branding and marketing ideas. With the help of my marketing communications consultant, Marie Swift, we finalized core marketing messages and produced collateral materials. Over the years, we have continued to improve those materials and refine the delivery of the message. It's a never-ending process, but well worth the investment.

Developing a strong company identity – even if you're just a company of one – is important. Do it earlier rather than later for the best results! I've included a Worksheet on the CD-ROM called "Key Branding Decisions" to help you through this vital process.

POSITIONING STATEMENTS

Every serious businessperson needs a series of positioning statements that can be communicated clearly and with passion – at will. It will take time and some thought to craft the right positioning statements for you. Remember, your positioning statement should be as unique as you are.

As you move through the process of creating your marketing plan and making essential branding decisions, jot down key words and phrases that lend themselves to verbal communications. You'll want to be able to gracefully – and authentically – answer these questions:

1. Who are you?

2. What do you do?

3. What makes you different from other financial advisors?

4. How does your company function? How do you serve your clients?

5. Who do you serve, and why?

6. What's your background? How long have you been doing this?

7. What drives or motivates you? *Why* do you do *what* you do?

8. Why should I trust / do business with you?

9. What benefits and solutions can you provide for me?

10. How are you compensated? What is the cost?

Of course, you wouldn't just plough down the list of questions in all of your interactions – that would send people running! But you need to be prepared to address each of these questions, as needed, in formal and informal settings. Most importantly, you need to *internalize* and, as the humorous Pier One shopping commercial with Kirsti Alley says, "become one" with your positioning statements.

I have to admit, I was slow to develop and adapt a *consistent* positioning statement of my own. When people asked me the questions above, or when I got up in front of a business or networking group, I felt I did just fine addressing them without going through the process of developing a series of formal positioning statements. But after being around other practitioners and hearing them speak about their practices (either powerfully or not-so-powerfully), and after my marketing coach nagged me long enough, I finally engaged myself in the process. Now I have *a series of consistent, compelling replies* that are a natural extension of who I am. It's a great feeling to know my strengths, my target market and my key selling points so well – and to be able to deliver them in a clear, compelling and consistent manner whenever needed.

Here are some tips to keep in mind as you construct your positioning statement and work on your delivery style:

- When we speak authentically, with forethought, clarity and passion, people are naturally drawn to us. They will either want to engage our services, or help us in other ways (e.g., by referring business to us, or by promoting us in the community).

- When we use lively words and try to draw "word pictures" in the listener's mind, we communicate with vivid power.

- When we anticipate and speak to the listener's needs and wants, we are persuasive.

- When we are sold on ourselves, our services and our business model, we are confident and allow our passion to show.

- When we practice saying our key messages aloud, we become both graceful and credible in our delivery.

I've included a number of other tips on developing a good positioning statement and verbal delivery style in Figure 6.5.

CREATING EFFECTIVE MARKETING COMMUNICATIONS TOOLS

Many small business owners think that one of the first things they must do is jump in and start creating their marketing communications tools right away. Financial planning entrepreneurs are no exception. They, too, may feel driven to begin creating and distributing their basic printed materials before they have done the real reflection and thinking described above. However, that is like putting the cart before the horse.

Even your basic collateral materials can help – or hinder – your communication and branding efforts. Every business card you hand out, every telephone call you make (or take), every letter or post card you send out, every seminar you present, every meeting you attend and network at, and every e-mail that you send out means that one more potential client has heard of you.

But what will their first impression be? And how will they remember you?

Make sure that your key messages and value propositions have been fully developed before you create your fundamental materials. You will (and should) evolve those essential messages and materials over time, but you'll want to start conveying the right image from the outset. In addition, it makes sense to start out with a logo and basic suite of collateral materials that you'll feel proud using – and won't outgrow – for two or three years. Once you're well-established as an expert in your community, you may decide to modify or evolve your brand; however, it is especially crucial in the start–up years to present a consistent

Figure 6.5

How to craft a good positioning statement and improve your verbal delivery:

1. Start by typing each question at the top of its own page. Place the pages in a three-ring binder (or in a tabbed section within your marketing plan binder). See the CD–ROM for a set of pre-typed questions in Word format.

2. As ideas and good phrasing occurs to you, jot these words down on the appropriate pages. Hone each reply until you've come up with a precise, compelling and genuine answer for each question.

3. Make an appointment with yourself to work on and improve your positioning statement each week. Re-type and clean up the pages. Create a long and a short answer for each question.

4. Practice speaking your responses *aloud.* Listen to the sound and rhythm of your voice. Vary your tone and emphasis. Envision yourself speaking to a specific person and intentionally *smile* while you practice aloud.

5. Use your hands and move around when you practice. Bend your knees. Gesture. Remember to smile. Watch yourself in the mirror.

6. Try out your verbiage on your spouse and other trusted friends and colleagues. Get feedback. Hone your wording and delivery skills.

7. Practice until you are essentially comfortable with your responses and verbal delivery. Notice I did not say "totally comfortable." Most of us never will be!

8. Now, forget about all your answers and preparation. Go out and meet people. Don't worry about "getting it just right." Practice "live," and discover what works and doesn't work. What feels right to you in a real-life situation?

9. Don't worry if you flub the wording when you speak. Let your light shine! It's who you are being *in that very moment* that matters most. Be comfortable with yourself, and others will be comfortable with you, too. Be more interested in the other person than you are in yourself.

10. Back at the office: Return to Step 3 above. Modify your verbiage and/or improve your delivery style.

visual image and deliver key marketing messages in a strategically-repetitive manner.

Your fundamental marketing tools are your letterhead, envelopes, business cards and brochures. Of course, you can extend that basic suite of materials to include personal note cards and matching envelopes, half-size note sheets, post cards and more. The possibilities are endless, but the good news is that today's technology is making production of these materials timelier and less expensive.

If you're starting your business on a shoestring budget, today's inkjet printers offer reasonably good (and sometimes exceptionally good) output, if the machine is maintained properly. Software such as Microsoft Publisher can offer you many do-it-yourself design options and attractive templates. Office Depot and other specialty paper suppliers (such as Paper Direct) offer a host of paper choices, including pre-scored brochure paper and precut business card sheets that are a bit heavier (and with less fuzzy edges) than previously available for office inkjet printer or laser printer output.

Once your practice is well-established, you may want to switch to professionally printed materials. You'll probably find that the cost-savings of in-office production dissipate as the quantity of the materials you need to produce increases. You'll want to assess the cost of the paper and the ink (the cost of which will increase for large areas of coverage). You should also factor in your time and the "hassle factor." For instance, if you need small quantities of tri-fold brochures, outputting them on an inkjet printer may be fine. However, if you need to run 50-100 (or more) brochures for a seminar or mailing, waiting for the ink to dry, monitoring the quality, running the second side, replacing the ink cartridge and folding the brochures yourself may be less than ideal.

Another option is using local "quick print" shops (such as Sir Speedy and Alphagraphics) and online "virtual print shops" (such as www.iprint.com and www.vistaprint.com), both of which can also produce decent printed materials. The online "virtual print shops" have basic templates that can be filled in and modified. Their online systems can be used for sending orders directly to one of their print shops. Sir

Speedy and Alphagraphics, which have provided traditional walk-in printer's services for many years, now also offer online self-design and/or ordering capabilities. The primary downsides of using these types of templated systems are that the choices may be limited, and there is little (or no) personal guidance. In addition, if you customize or modify the templates too much, you may be undoing the template designer's good work.

If you feel a professional's help would be beneficial in the logo design and layout process (I know I did), print shops like Sir Speedy and Alphagraphics typically have someone on staff to help you add a bit more flair and polish than you'd achieve on your own. Alternatively, you can visit a variety of online logo creation firms, such as www.logo-mojo.com, and determine whether their skills and design packages seem acceptable to you. Perhaps you know a talented graphic artist who'd be willing to barter design services for financial planning services?

When I established Garrett Financial Planning, Inc. in 1998, I hired a local graphic designer to help me create my logo and basic printed materials. Together we created an eye-catching, one-color logo. (The logo looked like it was two colors, light green and dark green, but this is a trick that smart designers use called "half toning." Actually, there's just one ink color involved, so printing costs remain low while potential visual impact is high.) I chose to print my materials on a beige colored, recycled paper that retains the characteristic specks most people associate with recycled paper. I wanted to make a subtle statement about my values and attract clients with similar values, as well as progressive, independent, thrifty and forward thinkers.

A few years later, I decided to have a logo "makeover." At the same time, I adjusted my signature tag line to better suit my target market and service model. I started by having one of my staff members work-up an idea based on the elements we liked from the old logo; then we incorporated a new piece of clip art we had on file. While you won't be able to see the logo color choices in Figures 6.6, 6.7, and 6.8 (because they are printed in black and white), we chose a hunter green for the burst, black for the company name and a deep purple for the tag line.

Figure 6.6

GARRETT FINANCIAL PLANNING, INC.
Hourly, As-Needed Advice for Everyday Life™

~ *Logo 1*

My staff member set the burst in hunter green, the company name in black, and the tag line in deep purple. Something was amiss, but we didn't quite know what or, more importantly, how to fix it. We tried moving the word "Garrett" out of the burst, but could not seem to find the right balance and typesetting.

Although the elements seemed to work together fairly well, there were a couple of things that didn't seem quite right. Because my staff members and I are not trained as graphic professionals, we weren't able to fully identify and solve the problem. So we turned our initial design idea over to our marketing consultant, whose professional design team took our concept, polished it up, and provided the three-part logo (icon, tag line, and some stylized text) in an assortment of graphic files that were optimized for a variety of applications. (See Figure 6.6 [Logo 1] for the original concept my staff provided to the design team. See Figure 6.7 [Logo 2] for the polished design.)

Figure 6.7

~ *Logo 2*

The designer uncoupled the company name from the burst, reset the font to some-thing with greater impact, re-focused the eye on the most important word, "Garrett" and moved the burst to the right of the company name. She simplified the color scheme, keeping just the hunter green and the black inks. We print this on bright, white linen paper. This is the long version of our logo.

As previously stated, a logo can be simple or fancy text set in a styl-ized font. It may or may not include some sort of graphic or icon as a visual identifier and branding tool. It can have either a tall or a wide footprint – or there can be two similar versions (one tall and one wide) that allow for many flexible placement options. (See Figure 6.7 [Logo 2] and Figure 6.8 [Logo 3] for samples of how I use both a wide logo and a tall logo.) The third element you may want to include as an integral part of your logo is a tag line.

Whenever possible, I include all three elements together: (1) my styl-ized font; (2) my graphic identifier; and (3) my tag line. If needed, I can use each element separately, in strategic ways. For instance, I may use just "the bug" (the burst graphic) as a watermark on a Power Point pres-entation or note pad. Alternatively, there are times when the stylized text, isolated from the rest of the logo elements, is what is called for. Mostly, however, I use the three elements in tandem.

Figure 6.8

~ *Logo 3*

Here is what the tall / centered version of our logo looks like. While we prefer to utilize the long / offset logo (see Logo 2) wherever possible, there are times when a long footprint is unwieldy. In that case, we utilize the tall / centered logo. We might also use just the burst or the company name in the specialized font (isolated elements).

A professional-looking, but simple one- or two-color design has worked well for me. It's been cost effective, and my validator and Middle Market clients have responded well to my materials. I've shied away from ultra-fancy concepts like gold foiling and embossing because I wanted to communicate to my target market that I'm cost conscious yet professional, just like they are.

Before you begin developing any of your collateral items, however, you need to work through the key branding decisions. What image do you want to convey? Progressive and slightly new? Conservative and classic? Old school veteran? Trendy and on the cutting edge? Your logo and collateral materials should help you communicate your company's image. The logo design and color, the layout and motif of your letterhead and business cards, the papers you select, and the tag lines you develop and attach to your logo or include on other items wherever possible – all of these things will work together to convey the type of planner and planning firm you are.

While a graphic designer can assist you by adding the visual flair and polish you might be missing without her help, you must be able to communicate your company's personality and focus so that she can offer appropriate options that communicate your image in the most effective way possible. The logo design process should be a collaboration. A good designer will listen to your goals, preferences and mission, and offer several choices that work to bring the concepts into visual reality.

A fourth element in my branding strategy has been to incorporate high quality photographs of local landmarks in my printed materials and on my web site. When we began building my first web site (www.GarrettFinancialPlanning.com), my marketing consultant suggested we create a simple "splash page" that would contain just the company name, logo, tag line and a photo of a quintessential Kansas City landmark. We wanted people to stop – just for a moment – to absorb these four elements and feel a subtle sense of "being at home." Kansas City is known as "the city of fountains" and we were delighted to find just the right portrait of the best-known fountain in the city.

We also had our web team at AdvisorSites create a home page collage of three other easy-to-identify (and easy-to-identify-with) Kansas City landmarks.[6] We carried the water theme over to a specially designed web logo, which included a swish shape reminiscent of a river.

Of course, we learned several lessons in building this first web site (which could be the focus of another chapter in another book). But, the web site continues to prove its weight in gold. Every penny I've put into it has been returned to me many times over. I have always used a double-pocket folder filled with single-sheets of targeted information, article reprints, and a full-color, tri-fold brochure to communicate my value to potential clients, centers of influence and the media. However, my web site has served as the quintessential "mega brochure." When prospective clients arrive for their initial consultation, if they've visited my web site they are already "sold" and ready to engage my services. The web site has also served as a valuable resource and another way for me to communicate with, and add value for, my clients.

Instead of sending quarterly newsletters, as many practitioners do, I send special reports and client letters three or four times a year. I'm also a big fan of post cards. I have used them to announce my web site's launch, remind clients that it's time for their financial check-up, encourage them to visit my web site, and to read my comments on the market. I also use e-mail to accomplish the same things, but I recognize that not all clients use e-mail. However, most clients do have Internet access and will visit my web site if prompted to do so.

Here are a few other tips for client communications:

- Find reasons to be in touch with, and to re-communicate your value to, your clients on a periodic basis. Special reports and market commentaries are a perfect way to do this.

- Encourage referrals by simply handing happy clients a business card, brochure or article reprint at the end of every meeting. Ask them to pass it on to someone who might be interested.

- Put a "P.S." at the end of every piece of correspondence that says that you welcome and appreciate their referrals.

- Hold a client appreciation event once a year. I host an annual open house at my office, complete with appetizers, beer, wine and soft drinks. Other ideas I may try in the future include having my local Schwab representative give an educational talk on how to fully utilize Schwab's website for research, placing trades and tracking investment portfolios. We've also considered hosting computer classes on how to use Quicken to track personal expenses.

DIRECT MAIL AND ADVERTISING

As mentioned above, I use marketing letters, stimulating e-mails, offers for special reports, seminar flyers and postcard campaigns for my advertising. I've never mailed "cold" to a purchased mailing list. Instead, I cull my own names and addresses from various community directories and lists. Over time, the list has grown and my e-mails and direct mail communications have rippled out to a larger body of people.

Besides purchasing what I think is a pretty darn good yellow pages advertisement (it must be because it pays for itself), I don't do any other form of display advertising (although colleagues of mine swear by small display advertisements in their Chamber of Commerce directories, church bulletins, neighborhood newspapers, and other similarly targeted publications).

If you plan to use direct mail or advertising, be sure to budget wisely. You'll need to invest in several mailings to the same list of people in order for it to pay off. You should place the same (or similar advertisements) in the same publication or directory for a number of months in order to build "share of mind."

Other tips include:

- Know to whom you are targeting. Create a compelling message that will appeal to the needs and self-interests of your target clients. Brand your advertisements and/or direct mail pieces.

- Be colorful. Stand out with something different. Have a special offer or reason for them to contact you.

- Work on your headlines and create an active "call out" to attract their attention. You've only got about three seconds to capture their attention, so make those three seconds count.

- Provide options for contacting you – telephone, e-mail, fax, pre-paid reply card, etc.

- Provide your web site address so that your target clients can check you out privately, on their own terms.

- Finally, don't despair if your advertisements and mailings do not produce immediate results. Marketing experts tell us that it takes multiple exposures to your message/offer before a prospective client may call. Ninety-nine percent of the recipients will never call; 1% is a reasonable response rate. However, if you think of direct mail and advertising as just one more tool in your tool belt, and diversify your marketing methods accordingly, you should eventually see your efforts working together over time. Who knows, you may even hit the stellar 3% reply rate that some direct mail companies tout.

- Don't be surprised if you receive inquiries from advertisements, post cards or articles that were sent out many months ago. It's not unusual for people to keep a postcard, or tear out an advertisement or article, and place it in the top desk drawer until a need arises.

Kathy Dollard, a CFP® professional who practices near Boston, told me that she consistently hears that people "see her everywhere." Although she uses some small, strategically placed advertisements, they are not the backbone of her marketing communications program. Instead, she focuses on: (1) providing educational seminars in the community (using flyers, postcards, e-mails, catalog listings or targeted advertisements to promote them); (2) networking with allied professionals; and (3) encouraging referrals from existing clients. The direct mail campaigns and display advertisements she uses simply bolster her credibility in the community and help build "share of mind." It's not unusual for someone to show up at one of her seminars clutching a postcard she sent or an advertisement she placed many months ago. Kathy sticks with her marketing and advertising plan, through thick and thin, knowing that it takes time to yield results.

BUILD AFFINITY GROUPS

While e-communications, direct mail, display advertisements and other more expensive forms of marketing communications can bolster your visibility and your credibility, in my experience a key element of success is to find a variety of opportunities to "meet and greet" people with whom you have common interests. If you've done the "hard work" of reflecting on which clients you want to serve and have taken the time to craft the right message, it will be easy to spot right-fit opportunities within your community.

For me, the best place to apply my time and talents was by volunteering in a leadership capacity for key industry groups. Through my activities and the relationships I built via my involvement in NAPFA (the National Association of Personal Financial Advisors), the IAFP (the International Association for Financial Planning), and the ICFP (the Institute for Certified Financial Planners) (IAFP and ICFP were the predecessors to what we now know as the Financial Planning Association), I established myself as "the go-to person" for anything related to serving validators or Middle Market clients.

Of course it didn't hurt that I left my company-branded pens in strategic places wherever I went. I also wore an eye-catching button on my lapel that stated, "Ask me about ___," followed by the tag line of my particular brand of financial planning. Even though I'm technically an introvert, I'm so passionate about my mission that I confidently put myself in the public eye. When the *Kansas City Star* partnered with the IAFP to produce the well-received MoneyWise Personal Finance Fairs for several years, it was fortuitous that I was the chapter president and served on the public relations committee during that time period.

Did I have to force myself to take on these leadership roles? No, it was a natural fit for me. I loved being able to contribute to the various committees and task forces. I also learned quite a bit about working with the media and being in the public eye. A natural by-product of my participation was enhanced visibility among my peers and increased stature in my community. As a result of the relationships I continue to build within my affinity groups, I enjoy continued referrals from other advisors and clients, repeat business from current clients, and continued media interest from local and national press partners.

What are your natural affinity groups? Where can you meet and greet "your people"? Look for ways to meet and greet key people in your community – whether it's serving on a foundation board, doing volunteer work for a non-profit, serving on an FPA public relations committee or in a leadership role with NAPFA, or sponsoring seminars at your local community college or church. Find those people who will introduce you to others – they may, in fact, become your apostles in spreading your key messages. They can open additional (and sometimes unexpected!) doors for you.

For example, a colleague of mine has decided that business expositions and community fairs are his "cup of tea." St. Louis-based financial advisor, Dave Ressner, scours community papers and specialty publications (e.g., *Parent and Child*) to find out where opportunities exist. He signs up for the event and pays little or nothing for his booth or table space. Dave may set up just a card table at a Parents' Fair at Babies 'R Us, or he may set up something more elaborate at an Earth Day Festival. The materials he brings for his information table are designed to be a custom fit for the affinity groups and people who'll be attending. He simply thinks about what he'd like to see or receive if he were in their shoes.

At Earth Day, Dave provided literature on socially responsible investing that he obtained from Calvert funds. Of course, he had some additional information to hand out, including a special report branded with his company logo, web site and telephone number. Not only does it "light him up" to attend these events (remember, he's looking for groups in which he has common interests), but he also meets a large number of people who immediately get to know and like him. Frequently, he's the only financial planner exhibiting at the event. Dave uses a clipboard to obtain contact information from people who'd like to hear from him. Many of them check the "call me for an initial meeting" box. Better yet, the folks who come in for that initial meeting almost always engage his services. There's no trick here, but there might be a little "magic" involved – due to the fact that Dave has already established a good amount of rapport and trust just by meeting and greeting these folks at an event tied to a matter they all care about.

Remember, people do business with people they like and trust. Being a model of good citizenship creates a positive image, allows you to get in front of key individuals and groups of people, and makes you a better person in one fell swoop. While it will take some time, you don't need a large budget to make networking and public relations become a large part of your marketing effort.

PUBLIC AND PRIVATE SEMINARS

One of the most effective ways to maximize your perceived value to current and prospective clients is by delivering informative seminars. Creating an intelligent presentation of thought-provoking material takes time, but it's well worth the effort. It doesn't have to be expensive, especially if you let a host organization provide the room, handle the promotional work and fill the room for you. An added benefit of a privately-sponsored seminar is that there is an instant implied endorsement of you and your firm.

There are many good financial services seminar modules available for purchase. However, I prefer to create my own unique seminar modules based on current events or books I like. For instance, I love:

- *Your Money or Your Life: Transforming your Relationship with Money and Achieving Financial Independence*, by Joe Dominguez and Vicki Robin.[7]

- *The Seven Stages of Money Maturity* by George Kinder.[8]

- *The Richest Man in Babylon* by George Clasen.[9]

- *The Millionaire Next Door* by Thomas Stanley Ph. D., and William Danko Ph. D.[10]

It's easy to come up with a seminar or workshop that focuses on the fundamental messages in books that you love, and it's cheaper and more authentic than buying prepared modules.

Of course, you'll want to give credit to your source. You could even include a copy of the book as a part of the tuition. Or you could sell the books as a courtesy at the back of the room at your cost. What author wouldn't love that? It's a win-win-win situation.

How about creating a seminar based on current events? As I write this book, the markets are plunging. Our country has been plagued by a horrific terrorist attack and continued threats. It appears as though we may be out of the woods as far as the economic slow down is concerned, but the crisis of confidence in corporate America continues to dog the stock market and wreak havoc on portfolios. Clients are calling – and so did my local NBC affiliate and National Public Radio (NPR).

So what should you do? Step up communications, of course. Offering a seminar on "How to Survive and Thrive in the Current Financial Environment" and posting a related article on your web site is a natural way to be of service to your clients. It also presents a nice marketing opportunity for you. Just letting people know that the article is there – and that you are there during trying times – gives you a reason to send an e-mail message or postcard that can stimulate a visit to your web site or a telephone call to your office. It's also a great way to reach out to the media (more about that later in this chapter).

On one occasion, I overheard a group of people talking in a small group about the problems couples often have communicating about and managing money. Voila! A seminar was born. I called the proper person at the church, drummed up some flyers, had a promotional blurb placed in the church bulletin and made up a Power Point presentation titled "Couples and Money." What was the result? With just a little work I received a great response, got new clients, made new friends, and enhanced my visibility.

One rule I always follow in my marketing communications is this: "seek first to be of service and to educate." With a "service first attitude," marketing opportunities and enhanced visibility will naturally occur. People (and especially the media) can smell it a mile away if you have a hidden agenda. My advice to you – don't.

As I mentioned before, whenever possible opt for a hosted seminar instead of a public seminar. Let the host organization do the promotional work and fill the room for you. Then you'll be free to simply show up, present yourself and your material in the best possible light, and provide a valuable and educational handout (which happens to be tastefully branded with your logo and company information). You'll also get instant credibility if a reputable organization is sponsoring your presentation.

A word of caution: don't go overboard on promoting yourself at your seminars, either from the stage or in your handouts. Pressing too hard makes you look desperate and unprofessional, and the attendees will question your motives. Instead, create an information table at the back of the room or in the lobby and provide a variety of interesting handouts or literature for people to take with them. They'll call you if you've made the right impression.

If you feel you must gather names, leave a clipboard out with forms for persons to sign up for your quarterly newsletter or request a special report. Provide a box on the form that says, "Call me to discuss [Topic]," and lines for them to fill in their address, telephone numbers and e-mail address.

Remember, be service-minded first and foremost to reap the best rewards.

When I speak to groups of people, I don't hand out my business cards. In fact, I don't even keep them in my pocket. I intentionally leave them in my purse. People always approach me afterward and ask for them. My response is "Sure, just a minute while I get one out of my purse." Even when you need business, don't act like you do. As one major marketing campaign stressed, "never let 'em see you sweat."

Executive coach and consultant Bill Swift points to these truisms:

"IF PEOPLE SEE YOU NEED MONEY, YOU'LL NEVER GET IT. SIMILARLY, IF YOU COMMUNICATE IN ANY WAY THAT YOU NEED CLIENTS, YOU WON'T GET THEM EITHER. YOU MUST LEARN TO UNDERSTAND HOW YOU SHOW UP FOR OTHER PEOPLE AND IMPROVE YOUR PUBLIC PERSONA. LEARN TO RECOGNIZE YOUR OWN FEELINGS OF

INADEQUACY OR SCARCITY AS THOSE FEELINGS ARISE. IN THIS WAY YOU CAN DISSIPATE OR COMPARTMENTALIZE THOSE FEELINGS RATHER THAN BROADCASTING YOUR "NEED" TO OTHERS UNCONSCIOUSLY. THEN YOU CAN WEAR THE CLOAK OF CONFIDENCE WHENEVER YOU ENGAGE PROSPECTIVE CLIENTS AND LET YOUR BEST SELF SHINE."[11]

CREATE A BUSY PROFESSIONAL PERSONA

Can you still be confident when the pipeline's less than full? With regard to setting up initial meetings or telephone calls with clients, I take the advice "never look too available" one step further. Here's what I tell all of the new planners I mentor:

"EVEN IF YOUR CALENDAR IS TOTALLY OPEN, BOOK THE APPOINTMENT OUT BY A WEEK OR TWO OR (GULP) EVEN THREE. APPEAR TO BE A BUSY PROFESSIONAL, AND TAKE ON THAT PERSONA. EVENTUALLY YOU WILL BE."

Is this a "fake it 'til you make it" strategy? To some degree, yes it is. However, if you're focusing properly on the development and implementation of your marketing plan, you should have plenty of "real appointments" filling your week, such as: meeting with other professionals; networking at industry events; scheduling time to work *on* your business (not just *in* it); making telephone appointments with your business coach, marketing coach, mentor or "Dream Team" (more about that later in this chapter); writing an article for the personal finance section of the local newspaper; revising your marketing plan; or preparing for a seminar.

What about answering the telephone? I know lots of highly successful consultants who still prefer to answer the telephone themselves. Even if they have a cadre of helpers supporting them behind the scenes, it is often the first, and only, chance they get to establish rapport with a potential client. There have been many times I've answered the telephone myself and been glad that I did.

For instance, a client who has become a very important partner in promoting my business told me that it was that first telephone call, and the manner in which I cordially listened and related to her concerns, that made all the difference. First of all, she wasn't expecting *me* to pick up the call on the third ring with a simple "Sheryl Garrett." When the prospective client began to explain why she called, she also belly-ached that she and her husband had just had a bunch of money "fall into their laps." It just seemed like I should say, "(pause) Well, darn." We both laughed out loud! She was "sold," and the rest is history.

I've learned to relax and be myself – and you should, too. I dress fairly casually every day of the week, whether I have client appoint- ments or not. (It used to be "business casual," but has progressed to "pretty darn casual" most days.) This is a strategic business decision, and a personal preference of mine. I know that some folks will respect me for being "the real me," and others will not. But because I need to get into intimate discussions with my clients about their goals in life, immediately, I feel that allowing them to get to know me as quickly as possible helps facilitate our initial connection. I want my clients (and prospective clients) to feel comfortable in my presence; therefore, I like to be comfortable in theirs.

The best thing about the niche that I serve – this great untapped market called the "Middle Market" – is that it contains so many people looking for what I've got to offer (or, who *will be* eager to secure my services once they learn what I'm offering). Consequently, I don't have to work with people that I don't like or enjoy working for. Nor do I have to work with people who *really* don't want to work with me. I decided early on to seek out those persons who would like and trust me, and not to worry about the ones who choose not to engage my services. As stated in Chapters 3 and 4, my service model isn't appropriate for all people – just the majority of them!

What's your strategy for answering the telephone and taking initial inquiry calls? Officing? Dressing? Working with clients? How can you improve your state of mind and enhance your listening and relationship- building skills to improve outcomes?

TURN UP YOUR MARKETING RADAR

Another valuable activity is talking to other financial planners who are serving the validator and Middle Markets. "Pick their brains" to determine what has worked best for them in promoting their services in their respective communities. I also recommend that you attend industry conferences, participate in industry study groups and discussion boards, and read industry periodicals. In other words, learn from the successes and failures of others.

Remember that marketing to Middle Market consumers in rural Tennessee will be different from marketing to Middle Market consumers in urban New York. While middle income folks and do-it-yourselfers nationwide do have common characteristics, needs and sensibilities, every community and market has its own subtle character. *You* also have your own persona, preferences and character, and it's important that you try to match your personality and skills with people who'll quickly grow to like and trust you.

In the words of William Shakespeare, "To thine own self be true."[12]

As you go about your daily business, start noticing what makes your community unique. Also take note of what makes *you* unique. Keep a notepad on your desk and jot down your observations for a couple of weeks. Where are the overlapping interests and values that could lead to affinity and opportunity?

Another great idea is scanning the free periodical racks in the front of the supermarket. Read the smaller community publications as well as the larger ones. There are tons of "meet and greet" opportunities you can glean from these periodicals. After a while, what you once saw as "junk" periodicals may take on a golden glow.

Begin attending a variety of business and social functions. Wherever you go, have your marketing radar turned up high so that you will be alert to "right-fit" opportunities. Once you hone this skill, you'll find endless opportunities to talk to people, share your mission, and tell your story.

What Works According to Other Advisors

When asked, experienced advisors almost always list the following marketing techniques in their "what works in marketing" lists. All of these are important to a well-balanced marketing plan, and you might want to test them out in your community.

- Craft several good verbal messages and positioning statements that you can "tap" on demand (based on the situation and with whom you are speaking).

- Speak with friends, family and acquaintances so that you spread the word and get referrals to potential clients and professional allies.

- Actively participate in your local Chamber of Commerce.

- Actively participate in formal networking, civic and service groups.

- Actively participate in local FPA or NAPFA chapters (or other industry-related groups).

- Write articles or do "Money Makeover" or "Financial Q & A" columns for the local metropolitan paper or smaller community newspapers.

- Produce and distribute an informative newsletter or timely special report.

- Publish a targeted yellow pages ad.

- Establish a good web site – one that is partly educational, and partly electronic brochure.

- Present at privately-hosted educational seminars (a host organization, such as a church, business or community college promotes the event and provides the meeting facility).

- Sponsor public educational seminars (you fill the room and incur all costs).

- Make "warm" and "cold" telephone calls. (*Hint:* you should have a "real" and valuable reason to call.)

- Canvass local neighborhoods with flyers or mailers, in person or using a targeted direct mailing. (I happen to like postcards best because they can be extremely efficient and they have a long shelf life.)

- Place small display advertisements in targeted community newspapers, church and school bulletins, senior citizen center newsletters, etc.

- Do a targeted direct mail campaign (U.S. mail or e-mail) using a "warm" list. (*Hint:* a compelling message/offer is the key here.)

WORKING WITH THE MEDIA

Getting local publicity is one of the fastest ways to become known in your town. Best of all, publicity is free. All you need is (1) an idea that will benefit the public or the publication's readership, (2) some time, and (3) a bit of writing skill. If you are lacking in the copywriting skills department, a ghostwriter can add the Midas touch. Or perhaps your spouse or a trusted colleague or assistant can help you polish your articles.

A secondary benefit of publicity is that you can use your published items in your sales and marketing materials. Every time you send a letter to a prospect or sponsor a seminar, give out copies of articles that have been written about you (or by you). Nothing builds your credibility faster than your being held up as an "expert" by the local newspaper. It's always fun when people approach me in the supermarket or some other public place and mention that they've seen my photo in the paper or read the "Money Makeover" I was featured in.

Recently, one of my staff planners was at a park with her son talking to another mother and the subject of financial planning came up. "Do you know ... Sheryl Garrett?" the other mother asked. After a smile and an appropriate response from my staff planner, the mother confided that she'd read an article I'd written, called my office, been scared off by the consulting fee estimate (remember, I'm fee-only), but was now ready to come in for a check-up.

Media coverage, like direct mail and display ads, sometimes has an incubation period before it bears results. (This is one reason why I like postcards. People tend to keep them in the top desk drawer until they have a need for advice, or a stimulating event prompts their call.)

When people call your office asking for information about your services, be sure to include any newspaper articles quoting you as an expert. It's wonderful credibility! And if the articles are not worth providing in their entirety, then create a news summary sheet (or web page as I have on http://www.GarrettFinancialPlanning.com). With positioning like this, when you make your follow-up call do you think that you will be treated as a solicitor? Or will you be treated as a professional, just as the prospect treats his attorney or CPA?

In addition, if you're trying to build business relationships with CPAs and attorneys, you'll have the edge over other financial advisors if you've been quoted or profiled in publications.

Another approach is to create a "Dream Team of Advisors," consisting of an attorney, a CPA, a mortgage broker, an independent insurance broker, and, of course, you. You and the other members of your team can write articles together, produce seminars, refer business to one another and ultimately open more doors. You could even add a small business coach, marriage counselor or other non-traditional experts to your Dream Team. People (including the media) love stories on personal finance and on maintaining balance in life. In fact, just after personal health, personal finance is the hottest topic on many publications' slates.

Why would anyone want to write about you? Well, the main reason is that journalists need to fill newspapers with content, and what you have to say can be very good content – especially now that you are focusing on serving the Middle Market (which most likely represents the bulk of their readership).

I've found the best way to start is to simply read a periodical and determine who is writing about what. It's easy to find out how to contact various journalists – either look at the publication's masthead or visit their web site. If in doubt, simply call the publication and ask the person manning the information desk which writer or editor would be most interested in what you have to say. Find out if that journalist prefers to receive her information via e-mail or U.S. mail. Then send a press kit or a letter of introduction along with a story idea and your business card.

Another great strategy: E-mail the writer when he's done a good job writing about something related to your field of expertise. Compliment the journalist in a sincere, non-patronizing way and mention some small aspect that might tie in with the previous article, or that might be a good topic for a follow-up article. And if you're a member of certain industry groups (e.g., FPA or NAPFA), participate in their press partner programs and respond to media requests.

Also, don't overlook industry publications. Focus some of your attention on becoming a resource for periodicals such as *Financial Planning, Journal of Financial Planning, Investment Advisor, Financial Advisor, Registered Representative, Bloomberg Wealth Manager, Morningstar Advisor, Inside Information, Ticker* and *Research* magazines. You'll probably be reading these publications and industry discussion boards anyway, so look for opportunities to add your thoughts and insights. Your local editor and other journalists will take note if they see you've been quoted in one of these respected industry publications. They are likely be favorably impressed and more inclined to contact you the next time they need a resource or story idea. Your clients and referral sources will also be impressed when they see "[Your Name] has been quoted in *XYZ Industry Journal*" in your biography and promotional materials.

FAVORITE PRESS SUCCESS STORIES

Here are a couple of media success stories that I can't resist sharing:

Rich Chambers, a CFP® and colleague of mine who practices in Palo Alto, California, had a goal – a burning desire to be quoted in the *Wall Street Journal*, *Newsweek* or some other major consumer publication. He determined to *religiously read* the personal finance columns in the targeted publications. After awhile he'd compiled a comprehensive list containing the names, titles and e-mail addresses of his favorite columnists. One of them was Jonathan Clements, who as you know writes the "Getting Going" finance column for the *Wall Street Journal*.

Whenever Rich read an article that he agreed with or thought was well done, but could have included some additional insight or piece of information, he sat down at his computer and composed a thoughtful, courteous and brief e-mail to the writer. He was always professional and helpful. Usually, he had a trusted colleague or his marketing communications coach look over his letters to make sure the tone was right, and that the "i"s were dotted and the "t"s were crossed. Most importantly, he didn't write to promote his business; instead, he wrote to provide food for thought or to add a new idea the writer might not have considered. He always ended his e-mails the same way – with a simple sentence inviting the journalist to call him with any questions or for more information. The signature area had his company tag line, contact information and a link to his web site automatically embedded at the bottom of every message.

Within a few months, Rich had the local newspapers calling him for his insight and expertise. He kept a folder of "hot topics," facts, figures, quotes and ideas next to his telephone. If he was caught off guard or was busy when the journalist called, he'd get some information about the article, find out what they were looking for, and determine what their deadline was. He'd ask if he could take 10 minutes to collect his thoughts and compile the information they were seeking. Then he'd call them back, composed and ready to provide his best answers.

He practiced speaking in sound bytes and quotable quotes. When the content of the article warranted, Rich would also offer to research additional details and call back within the hour.

The local media coverage enhanced Rich's local visibility and credibility. Clients and other professionals would say, "Hey, Rich. I saw the article you were in" and strike up a conversation; frequently, they'd bring a copy of the article to Rich's office. Within a year of starting his media communications campaign, Rich had been quoted on CBS.MarketWatch.com and featured as a financial planning expert in articles in the *Christian Science Monitor, Forbes,* and the *Wall Street Journal.* National Public Radio called, and Rich was one of three planners who provided comments on college funding options.

Rich had more than met his goal. He included reprints of the articles when prospective clients requested introductory material. He mailed and e-mailed copies of the articles to friends, colleagues and clients who might have missed the article. He noted the media coverage in his biography and on his web site. He placed reprints on information tables when he spoke.

But now the media communications bug was in Rich's system. He just kept reading the publications and sending notes to the journalists. One day Rich was discussing marketing strategies and joint endeavors with his Power Partner, Steve Bell, a CFP® based in Livermore, California. His cell phone rang and Rich picked it up promptly as always, with a lively "Investors Capital Management. This is Rich Chambers." (Remember, he was meeting with his Power Partner, *not* waiting by the telephone or sitting on his laurels.) When the very pleasant gentleman with an English accent introduced himself as Jonathan Clements and explained that he was working on a story and wanted to bounce some ideas around with Rich, Rich didn't miss a beat (although he *did* think for just a moment that it might have been a financial planning buddy playing a joke on him).

At the end of their discussion, Rich offered to provide some additional information that would help Mr. Clements with his article. He provided the information promptly (via e-mail) as promised, with a brief "thanks for your call, it was a pleasure" preamble. Subsequently, Mr. Clements wrote an informative article that happened to contain ideal content for Rich's client communications – Rich also happened to be quoted in the article. Since then, Rich and Mr. Clements have collaborated on additional story ideas and content, some of which are still pending publication (but probably not for long).

When Rich told me this story, I almost said, "It doesn't get any better than that!" But then you just never know what can happen with a little thought, some persistence, and the right relationships.

Another favorite media success story is that of my friend and colleague, Dean Knepper. Dean hails from the Washington, D.C. area. After practicing for 20 years as a C.P.A. and financial advisor for firms catering to affluent clients, Dean decided to start his own financial planning and tax practice serving middle America; he founded Lifetime Planning in January 2001. Dean took a course on effective marketing communications and returned home with a press release to send to his local newspapers. He customized the press release and sent a copy to each of the three periodicals in his community. One of those periodicals was the *Washington Post*. The business editor liked Dean's press release title and story idea so much that he sent a photographer out to capture Dean standing in front of his office signage, complete with his name and credentials in a clearly visible area.

What was so compelling to the Post editor? Consider the title of the article the *Post* ran: "For the Not-So-Rich, A New Kind of Asset – Financial Counselor Changes his Focus." The article began like this:

> *"AFTER YEARS SPENT FIGURING OUT HOW TO MANAGE MONEY FOR THE WEALTHY, [DEAN KNEPPER, CPA, CFP®] WANTED TO FOCUS ON HELPING MIDDLE-INCOME AMERICANS MANAGE THEIRS. … FINANCIAL PLANNING USED TO BE A TERM USED ONLY BY THE WEALTHY. BUT INCREASINGLY, THE NOT-SO-RICH HAVE SOUGHT TO FOLLOW THEIR EXAMPLE."* [13]

The article went on to describe Dean's practice and detail his services.

A year and a half after the article came out, Dean told me:

"I AM STILL GETTING CLIENTS WHO SAW AND SAVED THE ARTICLE. ONE LADY SAID SHE HAD THE ARTICLE ON HER REFRIGERATOR FOR WELL OVER A YEAR BEFORE SHE CALLED FOR AN APPOINTMENT. IT WAS AN ADDED BENEFIT THAT THE ARTICLE WAS CHOSEN BY THE POST FOR INCLUSION IN A PROMOTIONAL 'LOUDOUN EXTRA' SECTION THAT WAS DISTRIBUTED TO ALL RESIDENTS IN THE COUNTY (THE LOUDON EXTRA SECTION RAN A COUPLE WEEKS AFTER THE MAIN ARTICLE). I CAN ONLY IMAGINE WHAT THAT WOULD HAVE COST IF IT HAD BEEN A PAID ADVERTISEMENT," EXCLAIMED DEAN.

In addition to enhancing Dean's client acquisition efforts, and helping him to establish himself as an expert with other professionals, the *Post* article – in conjunction with Dean's continued media relations efforts – led to further media recognition. Dean enjoyed multiple quotes on TheStreet.Com. One year later, the *Post* ran a follow up article called "Where are They Now?" – which again described Dean's practice and how he focuses on serving the Middle Market. A few months later, he was quoted again in the *Christian Science Monitor*.

Dean continued to speak with journalists. Not all of his contributions were used, and sometimes he didn't get quoted at all. Sometimes he'd see his idea or contribution in the article, but without any attribution. No worries, Dean just kept on truckin'. First and foremost, his goal was to become a trusted and valued resource.

One day National Public Radio called Dean looking for a financial planner to interview on a breaking news story. Dean didn't have any experience working with the broadcast media. Having only an hour to prepare, he felt a little gun-shy telling Jacki Lyden of National Public Radio what his clients had been asking – and what he'd been telling them – about the market's recent plunge, and the crisis in investor confidence despite good economic news. It wasn't that Dean would have said something he'd regret; he just wasn't ready for that type of radio interview.

Dean is one smart cookie. You don't have to honor every press request. To Dean's credit, he provided the name and telephone number of a trusted CFP® colleague to the NPR staff person. What a nice surprise Dean's colleague had when NPR called her that day. And I imagine that colleague will think of Dean the next time *she* has a referral or a press request that she'd like to pass along.

But perhaps the nicest surprise of all for Dean was when the writer for *Time* magazine contacted him. The journalist was writing an article on retirement planning issues and how the bear market was affecting baby boomers' and retirees' lifestyle projections. Were people planning to work longer? What suggestions and advice did Dean have? Months passed after the interview, but the article didn't materialize. Then one day, five months after the interview, the writer contacted Dean to let him know that the article would finally be published. Dean would be quoted in a nice-size paragraph summarizing his observations. The article would be *the cover story* for the next issue of *Time* magazine. "The article got shelved before due to a breaking news story," Dean told me. "I thought that was the end of it until the reporter contacted me on Friday and said it was going to print the following week."

There are many more stories I'd share if I had room! But as these stories and my own experience show, once you get rolling with the media, things will start to snowball. Personal finance journalists read each other's articles. They want to know what the others are writing about and whom they use as resources in their articles. One writer will mention your name to another writer, and one day you'll get a (truly surprising) telephone call from a publication. I remember my first such call!

TIPS FOR WORKING WITH JOURNALISTS

I started "small" with my own local newspaper doing "Money Makeovers" and ended up in *Newsweek*, *Smart Money*, *Kiplinger's Personal Finance* and many more. After many years of personal press success, I've come up with the following tips for working with journalists:

- Be timely. Remember journalists are working on deadlines. Return their calls promptly.

- If you are called out of the blue, ask what's their topic and deadline. See if you may call back in 10 minutes. (Tell them you'd like a few moments to pull together some comments, additional quotes or resources).

- Internalize your message. Say something quotable. Practice speaking in sound bytes. Recognize that quotes often need to be bold statements. You are an advisor, so you must be definitive. Respond to the interviewers questions directly and with conviction.

- Don't be upset if you are misquoted, or if you don't get a chance to proof the article or make corrections before it comes out. I've rarely had the opportunity to "proof" any of the articles I've been in.

- Be helpful. Have a "real reason" to call or e-mail the journalist. (Test: project yourself to the journalist's desk and ask whether *you* would welcome your call?). Seek to be of service first and foremost.

- Be patient. Perfect your style, tone and content to become "media worthy."

THE ART OF STORYTELLING

Publicity is by far one of the most effective marketing tools you have at your disposal, but how do you promote yourself to the media so that they will give your growing practice the spotlight it needs? The answer – storytelling!

That's right, storytelling. Ultimately, personal finance stories are human interest stories and every reporter is looking for a good story. Here are the key things you need to give the press to help them tell your story:

PERSONALITY. A company is faceless without the people who run it. In addition, personal finance stories work best when you can tell a real-life story about one of your clients and how they overcame an obstacle or realized a better future because of the work you did with them. (Be sure to ask your client ahead of time if you may use their name and story.) You want the personality of the people to come through so that the reader gets a sense of who you are, and who your clients are. As impressive as numbers can be, they aren't the whole story. Real-life examples of how you solved a client's problems bring your story to life. Readers want to hear about real people. Tell the stories behind the facts and provide details that would make someone want to listen.

FACTS AND FIGURES. Reporters love facts and figures that anchor a story in reality. Provide a table that supports your key tenets. Give a third-party quote that anchors the article and lends credibility to your assertions. If you prefer not to divulge certain figures about your business, talk instead about its rate of growth. Say something like, "business has doubled in the last year," or "we've already met our objectives for this year, and it's only July." Other alternatives include, "The client makes an executive level salary" or, "he is on target to retire at age 58." You get the picture. Be honest and helpful, but finesse it if you should.

DETAILS THAT REVEAL. Reporters have their antennae up for interesting details about the people behind the companies. Increasingly, that's the approach that reporters are taking so you need to be open and share details with them. Maybe the contents of your refrigerator (or the fact that you work best when sipping tea on your veranda while working from your wireless network) reveals something insightful about your marketing strategy. Perhaps your spouse works with you in the business, or you are active in providing financial literacy classes on a volunteer basis at your local high school. Your motivation and vision for being in business is who you are, and what makes your story unique.

TIE IN WITH CURRENT OR SEASONAL EVENTS. Every journalist needs support to convince their editor why they should write *this* story *now.* Anticipate this need and provide reasons why the story is timely and should be covered now. For instance, at tax time create a list of "Financial Spring Cleaning Tips." During the holidays, write an article on "Gifts With a Purpose" or "Year-End Tax and Financial Planning." If the markets are turbulent, offer comments on what you're telling your clients, and what they're asking you.

In short, the media needs you! In addition, journalists are frequently just the types of clients we are looking for. I've lost track of the many times that reporters have told me something like, "it is so refreshing to hear from a financial planner who would actually work with a person making an average salary and driving a Toyota" (they are referring to themselves). Start your media outreach campaign today!

KEYS TO MARKETING SUCCESS

I'd like to recap what I consider to be the essential keys in marketing to the Middle Market. To be successful in our marketing efforts we need to:

1. **DEFINE OUR MARKETS.** Understand our clients' needs and tune in to what makes them tick. Discover and address what's important to *them.*

2. **GATHER INFORMATION.** Look at all the possibilities.

3. **FORMULATE A WRITTEN PLAN.** Set goals. State expected results in words and in numbers.

4. **MAKE DECISIONS.** Implement the plan. Measure results. Refine the plan.

5. **OWN THE PLAN.** Embody our mission.

6. **KNOW OURSELVES.** Understand how we are unique and the value we provide. Practice and refine how we communicate our value. Convey benefits, not features.

7. **BECOME A GOOD STORYTELLER.** Be passionate, courageous and authentic.

8. **BUILD AFFINITY GROUPS AND STRONG RELATIONSHIPS.** To reap the best outcomes, seek first to serve and the benefits will flow to us naturally.

9. **LEVERAGE ACTIVITIES BASED ON OUR STRENGTHS AND PERSONAL PASSIONS.** Pick three or four key marketing methods and then execute them well. The primary methods we select should suit our natural abilities and personalities.

10. **NEVER GIVE UP.** Remain true to your vision and sense of purpose. Be tenacious. Surround yourself with positive, energetic people who support your vision.

A lot of ground has been covered in this chapter, but I feel as though I've barely scratched the surface. An entire book could be written on just the marketing aspects of serving this special target market. But since that is not the sole purpose of this book, I'll save that for another day.

There are many good resources available in the financial planning industry and through general business channels to help you fill in any gaps regarding the effective marketing and day-to-day operation of your practice. I've provided some of my favorite resources on the Resource Pages in Appendix A.

ENDNOTES

1. This definition has been approved by the American Marketing Association Board of Directors and is included in the *Dictionary of Marketing Terms*, 2d ed., edited by Peter D. Bennett, published by the American Marketing Association. This definition of marketing first appeared in Marketing News, March 1, 1985. See: http://www.marketing.com. Click on the link "About AMA," and then click on "Marketing Definitions."

2. *Oxford Desk Dictionary and Thesaurus*, American Edition, p. 485 (Oxford University Press, In., 1997).

3. Marie Swift is the Principal of Impact Communications (http://www.impactcommunications.org/).

4. Id.

5. Thomas Kostigan "Rich Gen-Xers in Distress" *CBS.MarketWatch.com* (July 17, 2001), at: http://www.CBS.MarketWatch.com. This news release also resulted in a major article written by Cort Smith titled "X Marks the Spot" in *Investment Advisor* (October 1, 2001) at http://www.investmentadvisor.com.

6. AdvisorSites is an excellent web building resource for independent advisors, owned and run by professional journalist, Andrew Gluck, and web master, Steve Gordonson.

7. Joe Dominguez and Vicki Robin, *Your Money or Your Life*, (Penguin, 1999).

8. George Kinder, *The Seven Stages of Money Maturity* (Dell Books, April 11, 2000).

9. George Clason, *The Richest Man in Babylon* (Signet, January 2000).

10. Thomas Stanley, Ph.D. and William Danko, Ph.,D., *The Millionaire Next Door* (Simon & Schuster, 1996).

11. The Internet address for Bill Swift is: http://www.billswiftonline.com.

12. William Shakespeare, *Hamlet*.

13. Sarah Schafer, "For the Not-So-Rich, A New Kind of Asset: Financial Counselor Changes His Focus" *Washington Post*, p. T5 (February 8, 2001).

Chapter 7

CONCLUSION

EFFECTIVE PEOPLE ARE NOT PROBLEM-MINDED; THEY'RE OPPORTUNITY MINDED. THEY FEED OPPORTUNITIES AND STARVE PROBLEMS.

— Steven R. Covey

We've covered a lot of ground in this book. In the introduction, I invited you to join me in exploring the many wonderful possibilities that exist in serving the Middle Market. I asserted that you would:

- Gain some fresh perspectives on the financial planning industry and the profession's evolution.

- Learn about different practice models and opportunities.

- Discover a host of financial planning resources.

- Glean key marketing insights.

Whether or not you join me and become an "All-American Planner," I hope that I have fulfilled these promises. In writing this book, I've tried to communicate a strong sense of purpose and my sincere enthusiasm for serving the Middle Market. Providing quality, affordable financial advice to all people who seek it, is not "just a job" for me — it's a mission!

When I first established my practice, I asked myself a very simple, yet defining question: how would I want to work with a financial advisor if I were a consumer? I built my practice to serve consumers on the same basis I wanted to be served by other professionals – on an hourly, as-needed basis.

Within two years of establishing my practice, I realized that the demand for my services was much greater than I could ever meet on my own. It became clear that my staff and I would be able to affect the lives of only a few hundred people. I received inquiries from people all over the country wanting to engage my firm's services. At times I had a waiting list of up to eight weeks for new client engagements. What made "common sense" to me (i.e., serving people from all walks of life on an hourly, as-needed basis), also made sense to a lot of other people, too.

Now my primary, professional objective is to help make competent, objective financial advice accessible to *all* Americans. I've found that "if you build it" – and let people know about it – "they will come." I'm an example of this "new breed of planner," the ones who are profitably working with Middle Market consumers and do-it-yourselfers. By succeeding in this market, telling my story and mentoring other advisors, I can accomplish my primary, professional objective – to make competent, objective financial advice accessible to *all* Americans.

IMAGINE THE POSSIBILITIES

People from all walks of life need and want to work with you! With the right tools, techniques and mindset, you can make a *huge* difference for your clients and enjoy a different kind of success than you'd ever possibly imagined.

I've heard from many financial services professionals that they have actually dreamed *for years* of establishing this kind of practice, they've just never done it. Unfortunately, the problem has been that too many "veterans" in the industry repeatedly told us:

- "It can't be done."

- "You can't make a living working in the Middle Market."

- "In time, you'll realize that this altruistic attitude must give way to profitability."

- "Go where the money is."

- "You've got to sell products, gather assets, and develop a client base that will provide you with continual revenues."

- "If your approach were doable, people would already be doing it."

At the beginning of the twentieth century, many great minds believed that all of the significant inventions had already been discovered – but since then we've learned that the opposite is true. Like Julius Frontinus (Roman soldier, governor of Britain and author of a history and description of the water supply of Rome in 1st century A.D), some of the world's best thinkers of the early twentieth century also agreed that "inventions reached their limit long ago, and I see no hope for further development."

However, in my opinion Hungarian Nobel Laureate Albert Szent-Gyorgi Von Nagyropolt got closer to the truth when he said:

"DISCOVERY CONSISTS OF SEEING WHAT EVERYBODY HAS SEEN AND THINKING WHAT NOBODY HAS THOUGHT."

We as planners must step outside of the box and redefine our advisory relationship with clients. The problem is not with the clients – it's with the service model. It's very difficult, if not impossible, to provide the same services, in the same way, to Middle Market clients as we do for affluent clients.

For too long, many of us have deferred not only *our* dreams, but also the dreams of countless deserving and grateful clients. Today, more than ever, *all* Americans need sound financial planning and advice.

Serving the Middle and do-it-yourself markets is not the choice of most veteran practitioners. They have established practices that work for them and their clientele. Many can't fathom working any other way, and that's perfectly okay. Their clients obviously need and want what they have to offer. Fortunately, new or transitioning practitioners have vast, untapped opportunities available in serving the Middle Market.

Not every attorney wants, or needs, to be a high-powered litigator. Not every doctor seeks to be a neurosurgeon or cardiologist. Not every financial planner wants, or needs, to be an asset manager or top producer. Each of these professionals must decide what his or her definition of "success" is. We should, too.

BUILD YOUR BUSINESS AROUND *YOUR* VALUES

It's actually possible to build your business around your values. At the beginning of this book, I asked you to reflect on your goals and dreams. I also asked you to consider the possibilities and not to overlook this great opportunity that I call "serving the Middle Market."

Now let me ask you this:

"What does success mean to you?"

In a recent column on MorningstarAdvisor.com, David J. Drucker said:

"FINANCIAL-PLANNING MEDIA TRADITIONALLY FEATURE ADVISORS WHOSE SUCCESS IS PREMISED ON GROWTH — GROWTH OF ASSETS UNDER MANAGEMENT, EMPLOYEES, CLIENTS, OR ALL OF THE ABOVE. BEHIND THE SCENES, THOUGH, MANY OF THOSE 'SUCCESSFUL' ADVISORS, THOUGH ADMIRABLY CLIENT-CENTERED, WORK LONG, STRESSFUL HOURS, DISPLAY LESS-THAN-IMPRESSIVE BUSINESS ACUMEN OR ORGANIZATIONAL SKILLS, AND NEGLECT THEIR FAMILY AND COMMUNITY."[1]

By contrast, Dave's column:

"SEEKS TO DEFINE THE SUCCESSFUL ADVISOR AS ONE WHO HAS HIS OR HER TOTAL ACT TOGETHER, WHO IS CLIENT-CENTERED BUT WHO HAS ALSO DONE HIS OR HER OWN LIFE PLANNING AND IS MAKING THE TIME AND MONEY FOR ALL OF THE THINGS HE OR SHE TRULY VALUES."[2]

What about your life planning?

When I took a hard look at my career choices and decided to revisit *my* life planning in 1996 and 1997, it became apparent to me that serving the Middle Market and adopting my current service model were the two missing elements I needed to both build a successful, thriving practice *and* create the type of balance I needed and longed for in my life. I researched other planners who had similar inclinations, penchants and desires.

THREE HINTS FOR HAPPINESS

In the August 2002 issue of Investment Advisor, *business coach Steve Moeller provided these tips for happiness, saying "There are three things that researchers have discovered were common denominators of happy people...with your help your clients can modify their behavior to increase their happiness." I second his advice but I'd add, "How about you?"*

1. SURROUND YOURSELF WITH THE RIGHT PEOPLE.

Spend time every day with people who make you happy.

2. ENJOY YOUR WORK.

Do work that is meaningful and a good match for your skills.

3. ENJOY YOUR ENVIRONMENT.

Surround yourself with the things and people you like.

I became a student of the Middle Market mindset and the validator niche. After experiencing solid financial success and an amazing amount of personal satisfaction within the first two years of establishing my "All-American" practice, I began a professional outreach and peer-networking program. The outreach and networking program were aimed at increasing the number of practitioners who'd embrace with me the idea of providing independent, competent financial planning and advice to anyone who sought it, regardless of income, net worth, investable assets (or anything else). I worked on NAPFA's Middle-Market Task Force and spoke with dozens of industry and consumer journalists.

It's been quite an enlightening journey!

THE SUCCESS STORY SNOWBALL

At first the Middle Market success stories were far and few between. Now, as I travel the nation and exchange ideas with various other professionals within our industry, I hear more and more examples of planners who've built successful practices that not only support their financial goals, but allow them to embrace their personal goals as well.

I personally know hundreds of practitioners who are now (or who are in the process of becoming) "All-American Planners." By doing their own life planning, advisors are making the time *and* the money for all the things they truly value. Many of these planners are meeting, or exceeding, their financial and business development goals. Furthermore, they are happier and more satisfied with their work and their personal lives.

In addition, the industry is increasingly acknowledging and supporting this trend. On August 26, 2002, *Investment News* ran a front page story entitled "Asset-based fees falling out of favor: Competition forcing variation in payments." Writer Jeff Benjamin states:

"FEES BASED ON ASSETS UNDER MANAGEMENT MAY BE GOING THE WAY OF COMMISSIONS. THE TREND NOW IS TOWARD RETAINERS, HOURLY RATES AND VARIOUS FORMS OF A LA CARTE PAYMENTS FOR FINANCIAL ADVICE, ACCORDING TO INDUSTRY ANALYSTS. AFTER PUSHING FOR PAYMENT IN FEES FOR THE LAST FEW YEARS, INDEPENDENT ADVISERS ARE EVOLVING TOWARD NEW PAYMENT PLANS AS THE DEMAND FOR NEW KINDS OF SERVICES MOUNTS. THE TRANSFORMATION ALSO IS BEING DRIVEN BY THE ECONOMICS OF THE NEARLY THREE-YEAR BEAR MARKET AND THE NEED TO COMPETE WITH INCREASINGLY FEE-BASED WIREHOUSES, ACCORDING TO EXPERTS.

'I DON'T THINK THE DOLLAR AMOUNTS [ADVISERS CHARGE CLIENTS] WILL BE CHANGING, BUT THE PACKAGING OF THE SERVICES AND THE WAY THEY ARE PRICED WILL BE CHANGING,' SAYS MARK HURLEY, CEO OF UNDISCOVERED MANAGERS LLC IN DALLAS. 'IT'S A LOGICAL THING. THERE'S JUST NO RATIONAL REASON TO BE CHARGING CLIENTS BASED ON A PERCENTAGE OF THEIR ASSETS.' MR. HURLEY COMPARES THE PRICING EVOLUTION TO THE WAY MEDICAL DOCTORS TREAT AND CHARGE THEIR PATIENTS. 'WHEN YOU GO TO SEE A DOCTOR, THEY DON'T ASK YOU YOUR NET WORTH,' HE SAYS. 'THEY TREAT YOU AND SEND YOU A BILL FOR THE SERVICE.'

JUST AS COMMISSION-BASED BROKERS GRADUALLY HAVE GIVEN WAY TO FEE-BASED ADVICE, THE INDUSTRY NOW MAY BE ADJUSTING TO AN ENVIRONMENT IN WHICH TAKING A MORE HOLISTIC APPROACH TO PRICING AND SERVICES MAKES MORE SENSE.

MATTHEW MCGINNESS, A CONSULTANT AT CERULLI ASSOCIATES INC. IN BOSTON, HAS WRITTEN A RESEARCH REPORT ON THE REGISTERED INVESTMENT ADVISER THAT INCLUDES A PERSPECTIVE ON HOW 'FEE STRUCTURES ARE IN FLUX. THE SERVICES BEING PROVIDED ARE GOING BEYOND JUST ASSET MANAGEMENT, AND ADVISERS ARE TRYING TO ALIGN FEES ACCORDINGLY,' HE SAYS. 'IF AN ADVISER IS SPENDING MORE THAN HALF HIS TIME PROVIDING ADVICE AND SERVICES BEYOND ASSET MANAGEMENT, IT MAKES SENSE TO TAKE THE FOCUS OFF OF

*ASSET MANAGEMENT.' MCGINNESS POINTS OUT THAT AS ADVISERS
CONTINUE TO FOCUS ON THEIR CLIENTS' 'ENTIRE FINANCIAL PICTURE,'
SOMEHOW PUTTING A PRICE ON THE EXTRA SERVICES BEING
PROVIDED WILL BE IMPORTANT."*

These thoughts are similar to the opinions I've been voicing for years — and a part of the reason why I established my fee-only hourly practice in 1998. I am pleased to see this growing trend within the financial services industry – specifically that:

1. Planners want to be compensated for the total value they provide to their clients.

2. A growing number of planners want to provide services that work for a wider body of clientele.

3. Planners want to achieve a better balance between their professional goals and personal lives.

As Mr. McGinness said in the *Investment News* article, "It's more of an evolution than a revolution." My fellow "All-American Planners" and I expect this trend to continue, and invite you to join us. As Henry David Thoreau said:

"DREAMS ARE THE TOUCHSTONE OF OUR CHARACTER."

What do your goals and dreams say about *you*?

FOLLOW YOUR DREAMS

As you've made your career choices and business decisions, like me you've undoubtedly encountered various "naysayers" along the way. You'll undoubtedly hear plenty of well-meaning colleagues and mentors tell you that a practice centered on meeting the needs of Middle America is a fruitless and draining venture.

At a conference in 1998, a veteran financial services professional put his arm around my shoulder and with a concerned voice basically told me, "Sheryl, it just can't be done." This colleague was just one of many who voiced their concerns and asserted that:

1. "I couldn't make a living."

2. "Clients wouldn't pay for my services."

3. "I wouldn't be fully compensated for the value I provided."

4. "The implementation wouldn't get done."

5. "I'd have higher liability exposure. "

6. "I'd be developing a practice I wouldn't be able to sell."

I'm here to tell you that *not only can "it" be done*, but if you do "it" well – and surround yourself with other like-minded, positive professionals – "it" can be rewarding *both financially and personally.*

If you've forgotten the additional details of my journey and why I'm encouraging you today, please re-read my introduction at the very beginning of this book. Trust me – if I didn't have a certain personal mission and sense of purpose, I wouldn't be writing a book. I'd be happily serving my Middle Market clients instead. (Thank goodness I have wonderful staff to help "hold down the fort" while I finish up this book. Thanks, team!)

And if you're still thinking through the six concerns voiced by various colleagues, please review "Debunking the Myths" in Chapter 4.

This chapter is about inspiring and motivating you to become an "All-American Planner," so remember that:

- If you've got cold feet, remember that you don't have to dive into the abyss alone. Network with other advisors who share the same philosophy. Learn all you can from role models. Find a mentor or affiliate with like-minded peers who support each other.

- If you've still got "how-to-make-money concerns," review Chapter 4. Reconsider the viability of building your practice around the Middle Market. The opportunities are untapped. Remember, the problem is not with the clientele – it's the service models we use with the clientele.

- Maybe you've decided that becoming an "All-American Planner" is just not a good fit for you. That's okay, too. There's room for all of us. We can all be of service, each in our own chosen way.

But now I want to return to *your vision for yourself* and how you choose to serve people as a financial planning professional. Author Judith Duerk once said, "Sometimes dreams alter the course of an entire life." I concur with that statement, but I'd make the sentence plural to read:

"YOUR DREAM CAN ALTER THE COURSE OF MANY ENTIRE LIVES."

If this dream calls out to you, don't wait another day!

At a recent retreat for financial planners, a fellow advisor took the microphone during the closing session and said words to this effect:

"I'VE BEEN A SERIAL JOB HOPPER WITHIN THE FINANCIAL SERVICES INDUSTRY. I NEVER FELT HAPPY WITH WHAT I WAS DOING UNTIL NOW... SERVING THE MIDDLE MARKET, MAKING A DIFFERENCE FOR MY CLIENTS, HAVING TIME FOR MY FAMILY AND FRIENDS, MAKING A DECENT LIVING, WORKING WITH PEOPLE I LIKE AND RESPECT. I NEVER THOUGHT IT WAS POSSIBLE TO HAVE IT ALL. BUT THANKS TO MY MENTORS AND THE SHARING WITHIN GROUPS OF LIKE-MINDED PRACTITIONERS LIKE THIS, I SEE NOW THAT I'VE FOUND MY HOME. AND I CAN HAVE IT ALL."

PASSION WITH A PURPOSE

As you can tell, I'm passionate about sharing my success stories and the lessons that I've learned! If you've read these pages, but you're still on the fence, would you give me just a few more pages to restate my case? And, as you're reading these final pages, would you do me one more favor? Every time I make a statement about proven or potential success in this special market, please plug in this thought:

IF OTHER PRACTITIONERS CAN DO THIS AND ACHIEVE SUCCESS —
I CAN DO IT TOO.

Now, let's recap some of the top reasons you should consider catering to the Middle Market and do-it-yourself consumer.

ENJOY FULFILLING WORK

Since leaving the wealth management firm to establish my "All-American" practice in 1998, I've been *more than pleased* with the results. The experience of working with a broad spectrum of Americans — each with different needs and characteristics, but with overlapping (and what some would call "common") concerns — is immensely fulfilling. I never tire of "the work." In fact, I hesitate to even use the word "work" because I so greatly enjoy what I do, how I do it and how it helps people.

GAIN BETTER BALANCE IN YOUR LIFE

Not only do I make a substantial difference for a host of appreciative clients (and not "just another quarter of a percentage point"), but I've also gained better balance in my life, too! As I mentioned in Chapter 3, in the wealth management environment I felt I needed to be "on call" for my clients 24 hours a day, seven days a week. I also felt increasingly burdened by the amount of responsibility and ongoing commitments required to maintain the level of service that clients would continue to value over time.

Now, I not only enjoy my work and helping people who really need me, but I have the time, flexibility and mental freedom I need to enjoy other aspects of my family and personal life. The gross revenues my firm generates and the salary I draw are more than adequate, and growing each and every year.

DOING WELL WHILE DOING GOOD

Bette Davis, a favorite no nonsense personality of mine, once said:

"TO FULFILL A DREAM, TO BE ALLOWED TO SWEAT OVER LONELY LABOR, TO BE GIVEN A CHANCE TO CREATE, IS THE MEAT AND POTATOES OF LIFE. THE MONEY IS THE GRAVY."

This is exactly how I feel about my practice. What could be better than to do work that you love, have time and energy left over to see the folks you love, and do the things you enjoy – and still enjoy a healthy serving of "gravy" on your "meat and potatoes"?

Building a business is much more than building a clientele. It involves building a system of processes that will make it possible to:

1. Provide great service to our clients.

2. Make a fair profit.

3. Enjoy our lives.

To effectively serve the Middle Market, a planner must be very efficient and a good business operator, too. However, with the right systems and strategies, you can indeed capture the Middle Market and increase your profits. And, you'll enjoy virtually no competition. So refine your processes and systems for delivering your work product; then you can concentrate on your *clients*, their needs, objectives, hopes and dreams.

Planners can make a good living doing work we love if our service model enables us to be compensated for all of our work, and we can work efficiently enough to meet our income objectives.

Keys to success include one or more of the following. Depending on your personal goals and objectives, you may wish to consider incorporating all of them:

- Use technology and systems to their fullest. Streamline and systematize your processes to continually become more efficient.

- Outsource the tasks that are not part of your core competency. Leverage your time and focus solely on the activities that will build the bottom line. Meeting with clients, nurturing press partnerships and building other strategic relationships should always be a part of your job description.

- Add professional staff so that you can serve more clients and receive a portion of their billings. In essence, duplicate yourself.

- Mentor new planners. Surround yourself with self-directed professionals to build a business that will last.

- Contribute to and support other like-minded professionals. You'll be enriched and supported in return.

- Maintain a "service-first" attitude and a clear vision for your practice. Position yourself to "do well as you do good."

Money therapist and author, Olivia Mellan, recently said in her column in *Investment Advisor*:

"WHEN YOU LIVE YOUR VALUES, YOUR POWER WILL BE ENHANCED AS CLIENTS SENSE A CONGRUENCE OF YOUR WORK AND YOUR PSYCHE. AND DEEP INSIDE, YOU'LL FIND THAT A MORE INTEGRATED SENSE OF SELF WILL DO WONDERS FOR YOUR SERENITY AND SELF-RESPECT."[3]

Whether one is building a thriving All-American practice and serving the Middle Market (or even if one is not), perhaps author Ayn Rand said it best:

> *"HAPPINESS IS THAT STATE OF CONSCIOUSNESS WHICH PROCEEDS FROM THE ACHIEVEMENT OF ONE'S VALUES."*

CAPTURE THE MIDDLE MARKET AND INCREASE YOUR PROFITS!

As discussed in Chapters 2 and 4, the overwhelming majority of the American population falls within the Middle Market definition, so the opportunity is indeed vast. There are approximately 105,000,000 middle income households who are *not* the target clients of typical financial planners today. There's little or no competition in this market! Somewhere between 70% and 86% of the American population is being either overlooked or underserved!

The average consumer's awareness of the need for professional guidance with regard to the management of their personal finances is greater than ever. The information age and the proliferation of self-directed, employer-sponsored retirement plans have created top-of-mind awareness and a sense-of-planning urgency for average consumers. But even though the need and awareness are there, average Americans may feel that they have few palatable options for obtaining independent, affordable planning assistance and advice. Those of us who are adopting an All-American focus need to do a better job spreading the word that we are ready, willing and able to help average folks.

One way that I spread the word is simply by making comments like: "I'm a financial planner. I help regular folks, like you and me, make better money management and financial planning decisions." When people hear the words "financial planner" come out of my mouth, I see them go a bit hazy at first – probably because they think they can't afford to work with me, or that I only want to serve an affluent clientele (you know, account minimums and all that). But they usually perk up when I say, "I help regular folks like you and me make better money management and financial planning decisions." At that point, it's as if they mentally sit up and say, "Oh, really? How do you do that? Would you work with me? How can I find out more about you?" and so on. It's an easy conversation to have because I'm prepared with many positioning statement capsules to communicate my value and how I help "All-American Clients" reach their financial goals.

Marketing efforts are also greatly enhanced by the fact that the media loves objective advisors who cater to their readers, most of whom are middle Americans. The financial planning industry's top associations are increasingly supporting Middle Market initiatives and public relations campaigns as well. They're trying to raise public awareness regarding the importance of financial planning for all people.

Opportunities for referrals are greater because the majority of today's independent financial advisors are targeting a more affluent clientele and seeking supervisor-delegator relationships. These professionals are usually relieved to find qualified colleagues to whom they can refer Middle Market and do-it-yourself clients. As financial planners or "specialized participants" (see Chapter 3), we are by nature a group of helping professionals. If we can't help a consumer, we want to refer them to someone else we know and trust.

More and more practitioners are embracing the "All-American Planner" mindset. Although they may choose to structure their individual practices somewhat differently, there is undeniably a small, but rapidly growing movement catering to the Middle Market and the do-it-yourself client. As the trend continues (i.e., as clients tell friends, friends tell colleagues, colleagues tell journalists, journalists tell the world, and so on), the demand for our services will multiply. As the number of "All-American Planners" increases to keep up with consumer demand, our strength and support for one another will blossom and grow. Eventually, conversations about "How to Capture the Middle Market and Increase your Profits" will fade away.

Until then, I'll continue to build my practice, speak at industry conferences, write books and articles, mentor new and transitioning planners and "beat the drum" with the media. I look forward to many spirited debates and exchanges with you, and all my colleagues, in the months and years ahead as we build this new profession together.

Walt Disney said:

"IF YOU CAN DREAM IT, YOU CAN DO IT."

If you're ready to become an "All-American Planner" now, get going! Start building your own "field of dreams" today.

Imagine the possibilities!

UPPER CLASSES ARE A NATION'S PAST;
THE MIDDLE CLASS IS ITS FUTURE.

~ Ayn Rand, American Novelist and Philosopher ~

ENDNOTES

1. David J. Drucker, MBA, CFP®, MorningstarAdvisor.com "Building a Practice Around his Life" (August 21, 2002); see also *Virtual Office Tools for a High-Margin Practice.*

2. Id.

3. Olivia Mellan, "Walking Your Talk," *Investment Advisor* (July 31, 2002) at: http://www.investmentadvisor.com.

Appendix A

FAVORITE RESOURCES FOR FINANCIAL PLANNERS FOCUSED ON SERVING THE MIDDLE MARKET

BOOKS ON SALES AND MARKETING COMMUNICATIONS

Basic Desktop Design and Layout, by David Collier, Bob Cotton, and Chris Prior (North Light Books, October 1989) (www.amazon.com).

Creative Marketing Communications: A Practical Guide to Planning, Skills and Techniques by Daniel Yadin (Kogan Page, Ltd., February 1, 2001) (www.koganpage.co.uk/asp/bookdetails.asp?key=3212).

Effective Marketing by Peter Hingston (DK Publishing, June 2001) (www.dk.com).

Marketing Yourself, by Dorothy Leeds (Harper Collins, March 1991) (www.amazon.com).

On Writing Well, by William Zinsser (HarperCollins College Division, 1985) (www.amazon.com).

Relationship Selling: The Key to Getting and Keeping Customers by Jim Cathcart (HDL Pub. Co., October 1987) (www.amazon.com).

Selling for Dummies by Tom Hopkins (Hungry Minds, Inc., 1995) (www.amazon.com).

The 25 Sales Habits of Highly Successful Salespeople by Stephen Schiffman (Adams Media Corporation, June 1994) (www.amazon.com).

Zig Ziglar's Secrets of Closing the Sale by Zig Ziglar (Word Publishing, June 1984) (www.amazon.com).

BOOKS AND PUBLICATIONS FOR PRACTITIONERS
GETTING STARTED

Getting Started as a Financial Planner by Jeffrey Rattiner (Bloomberg Press, July 2000) (www.amazon.com).

Inside Information by Bob Veres (www.bobveres.com).

So You Want to Be a Financial Planner by Nancy Langdon Jones (Advisor Works, September 28, 2001) (www.amazon.com).

BOOKS ON PERSONAL FINANCIAL PLANNING TOPICS

4 Steps to Financial Security for Lesbian and Gay Couples by Harold Lustig (Fawcett Books, June 1999) (www.amazon.com).

The Millionaire Next Door by Thomas Stanley, Ph.D. and William Danko, Ph.D. (Simon & Schuster, October 1996) (www.amazon.com).

101 Tax Saving Ideas by Randy Gardner and Julie Welch (Wealth Builders Press, February 2002) (www.amazon.com).

The Richest Man in Babylon by George Clason (Signet, January 2002) (www.amazon.com).

Seven Stages of Money Maturity: Understanding the Spirit and Value of Money in Your Life by George Kinder (Dell Books, April 11, 2000) (www.amazon.com).

2002 Tax Facts 1 and *2002 Tax Facts 2* (National Underwriter Company) (www.nuco.com).

Who Gets Grandma's Yellow Pie Plate? by Marlene S. Stum (Minnesota Extension Service, February 1, 1999) (www.amazon.com).

Your Money or Your Life: Transforming your Relationship with Money and Achieving Financial Independence by Joe Dominguez and Vicki Robin (Penguin USA, September 1999) (www.amazon.com).

CONSULTANTS AND SPEAKERS

E-Myth Consultant, Certified and Accountability Coach, Kevin Poland (813-636-9181 or (KevinPoland@worldnet.att.net).

Marketing Communications and Writing Coach, Marie Swift, Impact Communications (www.impactcommunications.org).

Personal Communications / Public Speaking Coach, Bill Swift (www.billswiftonline.com)

Personal Productivity and Accountability Coach, Tom Werder, Author of *The Bull's Eye Principle: How to Lead and Manage People to Extraordinary Results* (www.tomwerder.com)

FINANCIAL PLANNING RESOURCES (FROM CHAPTER 5)

American Association of Retired People (www.aarp.org)

Advisor Intelligence
(www.AdvisorIntelligence.com)

Aging with Dignity
(www.agingwithdignity.org)

Ask Jeeves Search Engine
(www.AskJeeves.com)

Bank Rate
(www.BankRate.com)

Collegiate Funding Solutions
(www. http://www.collegiatefunding.com/faprofessional_index.html)

Consumer Credit Counseling Services (CCCS)
(http://www.cccsintl.org)

Credit Talk
(www.credittalk.com)

EquiFax, Credit Reporting Agency
(www.equifax.com)

Experian, Credit Reporting Agency
(www.experian.com).

Finance Center
(www.FinanCenter.com)

Insurance Commissioner's Publications: To assist consumers in making
decisions about Medicare, health, life, disability, homeowners',
auto and long-term care insurance.
(www.insurance.wa.gov/readonline.htm)

Medicare Information
(www.Medicare.gov)

MoneyTree's Easy Money
(www.MoneyTree.com)

Morningstar Principia Pro
(www.morningstar.com)

The Mutual Fund Education Alliance
(www.MFEA.com)

National Association of Insurance Commissioner's Shopper's Guide to
Long-Term Care Insurance
(www.insurance.wa.gov/readonline.htm)

NOLO "Law for All"
(www.NOLO.com)

My Vesta
(www.myvesta.org)

Quicken's Debt Reduction Planner
(www.Quicken.com)

Trans Union Credit Reporting Agency
(www.tuc.com)

USAA Foundation
(www.usaaedfoundation.org)

Web Ex Virtual Conferencing Service
(www.webex.com)

GROUPS - BUSINESS ASSOCIATIONS TO CONSIDER

Business Network International (BNI)
(www.bni.com)

LE TIP
(www.letip.com)

National Speakers' Association
(www.nsaspeaker.org)

Toastmasters International
(www.toastmasters.org/indexbk.htm)

GROUPS - INDUSTRY ASSOCIATIONS TO CONSIDER

The Financial Planning Association (FPA)
(www.fpanet.org)

National Association of Personal Financial Advisors (NAPFA)
(www.napfa.org)

GROUPS - PEER NETWORKS TO CONSIDER

Cambridge Advisors, LLC
(www.cambridgeadvisors.com/adv/index.html)

Dream Achieve Network
(www.dreamachieve.com/network.htm)

The Garrett Planning Network, Inc.
(www.garrettplanningnetwork.com)

MOTIVATIONAL TAPES AND MUSIC

"Be a Champion," motivational CD by Staci Michaels and Tom
Hopkins (918-446-3378)

"The Bull's Eye Principle," audio program and workbook by Tom
Werder (www.tomwerder.com)

"The Psychology of Winning" audio program by Dennis Waitley
(www.nightingale.com)

"The Science of Personal Achievement," audio program by Napoleon
Hill (www.nightingale.com)

"Universal Laws of Success and Achievement," audio program by
Brian Tracy (www.nightingale.com)

PRINT AND DESIGN RESOURCES

AdvisorProducts
(www.advisorproducts.com)

Alphagraphics Print Shops
(www.alphagraphics.com)

Impact Communications
(www.impactcommunications.org)

Iprint
(www.iPrint.com)

Office Depot
(www.officedepot.com)

Paper Direct
(www.paperdirect.com)

Sir Speedy Print Shops
(www.sirspeedy.com)

Vista Print
(www.vistaprint.com)

WEB BUILDING RESOURCES

AdvisorSites
(www.advisorsites.com)

Appendix B

RECOMMENDED PERSONAL FINANCE BOOKS FOR CLIENTS

Bogle on Mutual Funds: New Perspectives for the Intelligent Investor by John Bogle (McGraw-Hill Trade, September 1, 1993).

A Commonsense Guide to Mutual Funds by Mary Rowland (Bloomberg Press, March 1996).

The Dollars and Sense of Divorce by Judith Briles, Edwin Shilling and Carol Ann Wilson (Dearborn Trade, June 1998).

For Richer, Not Poorer — The Money Book for Couples by Ruth Hayden (Health Communications, September 1999).

4 Steps to Financial Security for Lesbian and Gay Couples by Harold Lustig (Fawcett Books, June 1999).

Getting a Life: Strategies for Simple Living by Jacqueline Blix and David Heitmiller (Penguin USA, January 1999).

The Millionaire Next Door: The Surprising Secrets of America's Wealthy by Thomas Stanley, Ph.D. and William D. Danko, Ph.D. (Simon & Schuster, October 1996).

The Motley Fool Investment Workbook by David Gardner and Tom Gardner (Fireside, January 1998).

The Motley Fool's You Have More Than You Think: The Foolish Guide to Investing What You Have by David Gardner and Tom Gardner (Simon & Schuster, January 1999).

The Richest Man in Babylon by George Clason (Signet, January 2002).

Seven Stages of Money Maturity: Understanding the Spirit and Value of Money in Your Life by George Kinder (Dell Books, April 11, 2000).

Simple Asset Allocation Strategies by Roger Gibson and Randal Moore (Marketplace Books / Trader's Library, January 1, 2000).

The Wealthy Barber: Everyone's Commonsense Guide to Becoming Financially Independent by David Chilton (Prima Publishing, December 1997).

Who Gets Grandma's Yellow Pie Plate? by Marlene S. Stum (Minnesota Extension Service, February 1, 1999).

Your Money or Your Life: Transforming Your Relationship with Money and Achieving Financial Independence by Joe Dominguez and Vicki Robin (Penguin USA, September 1999).

Appendix C

FREQUENTLY ASKED QUESTIONS

1. **PLEASE TELL ME ABOUT THE FINANCIAL PLANNING PROCESS.** Financial planning is a multi-step process that provides you with two important things: (1) An in-depth review of your current financial situation, and (2) a blueprint that shows you how to achieve your goals and objectives for the future. GPN Members believe the financial planning process consists of seven distinct steps (see *Building a Brighter Financial Future* for details on our unique financial planning process). It is important to remember that financial planning is a process . . . not an event.

2. **HOW DO YOU CREATE THIS BLUEPRINT?** First we focus on your goals, objectives, priorities and values. For instance: the reduction of current and future income taxes may be an immediate goal, funding a quality education for your children and/or grandchildren may be an intermediate goal, and enjoying a secure financial future in your retirement years is likely to be one of your most important long-term goals. Another great goal in life for some people is creating wealth and/or leaving a legacy for your chosen beneficiaries or charities. You may already be on the road to meeting these objectives and simply need a new strategy, professional insight, or to fine-tune your plan. You may just be starting out, or you may be somewhere in between. Whatever your unique situation may be, everyone needs a periodic assessment of where they are on the road to meeting their financial goals. That's why

we do an in-depth review of your current financial situation. Next, you need to know how you can set about achieving (or continue working toward) your financial goals. By focusing on cash flow, investments, taxes, pensions and retirement plans, estate planning, insurance issues, savings opportunities and other general financial matters, we design a customized financial plan for you. Finally, to achieve the intended results, you must implement and monitor your plan.

3. **Sounds like a lot of work!** It may seem like that at first, but the good news is, if you follow your plan and maintain a disciplined approach, you can rest well knowing you can reach your stated goals. GPN Members try to make the process as easy as possible for you. In addition to receiving professional advice on your most important financial concerns, we can also provide implementation and ongoing asset management services, if appropriate for your needs.

4. **Who can benefit most from your services?** Any individual seeking financial peace of mind can benefit from our services. We serve people at all income levels, from all walks of life. Clients have the flexibility to work with us on either a one-time, as-needed basis or an ongoing basis. We welcome clients who simply need a one-time financial consultation or a second opinion, as well as those who need comprehensive financial planning and possible ongoing asset management services. In addition, any corporation or organization seeking quality, unbiased financial education for their employees or members can benefit from our financial education programs

5. **What is "Fee-Only" financial planning and why should that be important to me?** Because we are Fee-Only financial planners, all conflicts of interest regarding compensation are removed. We do not accept sales commissions; we work solely for our clients. Because we do not sell financial products such as investments and insurance, there are no third-party relationships or outside influences to color our thinking and financial recommenda-

tions. For more information on Fee-Only financial planning, including our Code of Ethics, Fiduciary Code and member requirements, please visit www.NAPFA.org.

In addition, all GPN Member firms are Registered Investment Advisors (RIAs); RIAs must comply with a host of regulations designed to protect the consumer. One important question you should always ask when considering a financial planner's services: "May I please have a copy of your ADV Part II?" This document contains important information about the planner's qualifications, fiduciary duties, history of any past violations, etc. Any GPN Member would be happy to send you a copy of their ADV Part II.

6. **I UNDERSTAND THE BENEFITS OF WORKING WITH A FEE-ONLY FINANCIAL PLANNER, BUT I MIGHT NEED TO OBTAIN FINANCIAL PRODUCTS. HOW WILL I BE ABLE TO DO THAT?** While we do not sell financial products, we will offer specific recommendations and opinions regarding the purchase of the various financial products that may be appropriate for you. So, if you need to obtain an insurance policy or a new mortgage, invest into a portfolio of mutual funds, or find an estate planning attorney or tax professional, we can direct you to the resources you need and/or help you obtain these products and services. If appropriate, we can also help you implement your plan and set up your accounts.

7. **DO GPN MEMBERS PROVIDE ONLY COMPREHENSIVE FINANCIAL PLANNING?** No. Although a comprehensive financial plan can provide the greatest benefits, we can limit our advisory services to your specific needs, such as cash management and budgeting, investment analysis or college education funding.

8. **MY SPOUSE AND I ARE JUST BEGINNING TO BUILD FOR OUR FINANCIAL FUTURE. THERE IS SO MUCH TO LEARN! WE NEED HELP AND GUIDANCE TO GET STARTED. WILL YOU ACCEPT US AS CLIENTS?** Yes. Some firms have income levels and/or net worth minimums but GPN Members realize that everyone has financial needs. We are proud to work with people from all income levels, and all walks

of life. Remember, "You don't have to have a fortune to start building one." Click the *Find a Planner* button and get started today.

9. I HAVE ALREADY ACCUMULATED SUBSTANTIAL ASSETS AND THINK I AM DOING QUITE WELL. BUT AS I PROGRESS AND BUILD FOR THE FUTURE, THINGS SEEM TO BE GETTING MORE COMPLICATED. I WANT TO BE SURE I AM ON TRACK, BUT I DON'T ALWAYS HAVE THE TIME OR INCLINATION TO MANAGE THE MYRIAD DETAILS BY MYSELF. CAN YOU HELP ME? Yes. People who need more sophisticated financial planning or advice will find our services appealing and beneficial. If you have a desire to simplify your financial affairs, one of our Ongoing Client Programs may be right for you (see *Building a Brighter Financial Future.*) If you are looking for a professional review or a second opinion to ensure you are on track, we can provide that, too.

10. I'M IN CHARGE OF THE RETIREMENT PLANS AND EMPLOYEE BENEFITS AT MY FIRM. I WOULD LIKE TO INCREASE THE NUMBER OF EMPLOYEES WHO PARTICIPATE IN OUR BENEFIT PROGRAMS. HOW CAN YOU HELP US? Corporate education is key in building employee participation. Our financial planning team can help your people understand the benefits of your programs. Please call to discuss your specific needs. We can custom-build an educational program for your company.

11. WHAT TYPES OF SECURITIES DO YOU PROVIDE ADVICE FOR? We provide advice for all types of securities, including mutual funds, stocks (as they relate to your portfolio holdings), bonds, bank deposits, variable and fixed annuities, limited partnerships and tax shelters. We also provide advice on mortgages, budgeting and cash flow issues, 401(k), 403(b) and other retirement programs, stock options, life and disability insurance, etc. If it has to do with money and finances, we can provide counseling, guidance and/or resources for you. Because we want our clients to know that they can call on us with any and all of their financial concerns, we have developed the slogan "Financial Planning and Advice for Everyday Life." Clients are encouraged to call us when they have a major life event, such as a new job, a baby, a mar-

riage or divorce, or if they are planning to buy a new home or start their own business. We also encourage our clients to call us with more common everyday questions, such as: "How should I invest within my 401(k) or 403(b) plan?" "How can I reduce my taxes?" "What advice can you offer on refinancing my home?" "How can I maximize my Flex Spending Account, Cafeteria Plan or Section 125 Plan at work?"

12. **IF I USE A GPN MEMBER TO DEVELOP A FINANCIAL PLAN, AM I OBLIGATED TO PURCHASE THE RECOMMENDED PRODUCTS?** Absolutely not. We will offer recommendations which in our professional opinion will meet your needs and objectives, but you are under no obligation to purchase them. In today's competitive market, it makes sense to shop around for the best available product or service. For instance, if you need to obtain a life insurance or disability policy, we will suggest the kind of policy, which riders and what amounts may be best for you. We will then direct you to a choice of companies that can provide a quality product at competitive prices for you. If you wish, we can help you purchase investments and/or set up your accounts with a third-party custodian such as a discount broker.

13. **TELL ME ABOUT YOUR INVESTMENT PHILOSOPHY.** As financial planners and investment consultants, we believe in the following fundamental principals with regard to designing an investment portfolio and making specific recommendations: The purpose of a client's investment portfolio is to fund current and/or future financial objectives. The design of the portfolio must take into account the client's financial objectives, tolerance for risk, needs for current income or liquidity, and special considerations such as income and estate taxes. The important thing to remember is that *no one can predict the future*. It is difference of opinion that makes a market. Investment and economic "experts" provided with the same information often come to different conclusions. We do not suggest that we can, or that any of the money or mutual fund managers that we recommend, will make the correct decision every time. We do believe, however, that studying the historic trends and relationships of investment classes and the philosophies and

approaches of successful investment managers can provide valuable insight. The appropriate allocation of investment assets for your goals and risk tolerance is the most important component in developing an investment portfolio. We believe that having a diversified, well-balanced portfolio, following long-term buy-and-hold strategies, and having patience, will increase the likelihood that one will achieve their long-term financial objectives.

14. **HOW DO YOU SELECT INVESTMENTS FOR A CLIENT?** Before we recommend any investment, we consider the current economic conditions, the outlook for that asset class or type of security and how this investment fits within your portfolio given your objectives and tolerance for risk. For equity investments, we focus primarily on the philosophies, experience and track record of the management team. With fixed income investments, we look for the best yield available for a given quality of security. As fiduciaries for our clients, we strive to obtain the most appropriate investment vehicles to meet your objectives, while being very conscious of total expenses and risk exposure.

15. **HOW DO YOU PRICE YOUR FINANCIAL PLANNING SERVICES?** The fees are based on the actual time involved in meeting with you in person or over the phone, researching and analyzing your current situation, and providing specific recommendations and implementation assistance (if appropriate). Hourly rates vary from one GPN Member to another. An estimate of fees will be provided at the end of the Get Acquainted Meeting, when your needs have been fully identified.

16. **HOW MUCH WILL MY FINANCIAL PLAN COST?** Financial planning fees are determined on a project basis; the total fee for a financial plan will vary from client to client based on the specific needs and complexity of your situation (please see our diagram *Building a Brighter Financial Future* to learn about our financial planning sequence and the client service options available). An estimate is provided after the Get Acquainted Meeting, when your personal needs are fully identified. Once your financial plan is complete,

there are generally two or three levels of client/advisor relationships available to you (for more information, see *Building a Brighter Financial Future* diagram).

17. **ARE YOUR FEES TAX DEDUCTIBLE?** Yes. Section 212 of the Internal Revenue Code permits an itemized deduction for tax and/or investment advice in the miscellaneous section of Schedule A. It is subject to a 2% floor of the adjusted gross income on a personal tax return.

18. **ONCE MY FINANCIAL PLAN IS COMPLETED, WILL OUR RELATIONSHIP END?** Depending on your client track, the actual engagement of services may end (please refer to *Seven Steps to Building a Brighter Financial Future*), but the majority of our clients choose some sort of Continuing Client Program. Because financial planning is a *process*, not an event, we offer ongoing services, periodic reviews and day-to-day consultations as requested and/or needed.

19. **HOW CAN I GET STARTED?** The first step is an initial inquiry from you. Call us, toll free, at (866)260-8400 or email us at service@garrettplanningnetwork.com. Or, click the *"Find a Planner"* button on this site. All GPN Members offer an initial no-cost, no-obligation Get Acquainted Meeting, either on the phone or in their offices. For Get Acquainted Meetings, appointments are scheduled based on availability during regular business hours of 9-5, Monday through Friday. Expanded office hours are available to accommodate special needs or emergency situations. Should you decide to engage a GPN Member's services, they will discuss which of their services and client tracks is appropriate for you. Most clients find the financial planning process to be stimulating and enlightening. The end result, of course, is greater peace of mind. We look forward to helping YOU build a brighter financial future!

Appendix D

SEVEN STEPS FLOWCHART

BUILDING A BRIGHTER FINANCIAL FUTURE™
CREATE YOUR FINANCIAL BLUEPRINT

ADVISOR ACTIONS / RESPONSIBILITIES	FINANCIAL PLANNING SEQUENCE	CLIENT ACTIONS / RESPONSIBILITIES
When you contact us, we'll provide a brief description of our services, philosophies, methodology and fee structures. We'll direct you to our web site or mail you an introductory packet to help you learn more.	**Step 1: Community Outreach or Initial Inquiry**	If our services appear to fit your needs, we'll schedule a Get Acquainted Meeting (can be done on the phone or in person). You can review our introductory materials, or visit our Web site if you wish to learn more, then contact us for Step 2.
The Get Acquainted Meeting or Teleconference is an opportunity for us to exchange information about your needs and objectives, and further discuss which of our services are right for you. We will also provide an estimated fee quote.	**Step 2: Get Acquainted Meeting or Teleconference**	When you decide to engage our services, we will give you a list of additional data or information which we will need to begin formulating your financial plan. One-half of the estimated total fee is due at the time of this engagement.
When we receive your information, we begin to review and develop your financial plan. We prepare initial reports to discuss at our Step 4 meeting.	**Step 3: Data Gathering and Initial Preparation**	In Step 3, you gather the data requested, and complete your cash flow worksheet and risk tolerance questionnaire. You may fax or mail this information to us before our next meeting. Upon receipt of it, we will schedule our Step 4 meeting.

CLIENT ACTIONS / RESPONSIBILITIES	FINANCIAL PLANNING SEQUENCE	ADVISOR ACTIONS / RESPONSIBILITIES
In this Interactive Goal Setting Meeting, you have another opportunity to clarify your current situation, financial goals and objectives. Come with any additional questions or concerns you may have.	**Step 4: Interactive Goal Setting Meeting or Teleconference**	In this interactive meeting, we discuss and clarify the information you have provided thus far. We continue to refine your financial goals and objectives.
As we move into Step 5, you simply schedule a meeting or teleconference 1 or 2 weeks after our Step 4 meeting. The ball is in our court in the interim. Revisit our web site to stay current on the changing world of personal finance and investments.	**Step 5: Analysis and Plan Formulation**	We edit the initial information as needed and run additional scenarios if applicable. We conclude our research and analysis, and produce final reports for your personal financial plan. We add our observations and recommendations to the plan.
Congratulations! At this point, you will hold a personalized blueprint, custom designed to meet your financial goals. Full payment of the balance for actual fees incurred is due at the conclusion of your plan presentation meeting.	**Step 6: Presentation of Your Financial Plan**	In Step 6, we present and review your personal financial plan. We discuss all reports and provide you with a written summary of our observations and specific recommendations.
Proper implementation is crucial to reaching your financial goals. Whether you now implement and monitor the plan yourself, or engage us to provide a portion or all of these services for you, we urge prompt action.	**Step 7: Plan Implementation and Follow Up**	If you need and desire our help with plan implementation and follow up, at the conclusion of Step 6 we will discuss what might be an appropriate ongoing plan with you. Periodic update meetings and reviews are also recommended.

© 2001 The Garrett Planning Network, Inc. • 12700 Johnson Drive, Shawnee, KS 66216-1643
• Toll Free Phone: (866) 260-8400 • Fax: (913) 260-6195 • Email: service@garrettplanningnetwork.com
• Web: www.garrettplanningnetwork.com

Appendix E

INCOME TAX

INDIVIDUALS, ESTATES AND TRUSTS
(Tax Years Beginning in 2002)

Col. 1 Taxable Income $	Separate Return Tax on Col. 1 $	Rate on Excess %	Joint Return Tax on Col. 1 $	Rate on Excess %	Single Return Tax on Col. 1 $	Rate on Excess %	Head of Household Tax on Col. 1 $	Rate on Excess %	Trusts & Estates Tax on Col. 1 $	Rate on Excess %
0	0	10	0	10	0	10	0	10	0	15
1,850	185	10	185	10	185	10	185	10	278	27
4,400	440	10	440	10	440	10	440	10	966	30
6,000	600	15	600	10	600	15	600	10	1,446	30
6,750	713	15	675	10	713	15	675	10	1,671	35
9,200	1,080	15	920	10	1,080	15	920	10	2,529	38.6
10,000	1,200	15	1,000	10	1,200	15	1,000	15	2,837	38.6
12,000	1,500	15	1,200	15	1,500	15	1,300	15	3,609	38.6
23,350	3,203	27	2,903	15	3,203	15	3,003	15	7,990	38.6
27,950	4,445	27	3,593	15	3,893	27	3,693	15	9,766	38.6
37,450	7,010	27	5,018	15	6,458	27	5,118	27	13,433	38.6
46,700	9,507	27	6,405	27	8,955	27	7,615	27	17,004	38.6
56,425	12,133	30	9,031	27	11,581	27	10,241	27	20,757	38.6
67,700	15,515	30	12,075	27	14,625	30	13,285	27	25,110	38.6
85,975	20,998	35	17,009	27	20,108	30	18,219	27	32,164	38.6
96,700	24,752	35	19,905	27	23,325	30	21,115	30	36,304	38.6
112,850	30,404	35	24,266	30	28,170	30	25,960	30	42,537	38.6
141,250	40,344	35	32,786	30	36,690	35	34,480	30	53,500	38.6
153,525	44,640	38.6	36,468	30	40,986	35	38,163	30	58,238	38.6
156,600	45,827	38.6	37,391	30	42,063	35	39,085	35	59,425	38.6
171,950	51,752	38.6	41,996	35	47,435	35	44,458	35	65,350	38.6
307,050	103,901	38.6	89,281	38.6	94,720	38.6	91,743	38.6	117,499	38.6

CORPORATIONS†
(Tax Years Beginning in 2002)

Col. 1 Taxable Income	Tax on Col. 1	Rate on Excess
-0-	-0-	15%
$ 50,000	7,500	25%
$ 75,000	13,750	34%
$ 100,000	22,250	39% *
$ 335,000	113,900	34%
$10,000,000	3,400,000	35%
$15,000,000	5,150,000	38% **
$18,333,333	—	35%

† Personal Service Corporations are taxed at a flat rate of 35%.

* A 5% surtax is imposed on income above $100,000 until the benefit of the 15 and 25% tax rates has been canceled. Thus, taxable income from $100,001 to $335,000 is taxed at the rate of 39%.

** Corporations with taxable income over $15,000,000 are subject to an additional tax of the lesser of 3% of the excess over $15,000,000 or $100,000. Thus, taxable income exceeding $18,333,333 is taxed at 35%. See Ann. 93-133, 1993-32 IRB 12.

PERSONAL EXEMPTIONS –$3,000

Phaseout - 2% for each $2500 (or fraction thereof)
by which AGI exceeds the thresholds below:

Joint or Qualifying Widow(er) $206,000
Single $137,300
Head of Household $171,650
Married Filing Separately $103,000

FICA AND MEDICARE RATES

FICA . . . . .6.2% of first $84,900 of earnings
Medicare . . . . .1.45% of all earnings

ITEMIZED DEDUCTIONS

Phaseout – 3% of AGI in excess of
Joint or Qualifying Widow(er) $137,300
Single $137,300
Head of Household $137,300
Married Filing Separately $68,650

ALTERNATIVE MINIMUM TAX

For Individuals (except Married - Separate)

0	175,000	26%	0
175,000	. . . .	10,920+ 28%	175,000

AMT EXEMPTION

Joint or Qualifying Widow(er) $49,000
Single or Head of Household 35,750
MFS, Estates, Trusts 24,500
Before phase-out

STANDARD DEDUCTION

Joint or Qualifying Widow(er) $7,850
Single 4,700
Head of Household 6,900
Married Filing Separately 3,925
Additional for Elderly/Blind-Married 900
Additional for Elderly/Blind-Unmarried 1,150
Claimed as Dependent (or Earned Inc.) 750

Reprinted with permission from Meara, King & Co.

Appendix F

TRANSFER TAX TABLES

2001, 2011- GIFT AND ESTATE TAX TABLE

Taxable Gift/Estate		Tax on	Rate on
From	To	Col. 1	Excess
$ 0	$ 10,000	$ 0	18%
10,000	20,000	1,800	20%
20,000	40,000	3,800	22%
40,000	60,000	8,200	24%
60,000	80,000	13,000	26%
80,000	10,0000	18,200	28%
100,000	150,000	23,800	30%
150,000	250,000	38,800	32%
250,000	500,000	70,800	34%
500,000	750,000	155,800	37%
750,000	1,000,000	248,300	39%
1,000,000	1,250,000	345,800	41%
1,250,000	1,500,000	448,300	43%
1,500,000	2,000,000	555,800	45%
2,000,000	2,500,000	780,800	49%
2,500,000	3,000,000	1,025,800	53%
3,000,000	10,000,000	1,290,800	55%
10,000,000	17,184,000	5,140,800	60%
17,184,000	....	9,451,200	55%

2002 GIFT AND ESTATE TAX TABLE

Taxable Gift/Estate		Tax on	Rate on
From	To	Col. 1	Excess
$ 0	$ 10,000	$ 0	18%
10,000	20,000	1,800	20%
20,000	40,000	3,800	22%
40,000	60,000	8,200	24%
60,000	80,000	13,000	26%
80,000	10,0000	18,200	28%
100,000	150,000	23,800	30%
150,000	250,000	38,800	32%
250,000	500,000	70,800	34%
500,000	750,000	155,800	37%
750,000	1,000,000	248,300	39%
1,000,000	1,250,000	345,800	41%
1,250,000	1,500,000	448,300	43%
1,500,000	2,000,000	555,800	45%
2,000,000	2,500,000	780,800	49%
2,500,000	....	1,025,800	50%

2003 GIFT AND ESTATE TAX TABLE

Taxable Gift/Estate		Tax on	Rate on
From	To	Col. 1	Excess
$ 0	$ 10,000	$ 0	18%
10,000	20,000	1,800	20%
20,000	40,000	3,800	22%
40,000	60,000	8,200	24%
60,000	80,000	13,000	26%
80,000	10,0000	18,200	28%
100,000	150,000	23,800	30%
150,000	250,000	38,800	32%
250,000	500,000	70,800	34%
500,000	750,000	155,800	37%
750,000	1,000,000	248,300	39%
1,000,000	1,250,000	345,800	41%
1,250,000	1,500,000	448,300	43%
1,500,000	2,000,000	555,800	45%
2,000,000	....	780,800	49%

2004 GIFT AND ESTATE TAX TABLE

Taxable Gift/Estate		Tax on	Rate on
From	**To**	**Col. 1**	**Excess**
$ 0	$ 10,000	$ 0	18%
10,000	20,000	1,800	20%
20,000	40,000	3,800	22%
40,000	60,000	8,200	24%
60,000	80,000	13,000	26%
80,000	10,000	18,200	28%
100,000	150,000	23,800	30%
150,000	250,000	38,800	32%
250,000	500,000	70,800	34%
500,000	750,000	155,800	37%
750,000	1,000,000	248,300	39%
1,000,000	1,250,000	345,800	41%
1,250,000	1,500,000	448,300	43%
1,500,000	2,000,000	555,800	45%
2,000,000	....	780,800	48%

2005 GIFT AND ESTATE TAX TABLE

Taxable Gift/Estate		Tax on	Rate on
From	**To**	**Col. 1**	**Excess**
$ 0	$ 10,000	$ 0	18%
10,000	20,000	1,800	20%
20,000	40,000	3,800	22%
40,000	60,000	8,200	24%
60,000	80,000	13,000	26%
80,000	10,0000	18,200	28%
100,000	150,000	23,800	30%
150,000	250,000	38,800	32%
250,000	500,000	70,800	34%
500,000	750,000	155,800	37%
750,000	1,000,000	248,300	39%
1,000,000	1,250,000	345,800	41%
1,250,000	1,500,000	448,300	43%
1,500,000	2,000,000	555,800	45%
2,000,000	....	780,800	47%

2006 GIFT AND ESTATE TAX TABLE

Taxable Gift/Estate		Tax on	Rate on
From	To	Col. 1	Excess
$ 0	$ 10,000	$ 0	18%
10,000	20,000	1,800	20%
20,000	40,000	3,800	22%
40,000	60,000	8,200	24%
60,000	80,000	13,000	26%
80,000	10,0000	18,200	28%
100,000	150,000	23,800	30%
150,000	250,000	38,800	32%
250,000	500,000	70,800	34%
500,000	750,000	155,800	37%
750,000	1,000,000	248,300	39%
1,000,000	1,250,000	345,800	41%
1,250,000	1,500,000	448,300	43%
1,500,000	2,000,000	555,800	45%
2,000,000	....	780,800	46%

2007-2009 GIFT AND ESTATE TAX TABLE

Taxable Gift/Estate		Tax on	Rate on
From	To	Col. 1	Excess
$ 0	$ 10,000	$ 0	18%
10,000	20,000	1,800	20%
20,000	40,000	3,800	22%
40,000	60,000	8,200	24%
60,000	80,000	13,000	26%
80,000	10,0000	18,200	28%
100,000	150,000	23,800	30%
150,000	250,000	38,800	32%
250,000	500,000	70,800	34%
500,000	750,000	155,800	37%
750,000	1,000,000	248,300	39%
1,000,000	1,250,000	345,800	41%
1,250,000	1,500,000	448,300	43%
1,500,000	....	555,800	45%

2010 GIFT TAX ONLY TABLE

Taxable Gift/Estate		Tax on	Rate on
From	To	Col. 1	Excess
$ 0	$ 10,000	$ 0	18%
10,000	20,000	1,800	20%
20,000	40,000	3,800	22%
40,000	60,000	8,200	24%
60,000	80,000	13,000	26%
80,000	10,0000	18,200	28%
100,000	150,000	23,800	30%
150,000	250,000	38,800	32%
250,000	500,000	70,800	34%
500,000	....	155,800	35%

IRC Secs. 2001(c), 2502(a), 2210, as amended by EGTRRA 2001.

ESTATE TAX UNIFIED CREDIT

Year	Exclusion Equivalent	Unified Credit
2000-2001	675,000	220,550
2002-2003	$1,000,000	$345,800
2004-2005	$1,500,000	$555,800
2006-2008	$2,000,000	$780,800
2009	$3,500,000	$1,455,800
2010	NA	NA
2011	$1,000,000	$345,800

IRC Sec. 2010(c), as amended by EGTRRA 2001.

GIFT TAX UNIFIED CREDIT

Year	Exclusion Equivalent	Unified Credit
1977 (1-1 to 6-30)	$ 30,000	$ 6,000
1977 (7-1 to 12-31)	120,667	30,000
1978	134,000	34,000
1979	147,333	38,000
1980	161,563	42,500
1981	175,625	47,000
1982	225,000	62,800
1983	275,000	79,300
1984	325,000	96,300
1985	400,000	121,800
1986	500,000	155,800
1987-1997	600,000	192,800
1998	625,000	202,050
1999	650,000	211,300
2000-2001	675,000	220,550
2002-2009	1,000,000	345,800
2010	1,000,000	330,800
2011-	1,000,000	345,800

IRC Secs. 2505(a), 2010(c), as amended by EGTRRA 2001.

Maximum State Death Tax Credit (SDTC)

Adjusted Taxable Estate		Credit on	Rate on
From	To	Col. 1	Excess
$ 40,000	$ 90,000	$ 0	.8%
90,000	140,000	400	1.6%
140,000	240,000	1,200	2.4%
240,000	440,000	3,600	3.2%
440,000	640,000	10,000	4.0%
640,000	840,000	18,000	4.8%
840,000	1,040,000	27,600	5.6%
1,040,000	1,540,000	38,800	6.4%
1,540,000	2,040,000	70,800	7.2%
2,040,000	2,540,000	106,800	8.0%
2,540,000	3,040,000	146,800	8.8%
3,040,000	3,540,000	190,800	9.6%
3,540,000	4,040,000	238,800	10.4%
4,040,000	5,040,000	290,800	11.2%
5,040,000	6,040,000	402,800	12.0%
6,040,000	7,040,000	522,800	12.8%
7,040,000	8,040,000	650,800	13.6%
8,040,000	9,040,000	786,800	14.4%
9,040,000	10,040,000	930,800	15.2%
10,040,000		1,082,800	16.0%

For this purpose, the term "adjusted taxable estate" means the taxable estate reduced by $60,000.

Reduction in Maximum SDTC

Year	Multiply Maximum SDTC Above By
2002	75%
2003	50%
2004	25%
2005-2009	0%*
2010	NA
2011-	100%

*deduction for state death taxes paid replaces credit

IRC Secs. 2011(b), 2011(g), 2058, as amended by EGTRRA 2001.

Qualified Family-Owned Business Deduction

Year	Deduction Limitation
1998-2003	$675,000
2004-2010	NA
2011-	$675,000

IRC Secs. 2057(a)(2), 2057(j), as amended by EGTRRA 2001.

ESTATE TAX DEFERRAL: CLOSELY HELD BUSINESS

Year	4% Interest Limitation
1997	$153,000

Year	$1,000,000 Indexed
1998	$1,000,000
1999	$1,010,000
2000	$1,030,000
2001	$1,060,000
2002	$1,100,000

Year	2% Interest Limitation
1998	$410,000
1999	$416,500
2000	$427,500
2001	$441,000
2002	$484,000
2003	$484,000*
2004	$513,000*
2005	$507,000*
2006	$506,000*
2007-2009	$495,000*
2010	NA
2011-	$484,000*

*Based upon $1,100,000 as indexed for 2002. May increase.

IRC Secs. 6166, 6601(j). Calculations reflect EGTRRA 2001 changes.

SPECIAL USE VALUATION LIMITATION

Year	Limitation
1997-1998	$750,000
1999	$760,000
2000	$770,000
2001	$800,000
2002	$820,000

IRC Sec. 2032A(a).

QUALIFIED CONSERVATION EASEMENT EXCLUSION

Year	Exclusion Limitation
1998	$100,000
1999	$200,000
2000	$300,000
2001	$400,000
2002-2009	$500,000
2010	NA
2011-	$500,000

IRC Sec. 2031(c)(3).

GIFT (AND GST) TAX ANNUAL EXCLUSION

Year	Annual Exclusion
1997-2001	$10,000
2002	$11,000

IRC Sec. 2503(b).

GIFT TAX ANNUAL EXCLUSION
(DONEE SPOUSE NOT U.S. CITIZEN)

Year	Annual Exclusion
1997-1998	$100,000
1999	$101,000
2000	$103,000
2001	$106,000
2002	$110,000

IRC Sec. 2523(i).

GENERATION-SKIPPING TRANSFER TAX TABLE

Year	Tax Rate
2001	55%
2002	50%
2003	49%
2004	48%
2005	47%
2006	46%
2007-2009	45%
2010	NA
2011-	55%

IRC Secs. 2641, 2001(c), 2664, as amended by EGTRRA 2001.

GENERATION-SKIPPING TRANSFER TAX EXEMPTION

Year	GST Exemption
1997-1998	$1,000,000
1999	$1,010,000
2000	$1,030,000
2001	$1,060,000
2002	$1,100,000
2003	$1,100,000*
2004-2005	$1,500,000
2006-2008	$2,000,000
2009	$3,500,000
2010	NA
2011-	$1,100,000*

*Plus increases for indexing for inflation after 2002.

IRC Secs. 2631, 2010(c), as amended by EGTRRA 2001.

INDEXED AMOUNTS SOURCE

Year	Rev. Proc.
1999	98-61, 1998-2 CB 811
2000	99-42, 1999-46 IRB 568
2001	2001-13, 2001-3 IRB 337
2002	2001-59, 2001-52 IRB 623

Need Additional Copies?

Call **1-800-543-0874** to order and ask for operator BB or fax your order to **1-800-874-1916**. Order on the web at www.nationalunderwriter.com.

The
NATIONAL UNDERWRITER Company
PROFESSIONAL PUBLISHING GROUP

Orders Department
P.O. Box 14448 · Cincinnati, OH 45250-9798

2-BB

_____ Copies of *Garrett's Guide to Financial Planning, How To Capture The Middle Market and Increase Your Profits* (#2750000) $39.99
_____ Copies of *The Tools & Techniques of Financial Planning* (#2770006) $49.95

❏ Check enclosed* ❏ Charge my VISA/MC/AmEx (circle one) ❏ Bill me

*Make check payable to The National Underwriter Company. Please include the appropriate shipping & handling charges and any applicable sales tax.

Card # _____ Exp. Date _____

Signature _____

Name _____Title _____

Company _____

Street Address _____

City _____ State _____ Zip _____

Business Phone (_____) _____ Fax (_____) _____

May we e-mail you? ❏ e-mail _____

The
NATIONAL UNDERWRITER Company
PROFESSIONAL PUBLISHING GROUP

Orders Department
P.O. Box 14448 · Cincinnati, OH 45250-9798

2-BB

_____ Copies of *Garrett's Guide to Financial Planning, How To Capture The Middle Market and Increase Your Profits* (#2750000) $39.99
_____ Copies of *The Tools & Techniques of Financial Planning* (#2770006) $49.95

❏ Check enclosed* ❏ Charge my VISA/MC/AmEx (circle one) ❏ Bill me

*Make check payable to The National Underwriter Company. Please include the appropriate shipping & handling charges and any applicable sales tax.

Card # _____ Exp. Date _____

Signature _____

Name _____Title _____

Company _____

Street Address _____

City _____ State _____ Zip _____

Business Phone (_____) _____ Fax (_____) _____

May we e-mail you? ❏ e-mail _____

NO POSTAGE
NECESSARY
IF MAILED
IN THE
UNITED STATES

BUSINESS REPLY MAIL
FIRST-CLASS MAIL   PERMIT NO 68   CINCINNATI   OH

POSTAGE WILL BE PAID BY ADDRESSEE

ORDERS DEPARTMENT
THE NATIONAL UNDERWRITER COMPANY
PO BOX 14448
CINCINNATI OH 45250-9798

NO POSTAGE
NECESSARY
IF MAILED
IN THE
UNITED STATES

BUSINESS REPLY MAIL
FIRST-CLASS MAIL   PERMIT NO 68   CINCINNATI   OH

POSTAGE WILL BE PAID BY ADDRESSEE

ORDERS DEPARTMENT
THE NATIONAL UNDERWRITER COMPANY
PO BOX 14448
CINCINNATI OH 45250-9798